MORE THAN
SPECTATORS

Fulfilling Your Role in the Local Church

More Than Spectators: Fulfilling Your Role in the Local Church

© 2002 Paul W. Downey

Printed in the United States of America

Scripture refrences are from the King James Version

Ambassador Emerald International
427 Wade Hampton Boulevard
Greenville, S.C. 29609 U.S.A.

and

Ambassador Productions Ltd.
Providence House
Ardenlee Street
Belfast BT6 8QJ, Northern Ireland

www.emeraldhouse.com

cover design and page layout by A & E Media, Sam Laterza

ISBN 1 889893 79 X

MORE THAN SPECTATORS

Fulfilling Your Role in the Local Church

Paul W. Downey

AMBASSADOR
EMERALD INTERNATIONAL

Greenville, South Carolina • Belfast, Northern Ireland
www.emeraldhouse.com

Acknowledgements

I could not hope to properly acknowledge everyone to whom credit is due for the influence they have had in the production of this book. Decades of formal and informal instruction in the Word from pastors, teachers, and friends have helped to shape my thinking on many subjects. In most cases, it is impossible for me to recall precisely to whom I may be indebted.

I must mention a few, though, who have provided specific and direct assistance on this project. I offer thanks to Matt Olson for granting permission to use my adaptation of one of his sermons for much of chapter twelve. Early in the writing process, Dan Olinger made very helpful suggestions. Friends like Jack Bamford, Randy Shaylor, and Carl A. Varez read early drafts and provided valuable editorial critiques of my grammar, style, and content. Your help was invaluable, even though you will probably still cringe when you find places where I did not take your advice.

The most profound influence has certainly come from my father, James Downey, who has been involved in full-time ministry for nearly forty years, and is currently the pastor of Calvary Bible Church in Berkeley Springs, West Virginia. I am truly grateful for your editorial review of the manuscript and for a lifetime of emphasis on allowing God's Word to mean what it says and change what we are.

I also want to express my appreciation to Dr. Bob Taylor, whose pastoral influence during my undergraduate days set a high standard for us college students to emulate. Thank you for your instruction and example then and for your friendship today. And thank you for writing the foreword for this volume.

I am also indebted to the congregations of Bible Baptist Church in Kreamer, Pennsylvania, and Temple Baptist Church in Athens, Georgia, the two churches where I have served as pastor. Lessons I have learned in those ministries are reflected on these pages.

While this book is far from perfect, it would have been much worse were it not for the contributions of these people and others too numerous to mention. The errors that remain are all my own

FOREWORD

It gives me great pleasure to write the foreword to *More Than Spectators*, authored by my good friend and fellow pastor, Paul Downey. It is obvious from the beginning that this book comes from a pastor's heart to his congregation. I trust it will challenge Christians everywhere to be totally committed to the Lord Jesus Christ. This book addresses many current issues and presents the practical side of the Christian life and church membership. Many Christians profess to be disciples of the Lord Jesus Christ and know too little of what they ought to do. *More Than Spectators* sets a high standard of Christian excellence in a day of half-hearted dedication. The Bible describes itself as a two-edged sword, which will cut, burn, and sting. These chapters will often do the same. They are penned from a pastor's heart and my prayer is that they will awaken a renewed dedication to the great cause of the Lord Jesus Christ.

Of course, no work on this subject can be absolutely complete. The author is not aiming at an exhaustive work. He covers well the basic elements of the Christian life and church membership. You will find Dr. Downey's discussion to be thought provoking, honest, and worthy of deep consideration. He covers some very sensitive issues in a sane, scriptural way, which I believe will be of great help to the cause of Christ in this twenty-first century. I can highly recommend this book to you.

Dr. Bob Taylor, Pastor
Colonial Hills Baptist Church
Indianapolis, Indiana

TABLE OF CONTENTS

INTRODUCTION

These days one can find on the shelves of any Christian bookstore all manner of volumes offering to teach church leaders how to build larger churches. Depending upon the viewpoint of the author, churches are urged to employ various techniques to entice believers and unbelievers, often referred to as "seekers," to fill their pews. Much has been written on how to market a church, usually emphasizing some appeal to the tastes and interests of the Baby-boomers, Generation X-ers, or some other demographic group.

In order to develop this user-friendly atmosphere, a more casual approach to worship is being encouraged, with emphasis on activities and programs and an accompanying de-emphasis on expositional preaching of the Word of God. This is producing a generation of professing believers who practice what could be thought of as Christianity-Lite—a nominal form of Christianity which approximates the *flavor* of the genuine, but has little of the *substance*. We see churches filled with people who have no biblical understanding of what constitutes true worship of a holy God and who see no biblical imperative for their own personal holiness. It is this attitude that Paul described as "having a form of godliness, but denying the power thereof" (2 Timothy 3:5).

Due to the visibility of high-profile Christian speakers, writers, and entertainers through various media outlets, the average Christian has begun to question the relevance of the ministry of his local church. Often, the local church is perceived as little more than a social club whose purpose is to provide a forum for its members to meet to discuss the latest recording by their favorite musician, or the newest trend in church growth, or the currently popular ideas of their favorite Christian spokesperson, or to organize trips to the next big rally. It has been well said that while the post-modern church in America has become quite adept at making *celebrities*, it has forgotten how to make *saints*. This is even seen in the terminology being popularized as people are called to *celebrate* God rather than to *worship* Him.

In many circles the focus of the local church ministry has shifted. A great deal of money and effort are being expended in attempts to attract and keep church members by entertaining them rather than by training them. Preaching services have been replaced by concerts and dramas. Genuine Bible study, where the real meaning of the biblical text is sought out and practical application is made to daily living with personal growth in Christlikeness as the goal, has been displaced. What passes for Bible study in many churches is nothing more than speculative biblical commentary, in which people gather to express their own ideas about what any particular passage "means to me." This exchanging of biblical exegesis for practical existentialism has made *feeling close* to God seem more important than *knowing the truth* of God. For many Christians, the authority of the Word of God has been displaced, with personal experience becoming the primary measure of truth.

The potential effectiveness of the local church pastor is being eroded. A pastor who dares to challenge the views or the methods of an especially popular radio or television preacher or a particularly well-known writer may well find himself without a pulpit. While in many cases it is, no doubt, unintentional, these celebrity-status Christians have become the modern equivalent of Absalom to the local church's David. They are charming away the local congregation's loyalty and support of their duly appointed and God ordained leader. Far too many professing believers are opting to be church *goers* rather than church *members*. The trend seems to be for people to shop around for a church that pleases them, rather than search out a sound church in which they can serve.

Part of the solution to this growing problem is for pastors to guard against the temptation to adopt a consumer mentality to market their church. When we make the primary purpose of a church the development of programs to target the perceived needs of a community, we make our practical theology man-centered, rather than God-centered. We must remember that the church does not exist for the purpose of entertaining believers. The commission of the church is to glorify God by evangelizing the lost and discipling believers by the proclamation of the truth, "till we all come in the unity of the faith, and of the knowledge of the son of God, unto a perfect man, unto the measure of the stature of the fullness of Christ" (Eph. 4:14).

This book has come about as a result of my conviction that the crying need of the church is not more celebrities, more activities, or more programs to entertain us. *What we need are more saints committed to obeying their Lord, whatever the cost.* We will not develop righteousness in the lives of believers by pandering to their every desire, as if that were the biblical meaning of the exercise of Christian liberty. If we want the righteousness of Christ to be seen in us, we must emphasize Christian responsibilities. With this in mind, I set out over a period of several months, to preach to my own congregation a series of messages on the themes addressed in our church membership covenant.[1] As a local church pastor myself, I desired to remind my congregation of the promises they made to one another and to God when they joined our church. This book represents the bulk of the content of those messages. While I hope this book will be a valuable resource to other pastors, my desire is that it will be used of God to encourage the individual believer to grow in the likeness of Christ and to be faithful to the service of his Lord through the local church.

I admit that I write from a Baptist perspective, but I hope that any individual or church that believes the Bible and seeks to live by it will find that most of these principles are relevant in their church contexts.

Paul W. Downey,
Pastor

---

[1] The text of that covenant appears on the next page.

OUR CHURCH COVENANT

Throughout this book, I make frequent reference to the membership covenant of the church I pastor. The following is the text of that covenant:

Having been led, as we believe by the Spirit of God, to receive the Lord Jesus Christ as our Savior and, on the profession of our faith, having been baptized in the name of the Father, and of the Son, and of the Holy Spirit, we do now, in the presence of God, angels, and this assembly, most solemnly and joyfully enter into covenant with one another as one body in Christ.

We engage, therefore, by the aid of the Holy Spirit to walk together in Christian love; to strive for the advancement of this church in knowledge, holiness, and comfort; to promote its prosperity and spirituality; to sustain its worship, ordinances, discipline, and doctrines; to contribute cheerfully and regularly to the support of the ministry, the expenses of the church, the relief of the poor, and the spread of the gospel through all nations.

We also engage to maintain family and secret devotions; to religiously educate our children; to seek the salvation of our kindred and acquaintances; to walk circumspectly in the world; to be just in our dealings, faithful in our engagements, and exemplary in our deportment; to avoid all tattling, backbiting, and excessive anger; to abstain from the sale of, and use of, intoxicating drinks as a beverage; to be zealous in our efforts to advance the kingdom of our Savior.

We further engage to watch over one another in brotherly love; to remember one another in prayer; to aid one another in sickness and distress; to cultivate Christian sympathy in feeling and Christian courtesy in speech; to be slow to take offense, but always ready for reconciliation and mindful of the rules of our Savior to seek it without delay.

We moreover engage that when we remove from this place we will, as soon as possible, unite with some other church where we can carry out the spirit of this covenant and the principles of God's Word.

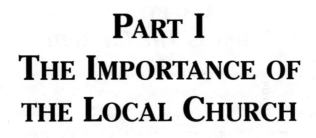

PART I
THE IMPORTANCE OF
THE LOCAL CHURCH

CHAPTER 1
WHAT IS *THE CHURCH*?

One need not move to a different country to encounter cultural nuances that can take some time for the newcomer to master. My first pastorate was in a church in a rural community in central Pennsylvania, a part of the country I'd traveled through but never visited for any length of time. One of the challenges I met there was simply learning to get around. In my teens, I had learned to drive a car in the suburbs of Washington, D.C., and most of my driving experience since then had been either on city streets or interstate highways. Traffic I could handle. I even found the road-clogging farm equipment and Amish buggies of central Pennsylvania a refreshing change of pace. But navigating unmarked mountain-country roads was another matter. I was used to travel directions including exit numbers, street names, and house numbers. I had trouble with landmarks. Over time, I learned to ask clarifying questions. For instance, if the directions included, "Turn left at Yoder's farm," I learned to ask if there was a sign, like a name on a silo or something, to identify it as "Yoder's Farm." The answer might be, "Nope. Yoder's don't own it any more. The farm's changed hands twice since Jacob Yoder sold the property back in '54." In that case, I'd need a clearer description.

In the second or third year of my ministry there, I needed to call on a family I hadn't visited before. I thought I had pretty good directions, with all the turns having either stop signs, "T" intersections, or identifiable landmarks. One of the directions said, "Turn right at the dump." I thought that seemed clear enough. But after driving back and forth along a particular country road for a while, I finally back-tracked to the service station at the last turn and asked where I might find the dump. The attendant was very helpful. He said I should go about a quarter of a mile back up the road I had just been traveling to the first road that goes off to the right. When I got there, and made the turn, I realized there had been nothing wrong with the directions. The problem was a misunderstanding of definitions. Sitting to my left was a collection of several green trash containers. I had driven past those dumpsters four times without ever considering they might be the *dump* I was trying to find. I was looking for a *landfill*.

The meaning of a given word can change significantly according to context, and even subtle differences can be important. Misunderstanding the meaning of "the dump" had been an inconvenience, costing me about half an hour. Misunderstanding the meaning of "the church" could have much more significant consequences.

The Lord Jesus introduces the concept of "the church" in Matthew 16:13-18.

> When Jesus came into the coasts of Caesarea Philippi, he asked his disciples, saying, Whom do men say that I the Son of man am? And they said, Some *say that thou art* John the Baptist: some, Elias; and others, Jeremias, or one of the prophets. He saith unto them, But whom say ye that I am? And Simon Peter answered and said, Thou art the Christ, the Son of the living God. And Jesus answered and said unto him, Blessed art thou, Simon Barjona: for flesh and blood hath not revealed *it* unto thee, but my Father which is in heaven. And I say also unto thee, That thou art Peter, and upon this rock I will build my church; and the gates of hell shall not prevail against it.

Without getting into controversy over Peter's role in the building of the church, we need to consider just what Jesus meant by "my church." What exactly did He promise to build?

Defining *The Church*

The word *church* is used in a variety of ways in our language today. It is most commonly used to refer to a *building* when we say things like, "we are putting up new lights in the church," or "meet at the church for a special activity." Sometimes we use it to refer to a *denominational group*, as in "The Free Presbyterian Church." It may be used in reference to *all Christians collectively within a nation*, as in "the Church in America." Or it may refer to *all the believers in the world*, sometimes known as the "Universal Church."[1]

If we would establish a true definition for the purposes of our study, we will need to use the Bible as our authority. We need to see what God has said concerning the church. To do that, we need to go the New Testament, because the church, as an organization, did not exist in Old Testament times.[2] It was a mystery, previously unrevealed, that was revealed by Christ Jesus in His ministry and more fully during the ministry of the Apostles (Rom. 16:25-26; Eph. 3:3-6).

The word translated *church* in the New Testament is the Greek word *ekklesia*. In its classical use, the word refers to a "summoned assembly," without necessarily any religious significance. It identifies an organization or institution having prescribed membership requirements, privileges, purposes, and policies. It is used in this way in Acts 19:39 and 41[3] to refer to the citizens of Ephesus who had gathered to protest Paul's teaching. It is not an *audience*, which implies a gathering of spectators, but is more accurately a *congregation*, a gathering of active participants. It may be applied to any summoned assembly, whether a religious body, a legislature, or a town meeting.

Much more commonly in the New Testament, *ekklesia* is used for believers in one of two senses. About ninety times it refers to local congregations, as in "the church which was at Jerusalem" (Acts 8:1), and "the churches of Galatia" (Gal. 1:2). At least twenty-three other times it is used to refer to the entire body of Christians, as in "Saul made havoc of the church" (Acts 8:3), and in Matthew 16:18 when Jesus said, "I will build my church." This is also how the word is used by Paul in Ephesians 3:21 when he said, "Unto him be glory in the church by Christ Jesus throughout all ages, world without end. Amen." In this sense, the church is made up of all true believers of the church age, past, present, and future, and is often referred to as the universal aspect of the church. It is not universal in the sense that everyone belongs, but that it transcends geography and time. Jesus Christ's glory in the church (singular) is evidenced "throughout all ages, world without end." Yet Paul also referred to the local assembly at Ephesus as "the church of God, which he purchased with his own blood" (Acts 20:28). Evidently, both the assembly of believers at a particular time and location, as well as all believers of all the world and all the church age can accurately be called *the church*.

We must be careful to avoid two extremes concerning the local and universal aspects of the church. Some overemphasize the local aspect, even denying the existence of a universal aspect. At times this represents mere semantics, but it still involves misconstruing several passages that refer to the church at large. This extreme position often leads to isolationism and elitism. It sometimes fosters a spirit of competition between local churches, because there is little or no sense of history or community among believers from other congregations. Also damaging to the ongoing work of the church is the opposite extreme: an overemphasis on the universal aspect that denies the significance of the local congregation. This is a weakness of some parachurch organizations and leads to detachment, apathy, and lack of accountability. It is this more prevalent extreme that has helped produce spectator Christians who are unwilling to become personally involved in organized, corporate ministry. These loose-canon Christians often drift from congregation to congregation without ever taking responsibility for ministry or accepting accountability under a local church's authority.

Describing the Church

Significantly, the symbols used in the Bible to describe the church at large have special application to the local assembly.[2] While each individual believer is called "the temple of the Holy Ghost" (1 Cor. 6:19), the entire assembly shares that designation. In 1 Corinthians 3:9-17 Paul describes the corporate body of believers as "the temple of God [which] is holy." Each church's *ministry* should reflect that truth. Tragically, many of us have rejected the corrupt theology and empty rituals of Roman Catholicism only to stoop to what amounts to profanity by introducing a carnival atmosphere to worship. When our church services take on the character of a side-show, using tricks and stunts and advertising gimmicks to attract an audience, we are neither thinking nor behaving like a holy Temple of God.

The assembly of believers is also called "the church, which is his [Christ's] body" (Eph. 1:22-23). Each church's *unity* should reflect that truth. Many churches do not stress the importance of official membership in their congregation, encouraging unbelievers to mingle anonymously among the believers, in some cases even permitting participation in the ministry functions of the church. In so doing, they have effectively established an unregenerate membership that corrupts the purity of the body of Christ and establishes an inappropriate union of "light" and "darkness" (2 Cor. 6:14).

The congregation is also called "the bride of Christ." This truth should be reflected in each church's *fidelity* to Christ. Paul said of the church of Corinth that they were "espoused" that they might be presented as a "chaste virgin to Christ" (2 Cor. 11:2). But he feared they would be unfaithful and corrupted by listening to those who preached "another Jesus," or by receiving "another spirit," or by accepting "another gospel" (11:3-4). In Ephesians 5:25-27, Paul illustrated the nature of a husband's proper love for his wife by describing the goal of Christ's selfless love for His Bride:

> Husbands, love your wives, even as Christ also loved the church, and gave himself for it; That he might sanctify and cleanse it with the washing of the water by the word, That he might present it to himself a glorious church, not having spot, or wrinkle, or any such thing; but that it should be holy and without blemish.

A church marketing program designed primarily to attract "seekers" is in danger of prostituting the church to the whims of the unregenerate community. The Lord Jesus did not give Himself for His Bride so she could be whatever she wants to be, much less what the unbelieving world wants her to be. When churches fail to require evidence of conversion and willingness to be held accountable in those who participate in their ministries, they become something other than the chaste virgins and spotless brides they ought to be. But even when believers *join* the church, they should be expected to become actively and faithfully involved in its ministry. If believers come and go with no real attachment to the local assembly, they fail to demonstrate the scrupulous faithfulness and undivided love that a bride vows to maintain toward her husband.

The church is also called "the flock of God" (1 Pet. 5:1-4). This emphasizes humility of spirit and submission to the leadership of the church. This truth should be reflected in each church's *conformity* to the image of Christ, in both obedience to Him and dependence upon Him. The pastor is called upon to be the under-shepherd representing the Good Shepherd. He is to feed, protect, instruct, discipline, and bind the wounds of the flock. The godly pastor will shepherd the flock with a firm but gently loving authority, without an inflated ego or heavy-handed tyranny. The faithful church member will follow the Good Shepherd through His appointed representative. This is not a mindless attitude that assumes the pastor is always right. It is the recognition of the proper roles within the church. Just as a godly pastor will rue God's call to lead an unruly flock, a godly flock will chafe under the leadership of an egotistical hireling.

For a church to be a *church* in a biblical sense, it seems evident that there should be some form of organizational structure, established membership requirements, and some measure of accountability.[5] Everyone who walks through the door and attends the services should be welcome, but not everyone is a part of the *ekklesia*. Rev. H. Ray Newman, former pastor of Temple Baptist Church in Glen Burnie, MD, provides the following definition of a local church:

> A body of baptized believers organized to gather for worship, fellowship, instruction in the Word, evangelizing the lost, observing the ordinances; to watch over and discipline its members for their good and the glory of God; which is governed by its scriptural officers…, and answering solely to Christ, its Head.

It is important to recognize that the universal and local aspects of the church are intimately related. The existence of the *universal* church is evident—every believer belongs to the Church that is the Temple of God, the Body of Christ, the Bride of Christ, and the Flock of God. That is the Church which will one day be assembled when called forth by the shout of the Lord, the voice of the archangel, and the sound of the trumpet of God (1 Thes. 4:16-17). But the importance of the *local* church is also clear. The local church is a miniature of the universal, a replica of the whole. It stands in the same relation to Christ as the universal church, giving visible and immediate expression to the invisible and eternal Church of Jesus Christ. Each congregation has an honored position as a group, representing Christ as a corporate body, with the responsibility to represent Him well. When a group of believers covenant together as one body in Christ, they reflect the *local* aspect of the *universal* church. They are not a social club. They are not an entertainment provider. They covenant to perform all of the functions of the whole Body of Christ in their geographic location and at their point in history.

---

[1] As will be explained, I've used the term "universal" in the sense in which it is generally understood in this context—that body composed of *all true believers of all the world and all the church age.* In no way should my use of this term be construed as belief in "universalism"—that salvation will be applied to all people.

[2] I realize that many of my Reformed brethren might dispute this assertion. Admittedly, the distinctions between a dispensational view of the church and a covenantal view are of theological importance. However, such distinctions do not seem to have any significant impact on the issue at hand—the relationship of the believer to the local church.

[3] These are the only times that *ekklesia* is translated "assembly" in the KJV. The word was usually translated "congregation" in the Geneva Bible, but that was thought by a majority of the Anglican clergy to undermine their ecclesiastical authority. Thus, when King James and Archbishop Bancroft established translation rules for the teams who would produce the KJV, rule #3 said: "The Old Ecclesiastical Words to be kept, viz. the Word *Church* not to be translated *Congregation* &c."

[4] The discussion that follows should be considered an introduction to these concepts rather than a thorough treatment of them. More will be said throughout this book that will be applicable to ideas mentioned here.

[5] This statement will be developed and defended in the next three chapters.

CHAPTER 2
DO I NEED TO BE INVOLVED
IN THE LOCAL CHURCH?

Three or four times a year, we have some sort of "food and fellow-ship" time for the entire church following the Sunday evening service. One of these is a mid-summer "pie and ice cream social." Those with the time and ability usually bring homemade desserts, while others buy ready-made ones. My wife is a fine cook—one look at her husband would tell any observer that he's not been on starvation rations—but she readily admits that baking pies is not her forte. The congregation knows that we usually purchase pies for this particular event.

On one occasion, one of the ladies in the church graciously volunteered to make a couple of extra pies to serve as our contribution. On the night of the social, my wife's thoughtful friend pointed out four beautiful pies and said, "I told everybody these two were yours." Sherry again expressed her gratitude—until she noticed what people were doing with slices of those pies. They would take one bite, then a tentative second bite, before leaving the rest untouched or tossing it in the trash can. She decided to try a piece herself. After tasting it, she went to her friend and asked, "Have you eaten any of the pie you brought?" Her friend said, "No; I eat my pies all the time. I thought I'd try someone else's tonight." So Sherry gave her a bite of the pie she had made. For a moment, her expression showed mingled shock and distaste, then came the dawning realization—"I forgot to put in the sugar!" For years after that, whenever it was time for a "pie and ice cream social," Sherry would jokingly tell her friend, "We're bringing ice cream this time!"

The difference between a pumpkin and a pumpkin pie is found in both the addition of other ingredients and in the work involved in its preparation. In a similar fashion, there are several ingredients essential for building godly individuals and godly families, and achieving that goal will take deliberate effort. Personal salvation is the foundation upon which the rest is built. Personal time in Bible study and prayer is also important. But there is also the need for faithful participation in the church. Omitting any of these ingredients from your lives may not be as immediately *noticeable* as leaving the sugar out of the pie, but it is far more *perilous*.

On occasion, a man will tell me that since his family is his first priority, and the church comes in at third or fourth on the list, he and his family will not attend church regularly because they have things they like to do on the weekends. He has, at best, revealed his misplaced priorities and a lack of spiritual discernment, and he may be deliberately wearing a pious façade. For all practical purposes, he has really placed *himself* first. He has things that he *wants* to do, even if it is just to please his family, and so he has decided that he will do what he wants regardless of what the pastor and the Scriptures say he *ought* to do. If his family were really first, he would recognize that the most important need in his family is a right relationship with God, and that involvement in a good local church is one of the ingredients necessary to accomplish that.[1]

Why You Need the Local Church

There are several ways in which the local church can help you develop into a strong and godly Christian. First, *the local church provides opportunities to worship with other believers*. In Acts 20:7 we find that the first century believers gathered together for worship. "And upon the first day of the week, when the disciples came together to break bread, Paul preached unto them..." These believers had a designated time, a designated place, and a designated activity for meeting together. The church gathered together as a body for the purpose of worship, fellowship, and instruction in the Word of God. You and your family need the corporate worship, fellowship, and instruction that are only available within the context of the local church.

A second reason you need the local church is that *it provides opportunities for spiritual growth and accountability* that are not found in solitude. There are believers today who insist that they can worship God in their own home, or at the lake, or on the golf course. In a sense, they are correct—it is not only *possible* to worship God in those places, we *ought* to worship God in those places. Worship is not restricted to a particular place or day of the week, and everything we do is to be an act of worship to the glory of God (1 Cor. 10:31). But God also *demands* that believers assemble to worship His Son (Heb. 10:25). A believer is not to be an island unto himself. Each of us has obligations to one another. In Hebrews 10:24, believers are challenged to "consider one another to provoke unto love and to good works…." To "consider one another" we have to know one another and care about one another, and that can only come through fellowship with one another. No one will ever be able to consider you and to provoke you to love and good works if they do not *know* you. You can only do that in the context of the local church assembly. You and your family need others to hold you accountable for your Christian testimony. If you and your family are not involved in a good local church, you deprive yourselves of contact with other believers who could encourage your spiritual growth.

Third, the local church *provides support in time of difficulty or distress.* The Apostle Paul says that believers are to "Rejoice with them that do rejoice, and weep with them that weep" (Rom. 12:15). In another passage, he elaborated a bit by saying: "And whether one member suffer, all the members suffer with it; or one member be honored, all the members rejoice with it" (1 Cor. 12:26). Notice that he did not simply say that *other* members suffer with the one who suffers or rejoice with the one who is honored. He said that *all* the members do so. Honestly, I do not know how many churches actually practice Christian sympathy and empathy to this degree, but a good local church will provide a far greater support base for the mitigation of personal suffering during the storms of life than will no church at all. The problem is that when you have money, good health care, and a busy schedule, it is very easy to conclude that you do not need the support of other believers only possible in a local church. You may be tempted to try to make it on your own, thinking that you and God alone at home are adequate. But when difficulty comes and tragedy strikes, you will suddenly find that there is nobody there for you. You have to go to the local hospital or call the local psychiatrist to see if he can set you up with a support group of some kind. If you remain shallow in your relationship to your local church, the support of other Christians will not be there for you when you need it most.

Fourth, you should be active in a good local church because *it gives you opportunities to help others.* Christians are not told to leave one another alone and mind our own business. Just as it is impossible for other believers to consider you and to provoke you to love and to good works if they do not know you, it is also impossible for you to do the same for others if you have little or no contact with believers in a local church setting. That is why Hebrews 10:25 adds, "Not forsaking the assembling of yourselves together, as the manner of some is; but exhorting one another...." There is a danger of assuming that all we need to do is gather on Sunday mornings and sit, expecting someone to entertain us or encourage us. We give little thought to our own responsibility to exhort one another. God commands us to be personally involved within the assembly. Each believer is to do his part, contributing to the overall working of the body of Christ.

The final, and most important, reason for your involvement in a local church is that *the local church provides you an opportunity to be obedient to the command of the Lord.* We are *commanded* to gather together for worship. This is something God *requires* of us, as we saw in Hebrews 10:25. There are several reasons for this, some having to do with our own spiritual benefit, while others are related to our usefulness in service. But the benefits of corporate worship to individual believers, or even to the entire congregation, are secondary to the ultimate purpose of bringing glory to God (Eph. 3:21). Each of the other benefits grows out of our obedient desire to glorify Him.

In Ephesians 5:25-27, we are told that Christ gave Himself for the church that He might sanctify and cleanse it with the washing of the water by the Word, and present it to Himself a glorious church, not having spot or wrinkle, that it should be holy and without blemish. Paul also writes of the gifts Christ gave to the church in order to assist in its purification. In this context, these gifts are not described as characteristics or abilities, but as individuals who are given to the church

for the perfecting of the saints for the work of the ministry, for the edifying of the body of Christ, till we all come in the unity of the faith and of the knowledge of the Son of God unto a perfect man, unto the measure of the stature of the fullness of Christ. That we *henceforth* be no more children, tossed to and fro, and carried about with every wind of doctrine, by the sleight of men, *and* cunning craftiness, whereby they lie in wait to deceive; But speaking the truth in love, may grow up into him in all things, which is the head, *even* Christ: From whom the whole body fitly joined together and compacted by that which every joint supplieth, according to the effectual working in the measure of every part, maketh increase of the body unto the edifying of itself in love (Eph. 4:11-16).

Paul is speaking of the church as a body, each member having his own responsibilities to fulfill, compacted together into the body of Christ. How does he say that is to be accomplished? It is through the influence of the local church. Paul is saying that God has given the local assembly gifted individuals for the purpose of guiding and instructing and equipping Christians for the service of the Lord within the church. Each believer brings to his local assembly something that no one else can bring. If he fails to function as he should within that assembly, then that local church suffers for want of that which he could have provided. Each individual can be used of God to help the whole body grow. It is impossible for you to fulfill these obligations by yourself at home, or on the golf course, or at the lake, or wherever you might be other than in the assembly with the believers. If you do not prioritize involvement in the local church, you will not only miss the blessing of what others can contribute to your spiritual growth, you will also lose the opportunity to contribute to the spiritual growth of others.

How You Can Become Involved in the Local Church

Psalm 1:3 says that believers are to be like trees, planted by rivers of water. Unfortunately, there are many Christian who are more like tumbleweeds. They roll from one church to another. The wind blows a little in one church, so they roll over to another church and stay until the wind blows a little there. Then they will roll on down the street to yet another church. Eventually, they roll up against a fence where they will stay for years. But they never put down roots. If you don't want to be like the tumbleweed, how do you plant your roots deeply into the local church?

The first and most obvious way to become involved in the local church is to *commit to it*. Prioritizing church involvement will require, first of all, that you be able to give a credible testimony of personal faith in the Lord Jesus Christ. Second, you should join the membership of a particular local assembly of believers, identifying with it and taking some responsibility for it. Your commitment should include faithful attendance to the services of that church, regular prayer for that local assembly and its particular members, financial support of the church ministry, helping with the conducting of the business of that church, and personal participation in meeting the spiritual and physical needs of its membership. You do yourself and your family a great service by taking your share of the responsibility for the sustenance and maintenance of the local church.

Having decided to which local church you will commit yourself, you should consistently *speak well of it*. The church has enough critics without its own members doing the job. Why would anyone else want to visit the church to which you belong if you never have anything good to say about it? First Corinthians 1:10 admonishes, "by the name of our Lord Jesus Christ, that ye all speak the same thing, and *that* there be no divisions among you; but *that* ye be perfectly joined together in the same mind and in the same judgment." The members of any church who are obeying this admonition will be speaking well of the church. That does not mean that we wink at misdeeds. We must never tolerate evil. However, if you are not defending the church, but are constantly running it down, people in the community will have cause to wonder why you go to that church. Your family and others need to hear you defend your church, praising its strengths and seeking positive ways to improve its weaknesses. If you cannot think of any strong points to praise, you should find another church.

Further, you should learn to speak of the church as "my church," or "our church." Others, your children in particular, need to hear you speak in terms of "our pastor," "our church leaders," "our Sunday school," "our church activities," "our missionaries." They need to hear that phrasing, so they will begin to think of it in those terms. In many local churches it is sad to see the number of children who are growing up *in* church without growing up *into* the church. Part of the problem is that they have never learned to identify with it.

Speaking well of your church should include inviting others to attend with you. That is not just the pastor's job. Technically, the pastor's job is to train the believers. It is the believers' job, in concert with the Holy Spirit, to bring people to Christ. The individual church member can often be more effective in inviting people to church than can his pastor. Given the visibility of television evangelists and the scandals that have been caused by sin in the lives of some, there is a strong tendency for the unchurched to assume that any preacher who invites someone to church has his own self-interest at heart. People tend to be skeptical of any preacher who is inviting others to come hear him speak. Some statistics indicate that the average church member currently invites others to church only once every twenty-eight years. Surely we can do better than that!

Another step toward becoming a vital part of the local church is for you and your family to begin to *minister within it*. Paul draws an analogy between the church and a body in which the hand, the foot and the eye all perform their particular functions for the good of the whole body (1 Corinthians 12:12-27). His point is that every member has a job to do and should contribute to the work of the whole church. Far too many believers show up on Sunday morning to occupy their space in the pew, stand up when they are told, sit down when they are told, sing (sort of) when they are supposed to, maybe even take a few notes on the pastor's sermon, close their eyes when someone prays, and then go home. That is the extent of their ministry within the church. The same people go to a ball game and behave much the same way, usually with considerably more enthusiasm. What a shame!

Rather than just looking for ways in which a particular church can meet your needs, find a way in which you can contribute to the min-

istry of that church. Since when is the church to be merely a religious
country club where you pay your dues until you find something more
interesting or exciting to do? Perhaps you could help by serving as an
usher or a greeter at the door, or assisting in a Sunday school class, or
working in the nursery, or visiting the elderly or the ill, or going soul-
winning, or helping clean the building or mow the lawn, or singing in
the choir. The list of possible areas of ministry involvement is virtually endless. If you see a need your church ought to be meeting, bring
it up and ask what you can do to help. The Lord may have put you in
that church for the purpose of identifying and meeting that need. No
one, least of all your family, will ever believe that the church is especially important to you if your idea of church involves nothing more
than sitting through sermons while letting others do the work of the
ministry.

A further way to become a vital part of a local assembly is for you to
give financially to the support of the church. God has first claim on your
financial resources, and He wants you to trust Him, not your bank
account, for your security. You need to develop the discipline of giving
abundantly, purposefully, and cheerfully (2 Cor. 9:6-7), and your family
needs to see you doing that. The amount you give is to be proportionate
to your ability to give. Some can give only ten percent, the tithe, but
others can give much more. We would do well to remember, though,
that how much we *give* reveals less about our attitude toward money
than does how much we *keep* for ourselves. God evaluates our giving on
the basis of our motives and our sacrifice, not so much on the amount.
Your giving should include regular contributions of tithes and offerings
necessary for the general budgetary needs of your church. In many
churches this would also include additional offerings for the support of
missions and other special projects through the local church.

Another element important to becoming involved into the local church
is to *support its ministers* with your love, respect, and loyalty. Support
the ministers by offering encouragement and expressions of appreciation
for their work in your church (Heb. 13:7). You also demonstrate your
love by giving the material support they need through the salary and
benefits package provided by the church. The church members must see
to it that their pastor is adequately compensated for his dedicated work
in the ministry. Paul said in 1 Timothy 5:17-18, "Let the elders that rule
well be counted worthy of double honor, especially they who labor in

the word and doctrine. For the Scripture saith, Thou shalt not muzzle the ox that treadeth out the corn. And, The laborer *is* worthy of his reward." It is the responsibility of the members of the church, perhaps through the agency of their elected representatives (i.e., deacons or elders), to see to it that the pastor's salary, insurance, and retirement benefits are adequate.

The loyal support that the church members owe to their ministers is also shown through their respect for his position of spiritual leadership. The members can do that by giving careful attention to the pastor's instruction from the Word of God and applying themselves to living by what they are taught. You also demonstrate respect by your refusal to make or listen to petty criticism and unfounded accusations against the pastor (1 Tim. 5:19-20).

If you are an apathetic spectator at the weekly meetings, irregular in your attendance, haphazard in your giving, often critical of the pastor and church officers, is it any wonder that others see little reason for becoming a Christian and joining your church? If you have a family, will your example encourage your children to desire to continue to be a part of such an organization when they become adults? If you want your children to place a high value on local church involvement, you must communicate to them that *you* consider local church involvement a priority.[2] Join the church, attend the services, speak well of it, participate in its ministries, give financially to its support, and support its ministers. You will become deeply rooted into the local church and you will help your family to do the same.

Think of how bad a pumpkin pie would taste without any sugar. Do not deceive yourself into thinking that spending time with your family on recreational outings is more important than taking your family to church. If you will commit yourself and your family to a sound local church, you will grow in worship, you will grow in spiritual maturity, you will receive support in time of need, and you will become obedient to the command of God in ministry.

---

[1] I am not arguing that a person must never miss a service in his home church. There will be circumstances that occasionally prevent attending. Nor am I suggesting that families should never vacation over a weekend.

I am talking about a pattern of behavior that fails to prioritize church involvement. Even when away from home on business or vacationing, believers will benefit from visiting a good church wherever they happen to be.

2 Of course, one's *first* obligation is faithfulness to Christ. There may come a time in which continued faithfulness to a particular local church constitutes *in*fidelity to Christ, in which case a believer should separate from that church in order to join one that shares his commitment to honor Christ first. See Chapter Twenty-four.

CHAPTER 3
HOW DO I FIND A GOOD LOCAL CHURCH?

Average attendance figures had dropped by about 5% over a period
of several years in a particular church. In the process of considering
strategies for increasing attendance, they decided to hire a church
growth expert to evaluate their ministry and make suggestions on how
their church could grow. After spending several days studying the
property and the community, evaluating members' responses to ques-
tionnaires, and visiting the services of the church, he made several
recommendations. These included cosmetic improvements like
adding flower beds to the grounds, upgrading the sound system, and
changing the colors in the auditorium. But his real emphasis was on
philosophical changes. His study concluded that the church should
incorporate contemporary music in the services despite the fact that
his own survey indicated that over three-quarters of the congregation
thought the traditional music program was fine or should be even
more conservative. He also said the church should require the youth
pastor to relax the dress standards for the youth group and to make
their activities more "culturally relevant." By that, he meant that teen
activities should include going to the movies and hosting dances. If
the youth pastor refused to modify his program accordingly, he should
be removed within a year and replaced with someone to whom

teenagers could "relate." None of his recommendations had anything to do with evangelism or spiritual growth. Basically, this expert had concluded that the church would attract more people if it would incorporate elements of religious liberalism and the Charismatic movement.

Such concerns and strategies result from a profound misunderstanding of what constitutes a *good* church. Too many believers want a church that promises to minister to their "felt needs" without expecting much in return. They place an undue emphasis on impressive facilities, extensive programs, and the personalities of the leaders. The committed Christian will want to prioritize finding a church home in which he can worship with integrity and serve enthusiastically. He should be alert to potential philosophical problems in the church's ministries, he should try to find a church that evidences the spiritual characteristics of a godly ministry, and he should look for evidence of a committed membership.

Philosophical Characteristics of a Man-centered Ministry

Pastors and churches today are facing pressures that require much spiritual discernment, commitment, and courage in order to maintain a Bible-centered, God-centered ministry. The desire to see numerical growth has sometimes led churches to adopt methods that may not please the Lord. There is much done in the name of church promotion that is neither biblical nor God-honoring. In looking for a good church, a believer should be alert for evidences of a philosophically carnal ministry—that is, a ministry whose theology and practice are man-centered rather than God-centered.

One indication of a man-centered ministry is seen in churches that seem to prefer popularity to purity. They have a passion for change in order to popularize the church and make it more acceptable to the world. The concept of the user-friendly, seeker-sensitive ministry is one example. The truth is, many good churches are struggling to survive and have been tempted to try to grow by attracting (or appeasing) a younger crowd. They have begun to replace services with social events. Godly worship is being displaced in favor of contemporary entertainment. Ministry plans are made on the basis of what unsaved and unchurched people in the community say they want, rather than on the basis of what God says they need. It has been well-said that if the world is like the ocean, the church should be like a boat. A boat is useless if you keep the boat out of the water, but it is also useless if you can't keep the water out of the boat.

Another evidence of man-centeredness is found in churches that exalt experience over doctrine. There is a growing notion that the primary responsibility of the church is to make people feel good. One's feelings about God are considered more important than objective truth. This is seen in the quality of the teaching and preaching of the church. First, Bible exposition has been replaced by personal perception. Instead of Bible study that emphasizes what the Bible actually says, there is group discussion about what the Bible "means to me." There is little acknowledgment that for your perception and your experience to be legitimate they must be rooted in truth. Additionally, godly sorrow is replaced by feel-good sentiment. There is less and less preaching on confession and repentance and more and more emphasis on finding "spiritual healing" and strength, encouraging self-esteem rather than self-abasement.

Some churches err by prioritizing growth over godliness. That is precisely the error that the church mentioned at the beginning of the chapter would have committed had they actually incorporated the philosophical changes recommended by the church growth expert. That is also the error made by churches who employ other marketing techniques to attract a crowd. There is certainly nothing wrong with churches desiring to grow. But doing so at the expense of godliness is not the answer. Churches that follow such trends have replaced confession (agreeing with God) with compromise (appeasing the world). They are more concerned with being perceived as friendly than with practicing godly love. They end up promoting programs rather than exalting Christ. Vance Havner got it right when he said,

> We are trying to make church members do a lot of things they don't want to do anyway. When the love of God is shed abroad in our hearts, it will not be necessary to encourage the saints by prizes and picnics and periodic shots in the arm to do the will of God.[1]

Another philosophical error is made by churches that emphasize man's "felt needs" over God's revealed Word. These churches often replace reverence with casualness, in their attire and in the tone and content of their worship, and they replace Word-centered preaching in favor of man-centered platitudes. Many churches have moved away from consecutive Biblical exposition and preach only topical, life situation messages. Such churches do not even attempt to equip their membership to handle the whole Bible with confidence and real understanding. They tend to treat the Bible as a collection of sayings rather than a unified body of truth with a sweeping scope and powerful themes.

A fifth misdirection in ministry comes when churches preach cultural relevance rather than biblical absolutes. You hear little or nothing about biblical separation, because it has been replaced by an emphasis on ecumenical unity. Separated Christians are accused of being "legalists," while compromising Christians are hailed as "tolerant." In churches that have made this error, Christians tend to resent being told they ought to live holy lives. They have replaced a proper emphasis on Christian responsibilities with an unbiblical emphasis on personal rights. Their people become more interested in defending their Christian liberty than in performing their Christian duty. Discernment and balance are needed. Standards for living are important for a person to become Christlike, but those standards will never make a person a Christian. Such a code of conduct should represent a practical implementation of biblical principles.

A final philosophical shift seen in many churches today is a growing dependence upon Christian counseling at the expense of pastoral guidance. Some churches have become infatuated with "counseling." When someone has a problem with sin or in a relationship, they look for a professional counselor to help. This is not to say that the pastor is the only person to whom one should go for counsel, but that the godly pastor is *qualified* to counsel, whether or not he is *certified*. Actually, any mature believer should be competent to admonish (counsel) a fellow believer in need of direction or instruction. I do, however, strongly object to the current trend that is turning Christian admonition into a profession reserved for trained experts.

Christians should be aware that the fact that a counselor is a Christian does not guarantee that his counsel is biblical. Good, sound biblical counseling is the application of scriptural principles to the life of an individual with the goal of leading to changes that result in greater holiness of living. Dr. Jim Binney, a professional counselor himself, claims that there are over 450 different counseling systems with over 10,000 specific methodologies. Much of modern Christian counseling is just secular humanism with some Bible verses appended. Many counselors neglect the Holy Spirit's power to change an individual, and many are ignorant of biblical theology. Thus, many counselors replace biblical theology with psychological therapy. Holy living has been replaced with happy feelings. For the believers, it is more important that our counselors base their advice on the authority of Scripture than that they be certified professionals.

When looking for a good church, seek out one that does its best to think and act like a holy temple of God that is His flock and is the body and bride of Christ. A church like that will not use promotional tools that reflect secular philosophy. A good church must not prioritize popularity over purity, experience over doctrine, growth over godliness, man's perceived needs over God's revealed Word, cultural relevance over biblical absolutes, or Christian counseling over pastoral guidance. Churches that have fallen into these traps have forgotten that the church's business is not to make people happy, but to make them holy. When faced with a choice, there is far greater reward in being *right* than in being *happy*.

Spiritual Characteristics of a God-centered Ministry

A couple of comments Paul makes to the church in Rome provide good summaries of the qualities that characterize a godly ministry. In Romans 6:17, he says of that church, "God be thanked, that ye were the servants of sin, but ye have obeyed from the heart that form of doctrine which was delivered you." He has listed four important characteristics of a good church in reverse order, starting with the result and working toward the cause. Outward obedience comes from the heart steeped in biblical doctrine that has been faithfully delivered. Paul has indicated that Christian ministry begins with delivering the message—evangelizing the lost and discipling believers. Before anyone can "obey from the heart," the Gospel and doctrines of Christ must be taught. So we see that a good church is concerned for the lost and demonstrates a desire to deliver the Truth to those who need to believe.[2] Paul has also indicated that a godly ministry is built upon an emphasis on sound doctrine—the leadership of a good church is preaching and teaching "all the counsel of God" (Acts 20:27), and the people of a good church are *learning the Word*. As the Bible is taught and learned, hearts are changed—the people of a good church are *loving the Lord*. The result is a congregation that gives evidence of consistent obedience to Scripture—the people of a good church are *living the Truth*.

Paul gives further commendation of the members of the church in Rome when he says, "I myself also am persuaded of you, my brethren, that ye also are full of goodness, filled with all knowledge, able also to admonish one another" (Romans 15:14). These people were first of all "full of goodness." This goodness includes characteristics like kindness, thoughtfulness, hospitality, charity, and evangelistic zeal. But the word Paul uses describes a quality of goodness that extends to their *moral* character. Not only did they do good deeds, they actually were good people. In this same letter Paul had made it very clear that this goodness is not part of the natural human condition (Romans 3:10-23.) What could never be true of these people on their own was now not only possible but mandatory because of the work of the Holy Spirit in their hearts. A church full of people who have been truly transformed by the power of the Holy Spirit will be doing good works and behaving with moral integrity.

Further, the believers in Rome were "filled with all knowledge." To be complete in knowledge, a believer must have an academic comprehension of both what the Scriptures say and what God expects of him. But beyond that, Paul's expression extends to a depth of knowledge that includes complete submission to the Word and will of God resulting in its life-changing application. Being filled with all knowledge includes having learned to *think* like Christ (Romans 12:1-2; Philippians 2:5) and to *act* like Christ (Ephesians 4:1; 5:1). One of the most significant reasons for the church's failure to make an impact in our world today is that too few Christians know the Word of God well enough to think like Christ. And if you cannot think like Christ, you will not be able to act like Christ. Churches all across America are filled with people who are, for all practical purposes, biblically

illiterate. They cannot find the books of the Bible, let alone describe
the theology that is taught in them. A church membership who is
filled with all knowledge will prioritize both knowing and living the
Word of God.

Finally, the members of the church in Rome are described as "able
[competent] to admonish one another." They were able to teach others the truths of Scripture, because they knew the truth well enough
that they could communicate it effectively. That is an interesting contrast to what Hebrews 5:11-14 says of the audience to whom that
book was written.

Of whom [Christ] we have many things to say, and hard to be
uttered, seeing ye are dull of hearing. For when for the time ye
ought to be teachers, ye have need that one teach you again which
be the first principles of the oracles of God; and are become such
as have need of milk, and not of strong meat. For every one that
useth milk *is* unskilful in the word of righteousness: for he is a
babe. But strong meat belongeth to them that are of full age, *even*
those who by reason of use have their senses exercised to discern
both good and evil.

The ability to admonish one another that characterized the believers
in Rome went beyond academic instruction. Paul says that they had
the power to effect a positive change in one another's lives by their
loving admonition. Just as the knowledge we are to have must get
beyond our heads and into our hearts, so our instruction in the Word is
to reach beyond the heads of others and affect a change of heart.
Such admonition includes an element of warning, to correct something that may be wrong. It includes the goal of building up to maturity, "Till we all come in the unity of the faith, and of the knowledge
of the Son of God, unto a perfect man, unto the measure of the stature
of the fullness of Christ" (Ephesians 4:13). It also includes communication in an attitude of loving humility (Galatians 6:1). A good
church is full of people who care enough about others to gently and
lovingly point them in the right direction and encourage them to grow
in the Lord.

A good church, then, will demonstrate the spiritual characteristics of
godliness in ministry. Obviously, these things will be true to varying

degrees among the people of any particular congregation. Spiritual growth is an individual matter, and every church will include a wide range of maturity levels among its members. But in a good church the general atmosphere among the people and the public ministry of the church should give evidence that they are making progress toward these goals.

Practical Characteristics of a Committed Membership

Ideally, your church home will show evidence of a committed membership. The people in a good church will, first of all, be *committed to the truth*. The most vital quality in a church is that they teach those things that are right. As Paul told Timothy, "but continue thou in the things which thou has learned and hast been assured of" (2 Timothy 3:14), every believer needs a church that will encourage continuity in the truth. But if the church is really biblical in its emphasis, and not just superficially so, its members will also be *committed to holy living*. God's purpose in breathing-out ("inspiring") His Word is "that the man of God may be perfect, throughly furnished unto all good works" (2 Timothy 3:17). The church that truly learns the Word will live by it. It should be fairly easy to tell if these things are true of a church, because the people will also be *committed to one another*. Many of us act as if we do not know how Jesus completed this statement—"By this shall all men know that ye are my disciples, if ye..." There are many things He *might* have said, but only one thing He *did* say. He told His disciples that the most important way they could demonstrate their love for Him was that they "have love one to another" (John 13:35). Authentic Christianity will be demonstrated among a people who are committed to one another.

When you have to look for a new church, you will not find a perfect one. Every church is made up of people at various stages of spiritual growth, and none of them are flawless. But some churches are better than others, and you should try to find a *good* one. Evaluate its strengths and weigh them against its weaknesses. Identify ways in which that church can help you and your family become better representatives of Christ, and be wary of ways it might exert a negative influence on your lives and in the community. Also, be alert to ways in which you can contribute to that church's fulfillment of its God-given responsibilities as you seek to glorify the Lord as you minister within the framework of the local church. Do your best to find a church that "seeks first the Kingdom of God, and His righteousness" (Matthew 6:33). Its priorities should be *eternal* prosperity and *genuine* spirtiuality.

---

[1] Vance Havner, *It is Time*, [New York: Fleming H. Revell, 1943], p. 35.

[2] See Chapter Twelve on evangelism and Chapter Thirteen on missions.

CHAPTER 4
IS IT NECESSARY FOR ME TO
JOIN A LOCAL CHURCH?

In February, 1980, a friend and I were on our way to pick up our wives from a teachers' convention. The Winter Olympics were nearing conclusion, and the gold-medal hockey game was to be played that night, so we stopped at a hotel early enough to watch the match on television. No United States hockey team had ever won an Olympic gold medal, and the all-amateur US team was badly overmatched by the experienced professional team from the Soviet Union. It promised to be another crushing victory for the Russians. But on this night the outcome would be different. I'll never forget the rush of excitement as the final buzzer sounded and the United States team was victorious. Tim and I screamed and yelled and jumped around the room like idiots. We were not alone in our euphoria—people throughout the hotel were going out into the halls to congratulate perfect strangers, celebrating an historic victory, shouting "We won! We won!" But for all of our joy, for all of the enthusiastic shouts, the truth is that none of *us* had won the game. We had fun watching, but the medals went to the men on the ice.

In the Olympic Games, or any other athletic competition, there are at least two categories of people: the participants and the spectators. The goal of the participants is to do their best as competitors in the various contests. The intent of the spectators is to enjoy the *thrill* of competition without the *commitment*. The spectators can enjoy victory without effort and can endure loss without cost. There may be interest, or even enthusiasm, but the prize goes to those personally involved. Much of professing Christianity today more closely resembles the spectators than the competitors. But God expects His church to be a well-run organization, with a regenerate and responsible membership which gathers to *participate in*, not just *watch*, real worship.

Evidence of Membership in the New Testament Church

When Luke recorded the events on the day of Pentecost, he concluded by saying, "there were added *unto them* about three thousand souls" (Acts 2:41). Those new converts were added to whom or to what? They were added to that invisible collection of all believers in the body of Christ, but they were also added to the local assembly in Jerusalem. Luke went on to say that those new converts "continued steadfastly in the apostles' doctrine and fellowship, and in [the] breaking of [the] bread, and in prayers" (2:42). Those new converts immediately began to study, fellowship, and worship with the other believers in an organized manner. In the days that followed, still more believed. After giving us a little information about their relationship with one another, Luke tells us that "the Lord added to the church daily such as should be saved" (Acts 2:47). The church continued to have new people added to its membership.

There are at least five general evidences that official records of membership were kept in the first-century church. As we have just seen, *the church kept track of its numbers* from the very day of its inception. As a matter of fact, numerical records were kept *before* Pentecost. Acts 1:15 says that at the prayer meetings that preceded Pentecost "the number of names together were about a hundred and twenty."[1] Not only did they keep track of how many were present, there seems to have been a list of names recording who belonged to the group. It is likely that it was to this roll that the new converts at Pentecost were added. It was with this group that the new believers mentioned in Acts 2:42 studied the Word ("continued steadfastly in the apostles' doctrine"), shared ("fellowship"), commemorated the Lord's sacrifice and resurrection ("[the] breaking of [the] bread"[4]), and prayed. Each of these activities implies both a high degree of organization and an official list of accepted participants.

By the time Peter and John were compelled to testify before the high priest (Acts 4:3-7), the number of members in the church at Jerusalem had swollen to about five thousand men. Evidently, *the church compiled detailed membership records.* These records included more than just names. This passage implies recording of gender, since there seem to have been either separate lists of men and women or a single list with gender indicated. Years later, Paul's instructions to Timothy as the pastor of the church at Ephesus included, "Let not a widow be taken into the number under threescore years old, having been the wife of one man" (1 Tim. 5:9). In this context, Paul is not talking about denying a younger widow church membership. He is talking about church support for elderly widows who have no living progeny (5:3-4). The significance of Paul's instructions to this discussion is that it seems to require that the church be keeping records of each member's age, probably including birth dates, each member's marital status, and information concerning their immediate and extended families.

Further evidence of official membership is seen in the fact that *the church held elections.* In Acts 1:16-26 the assembled believers elected one from among the group to serve as a replacement for Judas among the Twelve. In Acts 6:2-7 the church at Jerusalem elected[3] seven deacons from among their number. By that time, the total membership, which had been over 5000 in Acts 4, had multiplied. It is unlikely that in a body that large every individual would be well known and easily identifiable as a voting member without some kind of official list. Later, the church at Antioch elected representatives to accompany Paul and Barnabas to a church council meeting in Jerusalem (Acts 15:22). Such elections are possible only among an organized body whose membership is a matter of record. Those elected were nominated from a specific roll, and those appointing them were the rest of that specific group.

The fact that *the church disciplined its members* provides a fourth evidence of the keeping of official records. In 1 Corinthians 5, Paul chided the church at Corinth for having failed to maintain discipline in their church. He said, "It is reported commonly *that there is* fornication among you" (5:1), and told them that "he that hath done this deed" should be "taken away from among you" (5:2). He concludes by commanding, "put away from among yourselves that wicked person" (5:13). More will be said later about church discipline, but it is important now to see the recurrence of the phrase "among you." The sinner that was to be disciplined was one of their members, and the disciplinary action commanded seems to have involved removal of his name from their roll in order to officially remove his person from their fellowship (5:11).

A fifth general evidence of record keeping is that *church organization and structure required such records.* For the church to have officers, records must be kept so people would know who they were and how they lived, or they could not have examined their lives for specific qualifications (Phil. 1:1; 1 Tim. 3:1-13). For a church to have stated times for meetings there must have been at least some keeping of records in order to communicate with those involved (Acts 20:7; 1 Cor. 11:20; 14:26; 16:2). A church's practice of the ordinances of baptism (Acts 2:38) and the Lord's Supper (1 Cor. 11:23-26), implies the need to keep records of baptized believers who were permitted to fellowship in the Lord's Supper. For a church to have recognized customs and traditions providing some continuity among the community of believers, records would certainly be helpful, and perhaps necessary (1 Cor. 11:16; 2 Thes. 2:15; 3:6). For a church to have an order for worship, a structure for their meetings, they must have been comprised of a particular membership (1 Cor. 14:40; Col. 2:5). Further, the organization's functions in electing representatives (1 Cor. 16:3; 2 Cor. 8:19), in receiving or rejecting members (Rom. 16:1-2; 1 Tim. 5:9), in disciplining members (1 Cor. 5), and in recommending members to other churches (Acts 18:27; Rom. 16:1-2; 2 Cor. 3:1) strongly implies the church's authority over a specific membership, along with adequate records of who those members are.

While it may overstate it to *insist* that membership in a local church in the New Testament was a definite recorded relationship involving the use of a formal roll or register, the evidence supports such a conclusion. Membership is necessary for the church's ministry. Membership is necessary for the church's purity. Non-membership is irresponsible and disobedient. The concept of a believer who was not a member of a local church is completely foreign to Acts and the Epistles. Jesus' parable concerning the wheat and the tares indicates that the final judgment will sort out true believers from those among us who are not converted, and this may have application to unregenerate church members. However, the tares represent unbelievers who are present by stealth, hypocritically pretending to be something they are not. The commission to the church is to preach to all, and disciple the converts. That discipling is carried out primarily through the ministry of the local church as it nurtures its members, and the membership is assumed to be comprised *only* of believers. Further, Acts and the Epistles assume that *every* believer would join the membership of a local church.

Qualifications for Membership in the New Testament Church

The first requirement for local church membership is regeneration— the new life imparted to the believer, commonly called the new birth (John 3:1-21; 1 Pet. 1:23). The *ground*, or basis, for the new birth is the finished work of Jesus Christ: His death, burial, and resurrection (John 3:14-21; 1 Cor. 15:1-4). The *means* of the new birth is personal faith in the finished work of Jesus Christ (Rom. 10:9-10), accomplished by the inner working of the Holy Spirit in response to the Word of God (Rom. 10:17; Eph. 2:8-9). The *evidence* of the new birth is the fruit of the Spirit produced in the life of the believer. The change that occurs is called conversion and is the result of repentance (Gal. 5:22-23; Acts 3:19).

The fact that this regeneration is a necessary prerequisite for church membership is evidenced in several ways. First, it is implied in the commission the Lord Jesus gave the church.

> Go ye therefore, and teach all nations, baptizing them in the name of the Father, and of the Son, and of the Holy Ghost: Teaching them to observe all things whatsoever I have commanded you: and, lo, I am with you always, even unto the end of the world (Matt. 28:19-20; cf. Mark 16:15-16; Luke 24:46-48; Acts 1:8).

People must first believe and be baptized before they begin to be discipled as members of a church. Even the name *church* (*ekklesia*) implies the need for regeneration for membership. Those who are the summoned assembly are called out from among the general populace to a particular purpose in which they are each an active participant. The first church set the example of a regenerate membership in Acts 2:37-47. Before they were added to the church, the listeners had to believe the message and give evidence of conversion by publicly identifying with Christ through baptism. Further, if the universal church is made up of *all* believers, then the local church should be composed of *only* believers. Otherwise the local church could not function as a visible entity representing the whole. Finally, most of the New Testament Epistles were written to believers and addressed to local churches or their pastors. This implies that the believers were members of local assemblies and that only believers were members of the local assemblies.

The second requirement for local church membership is baptism. Historically, Baptists received their name because of the practice of immersion of the believer in water as a testimony of his faith in Christ and as a public identification with Christ (Acts 2:37-47). There are two primary reasons for practicing baptism by immersion. First, the undisputed meaning of the Greek word *baptizo* is "to immerse." It is a word that was commonly used for the process of dying fabric— which is not accomplished by sprinkling or pouring dye on the cloth, but by immersing the cloth in the dye. It is also used in classic Greek literature to describe what happened to a person who drowned or to a ship that sank. The significance of the word involves going completely into the water. Second, immersion best illustrates the believer's identification with Jesus Christ in His death, burial, and resurrection (Rom. 6:3-11). Coming out of the water is significant as a picture of resurrection.

Baptism is seen in the New Testament as a public testimony of personal faith in Christ—a sort of "pledge of allegiance" to the Lord. It is not necessary for salvation, but baptism is commanded by Scripture and required for local church membership. *Acceptance* by God is based on the blood of Jesus Christ, and we cannot add to that. *Pleasing* God involves obeying Him as the Bible directs us. Baptism has nothing to do with being made *acceptable* to God, but is the first step to *pleasing* Him. It also places the believer on record among the brethren as his testimony that they should be able to see an ever more complete reflection of Jesus Christ in him.

There are several indications in the New Testament that baptism was required for church membership. First, it is indicated in the commission given to the church. *Going* and *teaching* preceded *baptizing* (Matt. 28:19-20). Second, as we have already seen, this order is indicated by the example of the first local church in Jerusalem (Acts 2:37-47). The sequence of events was that they believed, then they were baptized, and then they were added to the church. Third, this order is indicated in virtually every New Testament reference to baptism. For instance, the conversion of the Ethiopian eunuch was followed by baptism (Acts 8:37); when Cornelius and his household believed, they were baptized (Acts 10:47-48); the jailer of Philippi was baptized after he believed (Acts 16:31-33); and Apollos and his company were *re*-baptized in Jesus' name after they believed the instruction they were given concerning Christ and the Holy Spirit (Acts 19:2-5). Fourth, baptism's requirement for church membership is indicated in its close relation to salvation as the outward expression of the believer's faith (Rom. 6:1-4), since members must be saved and publicly testify of their salvation. Fifth, since all believers are commanded to be baptized (Mark 16:16; Acts 2:38; 10:48), accepting as a church member a professing believer who was not baptized would amount to consciously bringing a disobedient believer into the membership of the church.

Barring some medical or physical factor that might prohibit it, as in the case of the thief on the cross, the only reasons one could have for refusing to be baptized would be that he is not truly saved or he is unwilling to obey the Lord's command. In either case, he should not be a member of the local church, which seeks purity among its members. If the applicant for membership is unbaptized only because he has not understood its importance, he should be willing to submit to baptism as a precondition of his membership upon receiving adequate instruction. Additionally, there is clear historical precedent beyond the biblical record of the first century. While denominational groups have varied in the *way* they have practiced this ordinance, the majority of church groups both past and present have required baptism for church membership.

Those who would join a local New Testament church must first of all be regenerated, born again by grace through faith in the finished work of Jesus Christ. They must testify of that faith by being identi-

fied with Christ in baptism. Only baptized believers are members of
the local church that follows the New Testament pattern, and every
believer ought to be baptized and an active member of a good local
church. The Olympic athlete is known by the uniform he wears.
Even so, a Christian is marked by the reputation of the local church
with which he is identified. If it is a sound New Testament church, he
will be recognized as a saved, baptized person who is seeking to be
obedient to the teachings of his Lord. If he refuses to join a local
New Testament church, he is seen as an observer, not a participant. If
he does join, he accepts responsibility for enhancing that church's reputation for Christlikeness.

---

[1] It could be argued that Luke's use of an approximate number ("about
120") implies that there was *not* a fixed register, especially since he
sometimes gives exact numbers, like 276 survivors of a shipwreck (Acts
27:37). However, it should be remembered that Luke was present at the
shipwreck described in Acts 27 and was not present at the meeting
described in Acts 1. When recording events in which he was not an eye-
witness, Luke often used approximate numbers, and that should not
imply that exact records were not kept. For instance, it should not be
assumed that there was no record of Jesus' birth date simply because
Luke 3:23 says Jesus was "about thirty years of age" when He began His
ministry.

[2] The definite articles I've inserted are in the Greek text but were omitted
by the King James translators. They are significant because the phrase
has special reference to the Lord's Supper. Without the definite articles,
the phrase may be misunderstood as if it simply referred to the congregation's dining together.

[3] The Greek word implies voting by lifting of the hand.

PART II
YOUR RESPONSIBILITIES
WITHIN THE LOCAL CHURCH

CHAPTER 5
THE ELEMENTS OF TRUE WORSHIP

It is not at all uncommon for professing believers today to explain that they rarely attend church because they can worship God in their own home, or at the lake, or on the golf course. Writing in *The Superstitions of the Irreligious* (Macmillan, 1951), George Hedley made the following insightful observation:

> It is possible to worship God while driving along the highway or sitting in a baseball park. But if we raise the question of statistical probability, the worship of God is scarcely as frequent in those places as in houses built in his honor. There is the story of the father who said, "Come on, we can sing hymns on the beach," to which the little girl replied, "But we won't, will we?"

Certainly, worship is not restricted to a particular place nor limited to a single day of the week, and everything we do is to be an act of worship to the glory of God. But a believer is not to be an island unto himself. Granted, there can and should be private worship, but corporate worship within the local church is also vital.

Much has been said in recent years about the worship of the church. In an attempt to emphasize the idea of worship in their services, many churches are simply changing the job title of their minister of music, calling him the "worship leader." While it is good for us to recognize that we are to gather for *worship*, few people have a clear idea of what that means. Most churches call their Sunday morning service a worship service. Does that mean that showing up for church and sitting through the hour (or so) means that we have worshipped? Not necessarily. There are many things done in churches that are not very worshipful—that do not redound to the glory of God. It is important for Christians to understand what the Scriptures teach are the *elements* of true worship. While it would be impossible to make a comprehensive list of every aspect of worship, there are at least eight specific elements of biblical worship that should be considered: prayer, praise, confession of sin, confession of faith, reading of Scripture, preaching, commemoration of Christ's sacrifice, and giving. While some of these elements could be practiced on the beach or in a tree stand, many of them require assembling with other believers as a church. Private worship is certainly possible, even commanded, but gathering with other believers for worship is also necessary.

Prayer

Prayer can be defined a number of ways. Obviously, if we are to "pray without ceasing" (1 Thes. 5:17), prayer in its broader sense must go well beyond that which we do when we gather together and bow our heads and our hearts to God. In this sense, prayer might be described as "an attitude of constant communication with and complete dependence upon God." But in the context of corporate worship, prayer should be defined in the narrow, specific sense of "petitions brought before God." In the Sermon on the Mount, the Lord Jesus told His audience that when they pray they should enter the closet and pray in secret (Matt. 6:6). His point was that prayer is not to be a spectacle to attract attention. There ought to be personal, private times of prayer to God. But the Bible also tells us that we are to pray together, as a body, joining our hearts in lifting petitions to God as a church family. It is obvious from even a superficial reading of the Book of Acts that corporate prayer was a foundational element in the worship of the early church.

In Acts 1:12-14 we find that when Christ ascended to the Father the disciples returned to Jerusalem, met in "an upper room," and "continued with one accord in prayer and supplication." While awaiting the coming of the promised Comforter, the believers were gathered for corporate prayer. The earliest activity of the assembled believers was

prayer. The first service of the assembled believers following the
Lord's ascension was a prayer meeting. A truly Christian service
without prayer is almost unthinkable. A church that gathers for
preaching, or programs, or meals, or for any other purpose, but does
not pray together, omits an essential element of their worship.
Corporate prayer is one of the cornerstones of Christian worship. And
we are not speaking of a ritualistic, formula prayer, but a genuine
"hearts in one accord" lifting of our petitions to God. This idea of
being in one accord is a recurrent theme throughout the Book of Acts.
It is important to note that "one accord" might also have been translated "single passion." This is more than merely a passive acceptance of
the majority's will. It involves each believer's active participation in
the unified mind and activity of the assembled believers.

In the aftermath of Pentecost, opposition to the fledgling church
grew. The more pressure the church experienced, the more they
depended upon prayer. The fourth chapter of Acts recounts the Jewish
council's reaction to the preaching of Peter and John. After they were
warned to stop their preaching and threatened with punishment if they
continued, Peter and John "went to their own company, and reported
all that the chief priests and elders had said unto them" (Acts 4:23).
The following seven verses (4:24-30) tell us that the assembled
believers immediately "lifted up their voice to God with one accord."
When faced with difficulty, they prayed—with a single voice and a
single mind. Prayer was not only practiced in the early church, prayer
was encouraged by the trials of the early church. People and churches
pray more when circumstances are difficult than they do when they
are easy. Sometimes God sends trials into our lives, and into the corporate life of the church, for the express purpose of forcing us to pray.
We cannot truly worship God unless we lift our hearts and voices in
prayer.

Praise

A second element of true worship is praise. In some churches the
congregations are quite reserved, and if someone were to shout
"Amen! Praise the Lord!" during the preaching, a dozen folks would
go into cardiac arrest. In other churches the walls fairly ring with the
shouts of the gathered believers. At first glance, it would seem that
the latter church is more faithfully including praise in their worship.

But that is not necessarily so. In many cases, energetic vocal praise during a church service may well be nothing more than showmanship, which would make it the antithesis of true praise. Further, genuine praise of God involves much more than simply shouting, "Praise the Lord!" *True praise of God involves confession of God's nature and works.*

God knows who He is and what He has done better than we do. Yet He tells us to praise Him for who He is and for what He has done. Why? Is it because God likes that swelled-head feeling that you or I might get from hearing nice things said about us? No! That would make God as prone to pride and as susceptible to flattery as we are. Praise is not for God's benefit, as if God, who is altogether perfect in every way, could possibly be benefited. God demands our praise so we will recognize and confess the truth about who He is for our own good. It is impossible to come to God for redemption without first recognizing the One True God. To worship in spirit and in truth, we must know the One True God who really exists.

The church offers this praise in prayer. The passage cited earlier from Acts 4 in which the church prayed following the report from Peter and John is a good example. The first five verses of that prayer involve adoration of God for having created all things, citation of the teaching of the Word of God that His servants could expect opposition, application of the Scriptures to the reaction of the leaders against Christ Jesus, and recognition that all of these events were a part of God's sovereign will. There is not really a statement of thanksgiving in this prayer, simply a recitation of the truth about who God is. All of that constitutes praise. They didn't ask for anything until they got to the last two verses of the prayer, and then all they asked for was boldness to preach the Word in spite of the threats of the authorities—and that request was immediately granted.

The church also offers this praise in song. The Psalms abound with examples of genuine and specific praise. Psalm 19:1 says, "The heavens declare the glory of God; and the firmament showeth his handiwork." The psalmist then goes on to list specific ways in which this is true. Psalm 100 identifies itself as a "Psalm of praise." Then it starts with commands to worship in song: "Make a joyful noise unto the LORD, all ye lands. Serve the LORD with gladness: come before his presence with singing." It continues with praise for God's creation and the fact that believers are His people. Similarly, the resurrected church is shown in Revelation 4 and 5 singing praise to God for the two greatest demonstrations of His power and love: creation and redemption. The Scriptures imply that praising God in song may be the highest means of expressing worship of God. You cannot worship God in spirit and in truth without participating in public prayer and songs of praise.

This has enormous implications for the kind of music we use. Too many of us select our music on the basis of carnal enjoyment rather than spiritual edification. When we criticize traditional church music as "boring," we reveal a great deal about our spiritual condition. What we call "exciting" or "boring" usually has little or nothing to do with its spiritual content and everything to do with our physical response to the music. We reveal ourselves to be controlled by the flesh rather than the Spirit if we make our personal likes and dislikes the primary criteria for determining what music we use. On the basis of Philippians 4:8 we can determine that our music must be excellent, true, honest, righteous, reputable, virtuous and praiseworthy. We should neither waste our time or talents nor harm our spirits with music that is false, dishonest, unrighteous, impure, ugly, disreputable, licentious, or shameful. We must not ask, "Will this music appeal to sinful men?" but "Is this music acceptable to a Holy God?"[1]

Confession of Sin

At the heart of true worship, and as the basis for all prayer and praise, is the confession of personal sin. When the worthiness of God is exalted, the unworthiness of man cannot go unnoticed. When confronted by Jesus in Luke 5:8, Peter said "depart from me for I am a sinful man, O Lord." When Isaiah "saw the Lord high and lifted up..." (Isaiah 6:1), he immediately confessed "woe is me for I am undone, because I *am* a man of unclean lips" (Isaiah 6:5). Jesus said that the prayer heard in the Temple was the penitent prayer of the publican, not the self-congratulatory prayer of the Pharisee (Luke 18:9ff). If you praise little, it may be that you believe yourself guilty of little sin and in need of only a little Savior.

This confession of sin is demonstrated in public, either when establishing your relationship with your church or in restoring your fellowship with the church. I am not suggesting a public recitation of a *list* of your sins, but a public admission of the *fact* that you are a sinner. Baptism, as introduced by John, was a response to a call to repentance and conversion. Peter called on the audience at Pentecost to be baptized as a public acknowledgment of personal repentance (Acts 2:38). A believer's baptism is a public confession that he is a sinner who needs to be identified with Christ's sacrifice for his sins. Public confession of *specific* sin is indicated in cases of church discipline (1 Cor. 5; cf. 2 Cor. 2:5-11). The one excommunicated for persistent sinful behavior, who wished to be forgiven and restored to fellowship, seems to have made public confession. There is also solid historic evidence that the post-apostolic church continued to practice public confession for restoration.

Confession of sin is also practiced in private. It is important throughout the life of the believer, not to continually revalidate his conversion, but to re-establish full fellowship with God. The Apostle John, writing to believers, says: "If we say that we have no sin, we deceive ourselves, and the truth is not in us. If we confess our sins, he is faithful and just to forgive us *our* sins and to cleanse us from all unrighteousness" (1 John 1:8-9). We cannot worship God in spirit and in truth without confession of sin.

Confession of Faith

Besides prayer, praise, and confession of sins, worship also includes a confession of faith. In its simplest form, the faith we must confess is "Jesus is Lord." Romans 10:9-10 tells us "That if thou shalt confess with thy mouth the Lord Jesus [or 'that Jesus is Lord'], and shalt believe in thine heart that God hath raised him from the dead, thou shalt be saved. For with the heart man believeth unto righteousness, and with the mouth confession is made unto salvation." But this confession of faith is not merely a magic phrase that communicates grace by its recitation. It is the conscious recognition and public profession of belief that the man known as Jesus of Nazareth is the sovereign Lord of the universe, the Messiah, the Son of God. You do not need to confess that this man is Jesus, but that Jesus is both Lord and Christ. That is precisely what Peter confessed in Matthew 16:16,

"Thou art the Christ, the Son of the Living God," and what Thomas confessed in John 20:28 when he called Jesus "My Lord and my God." That is also what John said we need to believe when he stated the purpose of his Gospel: "that ye might believe that Jesus is the Christ, the Son of God, and that believing ye might have life through his name" (John 20:31).

This confession of faith is necessary for salvation as an initial act of worship. Following our salvation, we confess our faith in Jesus as our Lord by the testimony of our public baptism, by our verbal witness, and by our actions. Every time we choose to resist temptation and do right, every time we make a decision to obey His will, we acknowledge His lordship over us. Conversely, every time we choose to give in to temptation, to disobey, we deny His lordship, just as Peter did. A consistent confession of faith, acknowledging Jesus as Lord, is essential to true worship.

Reading of Scripture

A fifth element essential for Christian worship is the reading of Scripture. The early church practiced the public reading of Scripture, but private study was also commended (Acts 17:11). The importance of the Word of God is stressed throughout Scripture. This emphasis was seen in Christ's ministry. When faced with temptation by Satan or when challenged by His detractors, Jesus responded by quoting Scripture. He was often in the synagogues teaching from the Scriptures. When praying for believers, Jesus asked the Father to "Sanctify them by thy truth; thy word is truth" (John 17:17). The public reading of Scripture was commanded by Paul and practiced in the church from the beginning. In 1 Thessalonians 5:27 Paul says, "I charge you by the Lord that this epistle be read unto all the holy brethren." Paul told Timothy, "Till I come, give attendance to reading, to exhortation, to doctrine" (1 Tim. 4:13). The church's worship must include the reading of the Word of God.

Preaching

While few would dispute the importance of reading Scripture to true worship, the preaching of the Word has become unfashionable. Many churches today gather for what they call worship services, "praise gatherings," or "celebrations," then neglect the preaching and teaching of the Bible. By calling their music director the worship leader, they have subtly identified the preacher as something other than a worship leader. As a consequence, the preaching of the Word of God is being marginalized by those who imply that it is less important than other elements of the service.

Preaching is essential to meet four great needs in the worship of the church: education, edification, exhortation, and evangelization. *Education* involves training the church in the Word of God. In 2 Timothy 2:2, Paul challenged Timothy by saying, "And the things that thou hast heard of me among many witnesses, the same commit thou to faithful men, who shall be able to teach others also." *Edification* involves strengthening the church by the Word of God. This is the significance of Paul's statement in Ephesians 4:11-13. God gave the church gifted individuals, identified as apostles, prophets, evangelists, and pastor-teachers. While accurately defining these functions is important, the significance to this discussion is that each of these is involved in the public ministry of the Word of God. They are given "for the perfecting of the saints for the work of the ministry, for the edifying of the body of Christ: till we all come in the unity of the faith, and of the knowledge of the Son of God, unto a perfect man, unto the measure of the stature of the fullness of Christ." God intends that the preaching of the Word be a part of our worship so that we will all become more like Christ. *Exhortation* involves motivating the church in the Word of God, challenging believers to change, to act, to exercise our faith. This is what Paul meant in 2 Timothy 4:2, when he said, "Preach the word; be instant in season, out of season; reprove, rebuke, exhort with all longsuffering and doctrine." *Evangelization* involves winning the lost through the Word of God. Romans 10:14 asks, "How then shall they call on him in whom they have not believed? And how shall they believe in him of whom they have not heard? And how shall they hear without a preacher?" We are also told that "it pleased God by the foolishness of preaching to save them that believe" (1 Cor. 1:21).

Those who insist that they can worship God privately are not entirely wrong. We can and should worship God in all our activities. However, we cannot worship God *adequately* without attending and giving attention to the preaching of the Word of God.

Commemoration of Christ's Sacrifice and Resurrection

Every Sunday when the church gathers for worship, we commemorate Christ's sacrifice and His resurrection. The whole point of worshipping on the first day of the week is that Sunday is Resurrection
Day. But another element vital to Christian worship is formal commemoration of Christ's sacrifice and resurrection in the service commonly referred to as Communion, or the Lord's Supper. The Apostle
Paul gives some instruction for this memorial:

> For I have received of the Lord that which also I delivered unto
> you, That the Lord Jesus the *same* night in which he was betrayed
> took bread: And when he had given thanks, he brake *it*, and said,
> Take, eat: this is my body, which is broken for you: this do in
> remembrance of me. After the same manner also *he took* the cup,
> when he had supped, saying, This cup is the new testament in my
> blood: this do ye, as oft as ye drink *it,* in remembrance of me.
> For as often as ye eat this bread, and drink this cup, ye do show
> the Lord's death till he come. (1 Corinthians 11:23-26)

This is an ordinance given to the local church. It is administered by
the local church during their worship services held on the first day of
the week. Some churches hold this memorial weekly, some monthly,
and some quarterly or even less often. Some limit participation to
their own membership; others permit anyone attending to participate
according to their own conscience. But the Lord's Supper is a com-
memorative service of the church that requires assembling the believers. It is not an aspect of worship that a believer can practice properly
apart from the community of a local church. And regular participation in the Lord's Supper is an important part of our worship.

Giving

"Now concerning the collection for the saints, as I have given order
to the churches of Galatia, even so do ye. Upon the first *day* of the
week let every one of you lay be him in store, as *God* hath prospered
him" (1 Cor. 16:1-2). God expects us to contribute financially to
Christian ministry as a part of our assembly for worship on the first
day of the week. Some churches pass an offering plate between the
song service and the sermon, others at the close of the service. Still
others do not pass an offering plate at all, using a collection box in the

foyer or in front of the pulpit. It is not the method of collection but the fact of it that is significant. God intends His work to be financed by the giving of His people. In Philippians 4:16-19, Paul commends the church at Philippi for having "sent once and again to my necessity." He describes their financial gifts as "an odor of a sweet smell, a sacrifice acceptable, well pleasing to God." Their giving was an act of worship. Giving to the support of the work of the church is an important part of our worship.

Worship is not to be limited to the eight elements just named. We must avoid reducing worship to ritual and restricting it to certain activities. Our worship is to be *comprehensive*. Every aspect of our lives is to be an act of worship. "Whether therefore ye eat, or drink, or whatsoever ye do, do all to the glory of God" (1 Cor. 10:31). We are to apply the elements of worship to life's situations. Every choice, every act, every thought is to be brought into subjection to Christ. When we do all things to the glory of God, we worship Him in all that we do. It would be impossible to make a comprehensive list of everything that is part of worship. All of our lives ought to be a symphony of worship to the Lord. But there are specific elements of worship that we are commanded to practice corporately. These are not rituals we perform to appease God. Rather, the elements that make up our Christian worship are aspects of our fellowship with God. They help us see His worthiness and our unworthiness. They help us know God.

---

[1] My undergraduate degree is in music education, so the music of the church is especially important to me. I've included as an appendix, "Why Cling to a Conservative/Traditional Music Standard?" This is a revision of a paper I originally prepared for presentation at the Georgia Association of Christian Schools state teachers' convention in September, 1999. An abbreviated version of it appeared under the same title in *Frontline Magazine*, Vol. 10, No. 5 (Sept/Oct 2000), pp. 8-10.

Chater 6
The Essence of True Worship

A friend of mine has a job that occasionally involves some travel. For several months, he was required to fly from Wilmington to Charlotte every Tuesday morning and return in the evening. He always took the same shuttle, and actually became pretty well acquainted with the crew on that particular flight. One Friday morning he had to go to Atlanta. He had an especially bad morning, including car trouble on the way to the airport that resulted in his having to hitch a ride the rest of the way. Arriving only minutes before his plane was to leave, he dashed to his usual gate, waved his ticket at the familiar attendant, and boarded the plane. He stowed his bags, settled into his seat, finally able to breathe a sigh of relief that he had made it. The pilot began his routine introduction, naming the airline, flight number, and destination. As he told the passengers that he hoped they would enjoy their flight to Charlotte, my friend suddenly realized that he was on the wrong plane. He had been so distracted by the circumstances of the morning that he had gone through his familiar routine without thinking about what he was doing, and nearly ended up in the wrong city.[1]

One of the greatest threats to our worship is the human tendency to fall into routines. In John 4:19-26 we find a portion of the conversation between Jesus and the Samaritan woman of Sychar:

The woman saith unto him, Sir, I perceive that thou art a prophet.

Our fathers worshipped in this mountain; and ye say, that in Jerusalem is the place where men ought to worship. Jesus saith unto her, Woman, believe me, the hour cometh, when ye shall neither in this mountain, nor yet at Jerusalem, worship the Father. Ye worship ye know not what: we know what we worship: for salvation is of the Jews. But the hour cometh, and now is, when the true worshippers shall worship the Father in spirit and in truth: for the Father seeketh such to worship him. God *is* a Spirit: and they that worship him must worship *him* in spirit and in truth. The woman saith unto him, I know that Messias cometh, which is called Christ: when he is come, he will tell us all things. Jesus saith unto her, I that speak unto thee am *he.*

The statements of the Samaritan woman indicate that she thought worship consisted of performing rituals in the correct location. In the same way, it is possible for the church to gather faithfully with the intent of worshipping the Lord, yet reduce the various elements of worship to mere ritual. Our prayers may be superficial and repetitive. Our praise may be meaningless or self-serving. Our confession of sin may be insincere. Our confession of faith may be done by rote. Our reading of Scripture may be unfocused and ritualistic. Our preaching may be man-centered and pointless. Our commemoration of Christ's sacrifice may be careless. Our giving may be half-hearted or resentful. We go through the motions, but we have not worshipped.

In John 17:17, Jesus asked the Father to "sanctify them by thy truth; thy word is truth." In the introduction to John's Gospel, Jesus is identified as the living Word, full of grace and truth (John 1:1-14), and John 14:6 records Jesus' claim to be "the truth." When considered in the context of Jesus' instruction to the Samaritan woman, it seems evident that worshipping God "in Spirit and in truth" has two applications. First, our worship must be a genuinely heartfelt desire to commune with God, not just a ritualistic practice of showing up at church. It must be based upon the true teaching of the written Word of God, not a subjective, feelings-oriented gathering for some kind of "encounter with God." Second, our worship must be a communion by the power of the Holy Spirit of God, accomplished through the Living Truth of God in Jesus Christ. Therefore, practicing and sustaining true Christian worship requires focusing on the Persons of the

Lord Jesus Christ and the Holy Spirit, and their relationships to the elements of worship.

The Essence of Christian Worship in the Person of Jesus Christ

We are to pray in the Name of the Son. In John 16:23 Jesus told His disciples, "And in that day ye shall ask me nothing. Verily, verily, I say unto you, Whatsoever ye shall ask the Father in my name, he will give it you." To pray "in Jesus' name" is not a magic formula that we tag on at the end of a prayer so God will have to do what we want. Praying in Jesus' name means that we recognize that we are Christ's ambassadors, acting on His behalf in His absence. God is not a cosmic genie who is obligated to grant our wishes. God has given His people certain responsibilities to fulfill for His glory. We have been promised anything we need to accomplish the glorification of the Father. Anything else I might ask for, I am requesting in my name, not Jesus' name.

We are to praise the works of God in the Son. In Ephesians 1:3-14, the Apostle Paul gives us a beautiful recitation of the spiritual blessings that are given to us by God.

Blessed be the God and Father of our Lord Jesus Christ, who hath blessed us with all spiritual blessing in heavenly *places* in Christ: According as he hath chosen us in him before the foundation of the world, that we should be holy and without blame before him in love: Having predestinated us unto the adoption of children by Jesus Christ to himself, according to the good pleasure of his will, To the praise of the glory of his grace, wherein he hath made us accepted in the beloved. In whom we have redemption through his blood, the forgiveness of sins, according to the riches of his grace; Wherein he hath abounded toward us in all wisdom and prudence; Having made known unto us the mystery of his will, according to his good pleasure which he hath purposed in himself: that in the dispensation of the fullness of times he might gather together in one all things in Christ, both which are in heaven, and which are on earth; *even* in him: In whom also we have obtained an inheritance, being predestinated according to the purpose of him who worketh all things after the counsel of his

own will: that we should be to the praise of his glory, who first
trusted in Christ. In whom ye also *trusted*, after that ye heard the
word of truth, the gospel of your salvation: in whom also after
that ye believed, ye were sealed with that holy Spirit of promise,
Which is the earnest of our inheritance until the redemption of the
purchased possession, unto the praise of his glory.

There are at least fourteen references to Christ in this passage, indicating that these spiritual blessings are ours through the agency of the
Son. This is also seen in Revelation 4 and 5, where we find the resurrected church praising God for His two most significant works: creation and redemption. The Lord Jesus is related to creation in that
"all things were made by him and without him was not anything made
that was made" (John 1:3). Paul underscores the role of Jesus Christ
in creation by saying, "all things were created by him and for him"
(Col. 1:16). The Lord's relation to redemption is seen in the fact that
John the Baptist identified Jesus as "the Lamb of God, which taketh
away the sin of the world" (John 1:29). We will spend eternity praising God for the two great demonstrations of His power, both of which
were accomplished in the Person of the Son.

We are to confess our sin on the basis of the sacrifice of the Son.
According to 1 John 1:7, it is "the blood of Jesus Christ his Son [that]
cleanseth us from all sin." We can only confess sin because Jesus
paid the penalty for our sin. Were it not for the sacrifice of the Son of
God, confession of sin would avail nothing. We obtain forgiveness
only on the basis of Jesus' blood shed for us (Colossians 1:13-14).

We are to confess our faith in the lordship of the Son. Confession of
belief in "God," as the "Supreme Being" of the New Agers (and others) or as the "Supreme Architect" of the Masonic Lodge, is inadequate. To be saved, you must profess faith in the Lordship of the only
begotten Son of God, the Lord Jesus Christ. "Neither is there salvation in any other: for there is none other name under heaven given
among men, whereby we must be saved" (Acts 4:12).

We find in the reading of Scripture the truth of the Son. Jesus said
that we should "search the scriptures...they are they which testify of
me" (John 5:39). Many cult groups, like the Mormons and the
Jehovah's Witnesses, claim to use the Bible as their foundation. But

they do not believe the revealed truth concerning the eternal Sonship and absolute deity of Jesus Christ, the Only Begotten of God. If you do not accept the truth about Christ Jesus, your use of Scripture is an abuse without merit (1 John 4:2-3).

We preach the revealing and reconciling work of the Son. Paul said, "all things are of God, who hath reconciled us to himself by Jesus Christ, and hath given to us the ministry of reconciliation" (2 Cor. 5:18). The central message of the Scriptures that we are to preach is that Christ has revealed the Father to us and has provided the means of our reconciliation with the Father. It is only Jesus' death and resurrection and His present intercession that give us access to the Throne of Grace (Hebrews 10:19-22). That is the heart of the message when we preach "Jesus Christ, and him crucified" (1 Cor. 2:2).

We commemorate the death and resurrection of the Son. In stating the purpose of the church's celebration of the Lord's Supper (Communion), Paul says, "For as often as ye eat this bread, and drink this cup, ye do show the Lord's death till he come" (1 Cor. 11:26). This is not what the Roman Church has blasphemously considered a ritual offering of Christ as a fresh sacrifice. This is not an observance to confer grace to the participants. Jesus is not present in the elements, but we commemorate His sacrifice. It is a worshipful reminder of the work of Jesus Christ in dying for our sin, rising from the dead, and ascending to the Father with the promise to return.

We give as God's gift of the Son and His gift in the Son. Our giving is an act of worship when motivated by our heartfelt, "Thanks *be* unto God for his unspeakable gift" of His Son for our salvation (2 Cor. 9:15). We also worship when our giving is motivated by sincere gratitude for the spiritual blessings that are given to us by God in His Son for our sanctification and glorification (Eph. 1:3). Our offerings will never even approach the value of what God has given us. We dare not be so bold as to suppose we have done God a favor by leaving a tip in the offering. If our giving is not offered in a spirit of genuine thanksgiving, we may be trying to buy merit with God or to obtain favor with man.

We must live all of life in the Son. In Romans 12:1-2, Paul writes,

I beseech you therefore, brethren, by the mercies of God, that ye present your bodies a living sacrifice, holy, acceptable unto God, *which is* your reasonable service [or 'spiritual worship']. And be not conformed to this world: but be ye transformed by the renewing of your mind, that ye may prove what is that good, and acceptable, and perfect, will of God.

A couple of chapters later, he adds, "For whether we live, we live unto the Lord; and whether we die, we die unto the Lord: whether we live therefore, or die, we are the Lord's" (14:8). Believers have been purchased by the blood of Christ Jesus. We are not our own. No believer has any business telling God, "It's my life; I can do what I want." It is *not* your life. It never was, and it never will be. You were once a slave to sin and Satan. When you trusted Jesus Christ as Savior, you became His bondservant. You were released from a situation in which sin had absolute control over you and entered into a relationship in which Christ has absolute authority over you. He has every right to expect full service, full surrender from each of us.

We can say unequivocally that any worship that omits the Son of God is not Christian worship; and any worship that exalts any person other than the Son of God is not Christian worship. This is an area where good churches can and do fail. When we heap praise upon Christian celebrities, be they musicians, writers, or preachers, we engage in a subtle form of idolatry. We must worship our Savior, not our heroes.

The Essence of Christian Worship in the Person of the Holy Spirit

We pray with the assistance of the Holy Spirit. Paul tells us in Romans 8:26 that we do not know how to pray. One aspect of the ministry of the Holy Spirit is to help us in this "infirmity" by making "intercession for us with groanings which cannot be uttered." God, who searches our hearts, knows the mind of the Spirit, because the Spirit makes intercession according to the will of God (Rom. 8:27). Without the Holy Spirit's intervention in our praying, we would never have any hope of having any of our prayers answered, for we would be praying according to our own will, not God's.

We praise by rejoicing in the Holy Spirit. This is not some ecstatic, emotional experience where we lose control and have no idea what is

going on. Neither is this the hilarious laughter nor the making of animal sounds that has been associated with a supposedly spiritual movement called the "Toronto Blessing." Rather, this is a conscious lifting
of the voice in praise to God for who He is and for what He has done.
We can only do that by the power of the Spirit of God. Three evidences of the filling of the Holy Spirit are described by Paul in
Ephesians 5:18-21. The first is verbal praise expressed in "psalms,
hymns, and spiritual songs," and internal joy expressed by "singing
and making melody in your heart to the Lord." The second is thanksgiving to God the Father "in the name of our Lord Jesus Christ." The
third is submitting to one another in the fear of God. Praise without
the presence of the Holy Spirit would either be empty or misdirected.

We confess sins under the conviction of the Holy Spirit. On the
evening before His crucifixion, Jesus told the disciples of the coming
of the Holy Spirit. He told them that one of the Spirit's ministries
would be to "reprove the world of sin" (John 16:8). It is possible to
feel remorse for one's sins, in a limited sense, without the prompting
of the Holy Spirit. But no one ever experiences genuine conviction
for sin, which leads to repentance and faith, apart from the ministry of
the Holy Spirit. We cannot even recognize our need to confess sin
without the working of the Holy Spirit in our hearts.

We confess faith in Christ by the Holy Spirit. According to 1
Corinthians 12:3, "no man can say [affirm] that Jesus is the Lord, but
by the Holy Ghost." Being "dead in trespasses and sins" (Eph. 2:1)
and "without Christ" and "having no hope" (Eph. 2:12), we have been
given access to the Father "by one Spirit" (Eph. 2:18). Without the
Holy Spirit's enlightenment and enablement, we would be incapable
of recognizing Jesus as Savior and submitting to Him as Lord (1 Cor.
2:9-14).

We read the Scriptures that were inspired by the Holy Spirit. Peter
tells us that there is one thing that we must "know...first" concerning
the Scriptures—that their clear message is trustworthy because they
were communicated by the Holy Spirit.

> Knowing this first, that no prophecy of the scripture is of any pri-
> vate interpretation. For the prophecy came not in old time by the
> will of man: but holy men of God spake *as they were* moved by
> the Holy Ghost (2 Pet. 1:20-21).

When we worship the Lord by reading the Bible, we are giving attention to the message delivered to us by the Holy Spirit. Further, we are only capable of understanding and believing that message by the illuminating work of the Holy Spirit (1 Cor. 2:9-14). As Peter pointed out, that does not give us license to assign to the Scriptures any meaning our imagination can draw out of them and blame our interpretation on the Holy Spirit. The illuminating work of the Holy Spirit is not to create fanciful "insights," but to help us see the sense of God's Word and its immediate application to our own lives.

We preach the Word as a demonstration of the Holy Spirit and of power. The demonstration of the Spirit and of power that Paul pointed to as authentication of his ministry among the Corinthians was not the miraculous sign gifts sought by modern charismatics. It was "my speech and my preaching" (1 Cor. 2:4). The believer's faith must not be attributed to "enticing words of man's wisdom," but to "the power of God" (2:5). Our churches languish, our worship is anemic, and professing believers are not being conformed to the image of Christ, not for want of eloquence in the pulpit, but for want of the Spirit's power.

We commemorate Christ's sacrifice as a fellowship of the Spirit. When the apostles preached at Pentecost, three thousand responded in repentance and faith and received "the gift of the Holy Ghost" (Acts 2:37-41). The immediate result was that they were baptized and added to the fellowship of the believers. The six verses that follow (2:42-47) mention "[the] breaking [the] of bread"—the Lord's Supper—twice, indicating that this commemoration of Christ's death and resurrection was an integral part of their fellowship in the Spirit.

We give in love as a fruit of the Holy Spirit. We have already seen that one of the evidences of the Holy Spirit's filling is a joyful and cheerful heart (Eph. 4:18-19). In 2 Corinthians 9:7, we are told to give "cheerfully" ("with abundant joy"). Paul also tells us in Galatians 5:22-23 that "the fruit of the Spirit is love, joy, peace, longsuffering, gentleness, goodness, faith, meekness, temperance...." Giving is not one of the characteristics mentioned in this list, but giving is intrinsic to several of them. Genuine love is a love that gives selflessly, without concern for recompense. On the other hand, when Ananias and Sapphira conspired to pretend to be more generous in their giving than they really were, Peter condemned them for their "lie to the Holy Ghost" (Acts 5:3). A joyful generosity of spirit is not part of man's natural disposition. The giving that God desires of us can only come from a heart made new by the Holy Spirit, and only then can our giving be truly worshipful.

We live godly lives by walking in the Holy Spirit. In Romans 8:1, Paul says, *"There is* therefore now no condemnation to them which are in Christ Jesus, who walk not after the flesh, but after the Spirit." In this verse and the eight that follow there are a total of nine references to the Holy Spirit's role in directing us in righteous living, and four references to the role of Jesus Christ. Paul is saying that we need to live in obedience to the will of God, and the only way we can do that is by the power of the Holy Spirit producing the likeness of Christ in us. Both the Holy Spirit and the Son of God are vitally involved in our daily walk and in our worship.

If we would worship in Spirit and in truth, we must incorporate the enumerated elements of worship while focusing on the essence of worship in the Persons of the Son of God and the Holy Spirit of God. In this way, true spiritual worship brings us into fellowship with all three Persons of the Godhead. True Christian worship is a conscious adoration of the Father, through the Son, by the Holy Spirit.

The Sustenance of Christian Worship in the Church

If you would contribute to sustaining and maintaining the worship of the Lord in your church, it will first require personal participation in the various elements of worship. You must pray. You must praise. You must confess your sin. You must confess your faith. You must attend to the reading of the Scripture. You must be involved in the proclamation of the Word of God, as a learner or a teacher or both. You must participate in the Lord's Supper. You must give financially to the Lord's work. If you show up at church and sit and watch somebody else do all those things, you are not a worshipper but a spectator. Many people attend church every week, yet do little more than watch other people be Christians. You can buy a ticket to a basketball game, get all excited about the action of the contest, and glory in your favorite team's victory or grovel in their defeat. But neither the victory nor the defeat is your own. You are not much more of a participant in the game than if you had stayed home. Going to church does not make you a worshipper any more than sitting in the gym makes you an athlete.

Second, contributing to the worship of your church will require a practical demonstration of Christianity in your daily life, obeying the teachings of God's Word. Of course some of the elements of worship you cannot practice daily, because they are the function of the assembled believers, the church. But there are people who will insist that they worship in prayer and praise, but they refuse to do so publicly. They do not return thanks for their meal in a restaurant. They will not participate in a corporate prayer meeting. They never give a public testimony to the goodness of God. There is little or no practical demonstration of worship in their lives.

Third, sustaining worship in your church will require your personal commitment that is both continual and comprehensive. You must be willing to become accountable for your contribution to the church's worship. Some folks seem to think that they are participants in worship because they taught a Sunday school class, or lead in prayer, or served as an usher fourteen years ago. Worship is not something that you do once and never again. It is a continuing activity.

Finally, maintaining your church's worship will require your energetic encouragement. Sustaining the worship of the church goes beyond personal participation to include holding it up and encouraging others to join in worship. There are two ways you can encourage others to worship. You can show them how to worship in Spirit and in truth by your example, and you can teach them by your exhortation. Others should learn to worship in Spirit and in truth by watching how you live and by listening to what you say.

Just as a traveler can do all the right things and still not make it to his intended destination, the churchgoer can go through all the motions and still not worship God. The focal point in our worship is neither the form of it nor the level of devotion, but that God in Christ has come in Person and fulfilled His work of grace. Spiritual worship is distinct from liturgical or ritualistic worship. It involves conscious participation and the inner ministry of the Holy Spirit in regenerating and sanctifying power. The person who is born of the Spirit and led by the Spirit will offer fitting and acceptable worship to God through Christ, both in organized worship and in all of life.

---

[1] Obviously, this took place before the terrorist attacks of 9/11/01 that introduced heightened security measures at US airports. Such a precipitous boarding would be unlikely at even a small airport today, and leaving a plane once you board would be even more difficult.

CHAPTER 7
THE NECESSITY OF SOUND DOCTRINE

A few years ago, I attended the funeral of a young man whose sister was a student in our church school. At one point, the pastor conducting the service encouraged people who knew the deceased to come down to the open casket and talk to the young man. The pastor said he believed that the spirit of the deceased was present in the room and would be encouraged and blessed by the kind words people would say to him. He said he believed that God would want the deceased to hear those things. It was getting a little spooky. I watched in consternation as dozens of professing believers made their way to the casket for their moment of communion with the dead. The pastor had no biblical basis for what he had suggested; he believed it simply because it made him feel good. His theology regarding the disposition of the soul following death was not developed biblically (Luke 16:19-31; 2 Cor. 5:8). What was disturbing was that so many people followed his lead without realizing that what they were doing was characteristic of occultism, not Christianity.

Professing believers are often woefully ignorant of biblical doctrine. If they belong to a local church there may be one or two denominational distinctives with which they are conversant, but it is the rare church member who can explain and defend the core doctrines of the Christian faith. We do not expect a new convert to have a thorough grasp of biblical doctrine, but it is inexcusable for a church member to have been a Christian for years and still be theologically ignorant. Charismatics distort doctrine in favor of emotionalism and sensationalism. Main-line denominations often emphasize form over substance. Evangelicals and fundamentalists have often been guilty of emphasizing evangelism to the exclusion of the rest of the counsel of God. In each group, there has been a tendency to consider theology too deadening, too intimidating, or too divisive. The mantra of ecumenical gatherings has become, "Let's not argue about doctrine; let's just be unified." They have forgotten that *truth*, by definition, is distinct and separate from error. They have ignored the clear teaching of Scripture that there can be no *biblical* unity apart from biblical truth. Much of the cause for the widespread corruption in the church today is due to the theological illiteracy of professing Christians. When people call themselves believers, but cannot articulate what they believe, they fall prey to popular movements and weird aberrations.

While this problem dominates our age, it is not peculiar to it. The writer of the Epistle to the Hebrews dealt with the same problem. He sternly rebuked his audience for their failure to have mastered fundamental doctrines of the faith and for failing to have grown to a more thorough understanding of doctrine.

Of whom [Christ] we have many things to say, and hard to be uttered, seeing ye are dull of hearing. For when for the time ye ought to be teachers, ye have need that one teach you again which *be* the first principles of the oracles of God; and are become such as have need of milk, and not of strong meat. For every one that useth milk *is* unskillful in the word of righteousness: for he is a babe. But strong meat belongeth to them that are of full age, *even* those who by reason of use have their senses exercised to discern both good and evil. Therefore, leaving the principles of the doctrine of Christ, let us go on unto perfection (Heb. 5:11-6:1a).

Lest we be included in the writer's condemnation of the believers for their theological ignorance, it is imperative that we examine the significance of our doctrine, a summary of our doctrine, and the sustenance of our doctrine.

The Significance of Our Doctrine

We are saved by believing doctrine. Acts 2:41 says, "Then they that gladly received his word were baptized: and the same day there were added *unto them* about three thousand souls." Those who were baptized and added to the assembly were those who believed the doctrine of Peter, particularly concerning Christ, man, and salvation. But some would object, claiming we are not saved by believing doctrine, but by "call[ing] on the name of the Lord" (Rom. 10:13). That is true, but Paul explains what it takes to get to that point.

> For whosoever shall call upon the name of the Lord shall be saved. How then shall they call on him in whom they have not believed? And how shall they believe in him of whom they have not heard? And how shall they hear without a preacher? And how shall they preach, except they be sent? ... So then faith *cometh* by hearing, and hearing by the word of God (Rom. 10:13-17).

Clearly, calling on the name of the Lord for salvation involves the understanding of and belief in the doctrines of the gospel. Everyone is a sinner and is worthy of death. Jesus Christ is the sinless Son of God. He died to satisfy God's righteous wrath, and rose from the dead to give us eternal life. Faith in Him is our only hope of salvation. Those are cardinal doctrines that one *must believe* in order to be saved.

We grow by learning doctrine. The new believers at Pentecost were saved when they "received his word" (Acts 2:41). The next verse says, "And they continued steadfastly in the apostles' doctrine" (2:42). They grew by learning the doctrines of the faith. Paul tells us that "All scripture *is* given by inspiration of God, and *is* profitable for doctrine, for reproof, for correction, for instruction in righteousness: That the man of God may be perfect, thoroughly furnished unto all good works" (2 Tim. 3:16-17). The church or movement that neglects or ignores doctrine, setting it aside in favor of experiential unity, does so at its peril and in direct contradiction to the express will of God. A believer's maturity is not measured in the years he has been saved, but by the doctrine he has learned and obeyed. Far too many of our churches teach little else than salvation, soul-winning, and tithing (and maybe interpersonal relations and dress codes.) Too many Christians are perfectly content spending their entire lives being spiritually bottle-fed. It is high time for church members to grow up and begin to chew the meat of the Word of God.

A Summary of Our Doctrine

We must know what we believe about the Bible. Every believer must know what the Bible teaches about its inspiration (it proceeded from God), its inerrancy (it is without error and absolutely trustworthy), its authority (it is the standard by which all men will ultimately be judged), its perspicuity (it is clear and understandable, not mystical and confusing), and its sufficiency (it is all we need to become what God wants us to be). (2 Tim. 3:16-17; 2 Pet. 2:20-21)

We must know what we believe about God. Every believer must know the biblical doctrines of God's triunity (three persons in one), His personality (a person, not an impersonal force), His transcendent imminence (separate from His creation, but present within it), His perfections (omnipotence, omnipresence, omniscience, et. al.), His glory, His sovereignty, His holiness, and so on. People have many different ideas about what constitutes God, but *there is only one true, living God.* The only way to discern between references to the One True God and references to any one of many false gods is to know the Bible doctrines concerning God. (Ex. 20:2-3; Mt. 28:19; John. 16:7-15; 17:5; Rom. 11:33; 1 Cor. 8:6; Eph. 2:18; 1 Tim. 4:11; Rev. 4:11)

We must know what we believe about the Person of the Father. Some use the doctrine of the Father to teach that God is only one Person. Others take the same doctrine and claim that God is the Father of us all. Theologically illiterate believers can easily be confused by representatives of either error. They must understand the biblical teaching that God is the Father of us all only in the sense that He created all people, but that He is the spiritual Father only of those who are brought to faith in God the Son by the agency of God the Holy Spirit. (Ex. 4:22; Mal. 2:10; John 20:17; Rom. 8:15-16)

We must know what we believe about Jesus Christ. Every believer must understand who Jesus Christ is (His Person) and what He has done and is now doing (His Work). It is too bad that many church members would find it difficult, and maybe impossible, to take an unbeliever to the Scriptures to show what the Bible teaches about the Person and work of Jesus Christ. (Mt. 4:1-11; John 1:1-18; 20:1-31;

Acts 1:1-11; 1 Cor. 15; 2 Cor. 5:21; 1 Thes. 4:13-18; Heb. 4:15; 9:1-28; Rev. 19 and 20)

We must know what we believe about the Holy Spirit. There are many false and confusing things being taught about the work of the Holy Spirit today. Many Christians are being led into error because they are ignorant of the Biblical doctrines concerning His ministry. Doctrines of the Spirit's permanent indwelling, His ministry of sealing until the day of redemption, His equipping for service and empowering for ministry, and His exaltation of the Son to the glory of the Father must be clearly taught and grasped. Charismatic confusion concerning the Holy Spirit's filling, baptism, and gifts are wreaking havoc in the churches. Believers must be equipped with a correct theology of the Holy Spirit. (Gen. 1:2; Mt. 28:19; John 3:5-6; 14:16; 16:7-13; Acts 5:3-4; Rom. 8:14-27; 1 Cor. 12:7; 2 Cor. 13:14; Eph. 1:13-14; 2 Thes. 2:7; Titus 3:5)

We must know what we believe about spiritual beings: angels, demons, and Satan. We have recently witnessed a renewed interest in angelic beings, and that could be either good or bad. It would be good if the emphasis were on the biblical doctrine of angels so the conclusions drawn would be consistent with the Word of God. But it is dangerous when biblical doctrine is ignored and experience is emphasized. Angels end up being studied or admired for what they do, rather than for whom they serve. It is Satan, an angel of light, who desires to draw attention to himself and away from God. Our popular culture's fascination with angels over the years has been seen in Michael Landon's portrayal of a good deeds angel in a television series, movies about angels helping athletes win games, and even John Travolta playing a scruffy looking, cigar smoking, disco dancing angel. These are just representative of many unbiblical views about spiritual beings that are leading believers to adopt a sort of "theology according to Hollywood." We must teach and understand what the Bible teaches about angels, demons, and Satan. (Ps. 148:2, 5; Is. 14; Ez. 28; Mt. 4:1-3; Col. 1:16; 2 Cor. 4:4; Heb. 1:14; Rev. 10:2-10)

We must know what we believe about creation. This doctrine is also under attack and being weakened or discarded by many professing believers. Some who insist that they believe orthodox doctrine concerning the atoning work of Jesus Christ will interpret the first three (and usually the first eleven) chapters of Genesis allegorically, in order to allow for some form of evolutionary theory of origins. They do not realize that belief in salvation by the blood sacrifice of Christ Jesus and belief in the evolution of man are irreconcilably contradictory. If the biblical account of creation is not true, but man evolved, even in some theistic scheme, over eons of time, then death was present from the beginning, and did not come as a result of sin. If the Genesis record of Adam's creation and rebellion does not tell the real story of how sin and death were introduced to creation, then the entire account of redemption—Christ's coming to take upon Himself the curse of sin and death that He might reconcile mankind to God—is meaningless. The whole point of the Gospel rests upon the assumption that the Genesis account of creation is literally true. (Gen. 1 and 2; Is. 43:1, 7; John 1:3; Col. 1:16-17)

We must know what we believe about man and sin. Much of what is wrong with our society today is directly attributable to unbiblical views of man and sin. Is man created for a purpose? Is man basically good, being corrupted by outside forces, or is he naturally corrupt? Is there such a thing as sin? If so, is it defined by absolute standards of right and wrong, or is it culturally defined? Is man capable of pleasing God by his own efforts? Is man searching for the truth in God, or is he running from the truth of God? Is there any remedy for man's condition? We need a strong biblical theology that identifies each person as a member of a fallen race. Each person inherits a sin nature from Adam and is completely enslaved to his own desires. Each person sins by choice every time his thoughts, words, or actions violate God's absolute standards of righteousness. Each person's sin is worthy of death, and his certain destiny is eternal damnation separated from God in the fires of hell. Each person is completely and utterly without hope apart from God's work of grace through the sacrifice of Jesus Christ for sin, and the inner prompting of the Holy Spirit to receive the free gift of salvation by faith. (Gen. 2:16-17; 3:1-24; Is. 53:6; 64:6-7; John 3:18, 36; Rom. 1:18-32; 3:9-19; 5:10, 12; Eph. 2:1-9; Titus 3:4-5)

We must know what we believe about salvation and regeneration. Church members are often timid in sharing their faith with others because they don't have a thorough enough grasp of the doctrine of salvation to be secure when challenged. Every believer who has grown at all should be able to explain the necessity for salvation, how it is provided, how it is obtained, and what its consequences (benefits and responsibilities) are. Important concepts are associated with this doctrine: propitiation (the satisfaction of God's righteous wrath), regeneration (those dead in sin being brought to life in Christ—the rebirth), adoption (becoming a member of God's family, rather than Satan's—receiving an inheritance in Christ), redemption (being bought back from slavery to sin unto a position of privileged service), sanctification (being set apart to God and growing in godliness), justification (having guilt removed and being declared to be righteous on the basis of the righteousness of Jesus Christ), glorification (God's glory revealed in believers, ultimately in the resurrection), etc. Far too few Christians can show someone the plan of salvation. And far too many of those who might try to explain their faith, demonstrate by the way they live that salvation has made little difference to them. (John 3:3, 16; 16:7-8; Acts 16:31; Rom. 3:24; 8:33-39; 11:6; 2 Cor. 5:17; Eph. 2:8-10; Phil. 2:5-8; Titus 3:3-7; Heb. 4:15; 1 Pet. 3:18; 1 John 2:2; 5:13)

We must know what we believe about the church. Every believer should learn what the Bible teaches about the beginnings of the church and the composition of the church (who is included). While there is room for some variety among sound churches, a believer must understand the biblical basis for the polity of his church. This would include such matters as membership, officers and their qualifications, organizational structure, and conducting of business. Members should also understand the church's ordinances, its ministries, and its discipline. A theology of missions is often discussed under this heading, as well. (Mt. 16:18; 26:26-29; 28:19-20; Acts 1:8; 2:38-42; 15:1-41; 20:17-18; 1 Cor. 5:1-6:11; 11:2, 23-28; 12:12-28; Eph. 1:22-23; 4:11; 5:23-24; Col. 1:18; 1 Thes. 4:13-18; 2 Tim. 3:1-13)

We must know what we believe about things to come. This would include the biblical teaching concerning the imminent return of Jesus Christ for believers, the resurrection of the saints to eternal reward and fellowship with God, the resurrection of unbelievers to eternal torment in the fires of hell, the judgments on Satan and antichrist and their followers, the establishment of the Millennial Kingdom, and its transition to the Eternal Kingdom. This is another area where there is room for difference among good churches. We recognize that not all

of us have identical understandings of the meaning of certain prophe-
cies or of the order of events. But we must agree that the Lord is really coming back to receive and reward the resurrected saints and to
condemn to everlasting punishment those who did not believe. [1] (Mt.
25:31-46; Luke 16:19-26; 21:31-32; John 14:3; 1 Cor. 15:12-58; 1
Thes. 4:13-18; 5:9; Rev. 3:10; 19:11-20; 20:11-15; 21:1-22:5)

The Sustenance of Our Doctrine

In 2 Timothy 3:14-15, Paul challenged Timothy to

continue…in the things which thou hast learned and hast been
assured of, knowing of whom thou has learned *them*; And that
from a child thou hast known the holy Scriptures, which are able
to make thee wise unto salvation through faith which is in Christ
Jesus.

Notice Paul's reference to the things Timothy had "learned", and
had "been assured of." That which Paul considered significant about
Timothy's doctrine was that he *knew* it. That is, Timothy's belief system had been established, confirmed, and made secure. But even
then, he is told to "continue in" those things. We are to study, review,
and master the doctrines of the Bible to the point that they have mastered us—made us like Christ.

Sustaining our doctrines also involves *defending* it. Paul's charge to
Timothy continued in the next chapter:

I charge *thee* therefore before God, and the Lord Jesus Christ,
who shall judge the quick and the dead at his appearing and his
kingdom; Preach the word; be instant in season, out of season;
reprove, rebuke, exhort with all longsuffering and doctrine. For
the time will come when they will not endure sound doctrine; but
after their own lusts shall they heap to themselves teachers, having itching ears; And they shall turn away *their* ears from the
truth, and shall be turned to fables (2 Timothy 4:1-4).

Paul has worded this charge as strongly as possible. He began by
reminding Timothy to whom he would give an accounting for how
faithfully he fulfilled this charge. Notice the centrality of doctrine.
Ministry is all about making people what God wants them to be by

the application of sound doctrine. But we are surrounded by, and sometimes contributing to, the fulfillment of the prophecy that people will not tolerate sound doctrine, but follow after teachers who will tell them what they want to hear.

If we would sustain our doctrine, we must be able both to state it and defend it. Many nominal Christians can tell someone what *their church* teaches, but that is not necessarily the same thing as telling someone what *they* believe. Our faith must go beyond memorization of a creed. The creed we are able to articulate, we must also be able to defend and demonstrate.

This chapter has merely provided a sketchy overview of biblical doctrine. Its purpose has not been to teach doctrine, but to raise some important questions for consideration. Have you been diligent in your study of Scripture that you might "rightly divide the word of truth" (2 Tim. 2:5)? Do you faithfully "search the Scriptures daily" to see whether these "things are so" (Acts 17:10-12)? Are you "ready always to give an answer" (1 Peter 3:15) that you might guard against the "false teachers among you who…would make merchandise of you" (2 Peter 1:19-2:3)?

If you had to answer "No" to any of these questions, then we must also ask, "What will you do about it?" Please do not protest, "I am not a theologian." That is simply not true. *Everyone* is a theologian of some sort. Some are careful theologians, and some are careless, but all are theologians. And don't be frightened by the terminology. You do not need an immense vocabulary or a towering intellect to be a good theologian. That was the argument used against the Apostles, "These fellows are not smart enough to teach theology. Their spokesman is a professional fisherman, of all things, who never went to seminary!" If the list of doctrines reviewed seems a bit over-whelming, it simply indicates a need for more diligent study. You do not need more intelligence. The two things you need are a willing-ness to be taught by God, and a willingness to prioritize the time and effort to study the Word of God. Therein lies the major problem. You will never become a good theologian without inconveniencing your-self and leaving out something else you want to do. As a believer in Christ you have an obligation to God to be careful and accurate in

your theology. As a member of your church, you also have an obligation to that body to become a careful and accurate theologian.

---

[1] Through at least the last half of the twentieth century, the majority of
evangelicals and fundamentalists have taught what is commonly referred
to as a "pre-Tribulation rapture" position, as I do. However, I hesitate to
make this a test of orthodoxy. *Historical* honesty demands that we admit
that few of our forebears held that view before the late nineteenth century, and that some disagreement remains today. Likewise, *theological*
integrity requires that we acknowledge that prophecy, by its very nature,
is difficult to fully grasp prior to its fulfillment, and that precise *means* of
fulfillment are often impossible to anticipate with a high degree of certainty. While I believe the weight of biblical evidence overwhelmingly
supports the pre-Tribulation rapture position, there are good brethren
who disagree.

CHAPTER 8
THE IMPORTANCE OF
PERSONAL BIBLE STUDY

When my son, Brandon, was about ten years old, he began to develop a keen interest in deer hunting. He watched hunting shows and read hunting magazines and talked constantly about guns, wildlife, guns, camouflage, and guns. Not being a hunter myself, he has had an uphill battle convincing me it would be a worthwhile and enjoyable pursuit. I have nothing against the sport, but getting up two hours before daylight so you can get into the woods and mount your tree stand where you may find yourself spending the day sitting in the sleet never sounded like a lot of fun to me. I was even less inspired by thoughts of what a hunter has to do if he actually shoots a deer (gutting the animal, dragging the carcass out of the woods, and so on).

When Brandon turned thirteen, one of the men in the church offered to take him hunting in the fall. To be able to go, he would first have to take a hunters' safety course that required several hours of class instruction and a final test over a hunters' manual. I surprised him by signing up to take the course with him. We spent two Thursday evenings listening to a rather disorganized and rambling lecture on hunting laws and safety rules, liberally laced with exciting stories, videos, and gun displays. During the week between the classes, my son often told me that he already knew all the stuff the instructor was covering. I believed him—he had been the first person in the room to recognize that a particular shotgun the instructor held up was designed for a left handed hunter. On the last night of instruction I spent every break reviewing the manual I had read that week, while my son got a kick out of the fact that I actually needed to study. Then came the examination. When Brandon returned from having his test scored, he boasted, "I only missed four questions. How many did you miss?" When I said I hadn't missed any, he asked incredulously, "How could you not miss any, and I miss four, when I know all this stuff?" I explained that while he had watched a lot of shows and listened to the instructor, I had actually read and studied the book on which the test was based.

Several organizations have taken polls on religion in America. Among their findings is evidence that 60% of all Americans claim to attend church at least once a month, but of those, only 12% read their Bibles. That means that about 7% of all Americans claim to read their Bibles. The International Bible Readers Association reported that 85% of professing Christians have never read through the entire Bible. While the accuracy of these statistics may be open to dispute, the fact remains that relatively few professing believers are the diligent students of Scripture that God has commanded us to be.

The thrust of this book has to do with the interdependence of the individual believer and the corporate fellowship of the church. It is important to be actively involved in a good local church, to truly worship as a part of that church, and to gain a thorough understanding of the basic doctrines of the Christian faith. But it is possible to do those things and still not give attention to your own personal, private growth in the Lord. When people join the church I pastor, they pledge themselves to a covenant that includes the promise to "maintain family and secret devotions." If you would be the kind of church member you ought to be, you need to go beyond the instruction in the Word you receive at church and engage in your own careful study of the Scriptures.

In 2 Timothy 2:15, Paul admonishes the believer to "Study to show thyself approved unto God, a workman that needeth not to be ashamed, rightly dividing the word of truth." The word translated "study" is not limited to meaning "an effort to learn by reading," even though that meaning is implied by its application to the "word of truth." The emphasis of the word is on diligent effort. Paul is saying that we must apply ourselves diligently and single-mindedly to pleasing God, mastering the Scriptures to the degree that we understand them thoroughly and apply them correctly, so we can serve God faithfully in complete obedience to His Word. A dire warning for failure to do so is found in the words of God through the prophet Hosea— "My people are destroyed for lack of knowledge: because thou hast rejected knowledge, I will also reject thee,...seeing thou hast forgotten the law of thy God, I will also forget thy children" (Hosea 4:6). If we would have the kind of private growth within the church that we need, the Scriptures must saturate our lives, and our lives must absorb the Scriptures.

The Bible Must Saturate Our Lives

As we have already seen, true worship requires obedience to Scripture. "True worshippers shall worship the Father in spirit and in truth: for the Father seeketh such to worship him" (John 4:23). But it is impossible to obey what we do not know. The level of knowledge necessary for complete obedience will not be achieved by merely attending church services. You must read and study the Bible. Reading the Bible through once or twice, reading it casually, or reading it only occasionally will not be enough. *Continual exposure* to the Word is necessary for mastery of the Word, and that must be our goal.

When God was preparing Joshua for the responsibility of replacing Moses as Israel's leader, He gave the following instructions:

This book of the law shall not depart out of thy mouth; but thou shalt meditate therein day and night, that thou mayest observe to do according to all that is written therein: for then thou shalt make thy way prosperous, and then thou shalt have good success (Joshua 1:8).

Joshua's success as Israel's new leader was dependent upon his mastery of and submission to the Word of God. And that is all he needed. Paul echoes this emphasis upon the authority and sufficiency of Scripture, saying, "All scripture *is* given by inspiration of God, and *is* profitable for doctrine, for reproof, for correction, for instruction in righteousness: That the man of God may be perfect, throughly furnished unto all good works" (2 Timothy 3:16-17). If we would be

complete and mature, fully equipped to do every good work, we must
gain a thorough knowledge of the Scriptures. Nothing less will suf-
fice. This is not just the responsibility of the pastor. It includes
everyone who would be a disciple of Jesus Christ. The mastery of the
Word of God must be our goal, but not simply for the intellectual satisfaction of *knowing*.

The knowledge of the Scriptures provides us the wisdom to come to
faith in Christ and to live by faith in Christ. In 2 Timothy 3:14-15,
Paul challenged Timothy to:

> Continue thou in the things which thou hast learned and hast
> been assured of, knowing of whom thou hast learned *them*; And
> that from a child thou hast known the holy scriptures, which are
> able to make thee wise unto salvation through faith which is in
> Christ Jesus.

God has also commanded us to be holy (Leviticus 20:7; Romans
12:1; 1 Corinthians 3:17). "Holiness" is an attribute of God that
emphasizes His *separateness* even more than His *sinlessness*. It is
more closely synonymous to *sanctification* than to *righteousness*.
Sanctification has to do with being separate from sin and dedicated to
God. Righteousness has to do with actively obeying God's commands. Both are essential, and both are accomplished by knowing
and heeding the Word of God. Jesus prayed that the Father would
"Sanctify them by thy truth; thy word is truth" (John 17:17). Moses
instructed Israel saying,

> And now, Israel, what doth the LORD thy God require of thee,
> but to fear the LORD thy God, to walk in all his ways, and to love
> him, and to serve the LORD thy God with all thy heart and with
> all thy soul, To keep the commandments of the LORD, and his
> statutes, which I command thee this day for thy good?
> (Deuteronomy 10:12-13).

If we would obey the command to be holy, we must know and obey
the Word of God. If we would please God with our lives, we must
know and obey the Word of God. If we would be the kind of church
members God desires and our churches need, we must grow in the
Lord by our personal comprehension of the Word of God, allowing it

to saturate our lives, affecting every thought, every word, every choice, and every act.

Our Lives Must Absorb the Bible

If we want our families to grow in the Lord, it is not enough to take them to church. While that is certainly an essential ingredient for their spiritual growth, it is insufficient by itself. There must also be daily Bible study in the home. For our homes to absorb the Bible there must be both formal instruction in the Word and informal demonstration of the Word.

The home was established long before the church. The forming of the church by Jesus Christ, and its inauguration as the visible expression of His body, complements the purpose of the home, it does not replace it. Before the establishing of the church, fathers were to teach, or give formal instruction to their children. God said of Abraham, "For I know him, that he will command his children and his household after him, and they shall keep the way of the LORD, to do justice and judgment; that the LORD may bring upon Abraham that which he hath spoken of him" (Genesis 18:19). Concerning the word of the Lord, Moses said to the men of Israel, "And ye shall teach them your children" (Deuteronomy 11:19). But this is not just an Old Testament command. Paul also commands fathers to "bring [your children] up in the nurture and admonition of the Lord" (Ephesians 6:4). Fathers are to teach their children what God has said and done, and what that means when applied to their lives. Husbands must also teach their wives (1 Corinthians 14:35). This will, of course, require a lot of personal preparation. The instruction need not be an hour-long class every day. But what men are learning in their private study of the Word, they must communicate to their families.

This instruction in the Word goes beyond a few minutes of formal explanation of whatever topic or passage may be the subject at hand. It includes informal demonstration of the truths of Scripture in our daily lives. Deuteronomy 11:18-21 says,

Therefore shall ye lay up these my words in your heart and in your soul, and bind them for a sign upon your hand, that they may be as frontlets between your eyes. And ye shall teach them your children, speaking of them when thou sittest in thine house, and

when thou walkest by the way, when thou liest down, and when
thou risest up. And thou shalt write them upon the door posts of
thine house, and upon thy gates: that your days may be multiplied, and the days of your children, in the land which the LORD
sware unto your fathers to give them, as the days of heaven upon
the earth.

People always seem to be looking for a little bit of "heaven upon
earth." Moses has told us how to have that: by allowing the Word of
God to permeate every aspect of our lives and our homes. We are to
instruct our families in the Word when we are sitting at home and
when we are walking by the way. We are to give this instruction
before bedtime and at, or before, breakfast. The Word is to be as if it
were bound upon our hands (affecting whatever we do) and between
our eyes (affecting whatever we see). It is to be on the doorposts of
our homes, which we would see when entering the house, and on our
gates, which would be on the edge of our property and seen when we
leave. So whether you are sitting at home or going somewhere,
whether you are going to bed or getting up, whatever you do, whatever you see, when you enter the house or when you leave, you are to be
thinking about and living the Word of God. That is pretty comprehensive.

Such single-mindedness must rest on a firm foundation of understanding what God has done in the past, what He is doing now, and
what He will do in the future. God's Word is to be heard and seen
wherever one looks while going about life. If you rely upon the pastor and Sunday school teachers, the youth leaders, or the Christian
school to do the job of instructing your family in the Word, you fail in
the most important responsibility God has given you: spiritual leadership in your home. Dads, if you are honest, you have to admit that at
least occasionally you have trouble withstanding temptation and the
constant bombardment of worldly influences. Can you possibly
believe that your children can successfully stand against the influence
of the world without the daily exposure to the Word described in
Deuteronomy 11:18-21? The problem is not that the message of
God's truth is less attractive than the message of the world—if you
believe it is, you have accepted the propaganda that Satan spreads so
effectively. The problem is that we allow every other influence to

have access to our homes and to be impressed on our family's thinking, so that God's Word goes unheard.

Two of the many contemporary challenges facing the church are
young people forsaking the professed faith of their parents, and
women taking over leadership in the church. A large measure of
responsibility for these problems can be laid at the door of husbands
and fathers who have failed to equip themselves with a thorough
understanding of the Word of God so they can be faithful and effective teachers of the Word in their homes.

Bible Study Methods

Part of the solution to these problems is to have regular times of personal and family devotions, including Bible study and prayer. There
are many Bible study methods individuals or families might employ.
Some are more effective than others.

Probably the most used and least adequate approach to Bible reading
could be called *hit or miss.* This is merely reading a passage of
Scripture or a devotional when you have time. It is haphazard, so it
really doesn't deserve to be called a method, but this is what most
Christians who claim they read their Bible actually do.

Another popular method is to *read your Bible in a year.* In this
approach a schedule is laid out in which you read a few chapters a
day. For many people this is an effective tool for accomplishing the
reading of the entire Bible, and that is something *every* Christian
should do. Obviously, you are unlikely to ever read all of the Bible
unless you set out to do just that. This method has the advantage of
taking the time to read large portions of Scripture. Paul tells us that
Christ intends to cleanse the church "with the washing of water by the
word" (Ephesians 5:26). Generally, when one cleans himself by
washing with water, it helps to have more than a few drops of water
with which to wash. The greater the quantity of the water, the more
likely he is to be cleansed. A disadvantage to this method, though, is
that *finishing* may become the goal and *learning* suffer. You may
make it through the Bible, but learn very little. If this is the only
method you ever use, many important applications will be missed. It
is possible, and probably desirable, to occasionally modify this
method in combination with some other method, so you can take the

time to think about what you are reading as you work your way
through your Bible.

Many people opt for a method using *Bible story books or devotional
guides*. This has the advantage of simplicity, usually including a passage of Scripture with an application. While this method has some
merit, it is not without weaknesses. Most devotional guides use only
brief, isolated passages of Scripture in which the reader gets little or
no sense of context. Illustrations and applications are often weak,
inappropriate, or incorrect. Also, many such books do not print the
Bible text from which the story comes or the devotional thoughts are
being drawn, giving only the reference, and the reader may be tempted to read only the author's thoughts and never actually read the
Scripture. If you use this method, choose your devotional guide carefully, read critically, and make sure you read the Bible text.

A similar method that would be more effective would be to use
Bible study books or commentaries. These will give a more detailed
explanation of the Scriptures, usually taking the reader systematically
through a topic or a book of the Bible. Many books designed as Bible
study helps will direct you to specific passages of Scripture and
include questions for you to answer. Commentaries often print the
passage under consideration and then offer explanatory comments,
illustrations, and/or applications. While this is an excellent method,
one should use it cautiously. Commentaries may be too shallow or
too deep, too simple or too technical, or may simply interpret the
Scriptures incorrectly. As with the devotional books, you should
choose carefully. Ask your pastor for help in selecting books and
authors that will be especially beneficial to you.

Besides these, or as a supplement to one of them, there are several
different *devotional methods* you might employ in which you read
your Bible through using a notebook and pen. A short, simple devotional Bible reading time might include the following steps:

1. Read a passage (a few verses or chapters, working through a
   book), recording the section read for that day in your notebook.
2. Mark in the text as you read, underlining important thoughts.
3. Identify the one most significant thought you marked.

4. Summarize the thought, writing it in your notebook in your own words.
5. Make a note of some way you can apply this thought to your life today.

If you want to take a little more time with your devotional reading you might read the selected passage more than once, having a work-sheet in a notebook for each passage on which you would write the answers to the relevant questions from a series like the following:

1. What is the subject of this passage (one sentence)?
2. What lesson(s) is (are) here for me to learn?
3. What is the best or key verse?
4. Who are the principle persons?
5. What can I learn about Christ (or God, or the Holy Spirit) here?
6. What example is there for me to follow?
7. What error(s) is (are) there for me to avoid?
8. What command(s) is (are) there for me to obey?
9. What promise(s) is (are) there for me to claim?
10. What prayer is there for me to pray?

Yet another Bible study method that bears mentioning could be called a *topical method*. For this you will need a good concordance. Strong's Exhaustive Concordance lists every Scripture reference in which any given word (KJV) may be found. It also uses a numbering system to identify the Hebrew or Greek word from which the English word was translated, and includes a dictionary giving brief definitions and etymologies of those words. Several companies have produced Bible study materials for use with a personal computer. Some of them include immense libraries of resources at a fraction of the cost of hard copies of the volumes. The word-search functions make it possible to quickly do much more thorough research than would be possible with a shelf full of books. Using any of these tools, the Bible student can do all sorts of individual studies. You may learn a great deal by investigating words like peace, joy, sin, grace, love, righteousness, salt, light, and so on. You can use the concordance to do biographical studies of patriarchs, apostles, prophets, Bible women, mighty men, church leaders, or kings. Doctrinal studies of

subjects like salvation, Satan, heaven, hell, angels, judgment, or creation can be very beneficial.

In general, the Bible study methods above have been described in
terms of personal Bible study. But each is easily adaptable to family
study. Some will require more advance preparation than others.
Some will require a larger time block than others. Choose one that
will work now, then adapt and change as your family's needs change
and your children mature. No one method of Bible study will be adequate for a lifetime. You will need to vary your methods. But most of
us need a system to be disciplined in our study and to profit by it. If
you are just getting started in personal or family Bible study, don't
start with the most complicated or time-consuming system. You may
get discouraged and give up. Start simply and build over time. But
whatever method you use, you and your family need to spend time in
God's Word and prayer daily. You owe it to the Lord, your family,
and to your church to be a Christian who is growing in his knowledge
of the Word of God.

CHAPTER 9
THE SIGNIFICANCE OF PRAYER

Another element important for the growth of the believer and the well being of the church is prayer. You may be a diligent student of Scripture and an energetic participant in the worship and ministry of your church and still lack the power of God in your life because you are not a person of prayer. In Chapter Five, prayer is described as, "an attitude of constant communication with and complete dependence upon God." That is the meaning Paul seems to have had in mind when he commanded that we "pray without ceasing" (1 Thes. 5:17). However, in a more practical and immediate sense, prayer can be thought of as simply "talking to God." That is basically what Paul meant when he wrote, "Be careful for nothing; but in every thing by prayer and supplication with thanksgiving let your requests be made known unto God" (Phil. 4:6). In giving his instructions to Timothy concerning pastoral leadership of the church at Ephesus, Paul *prioritized* the ministry of prayer, saying, "I exhort therefore, that first of all, supplications, prayers, intercessions, *and* giving of thanks, be made for all men" (1 Tim. 2:1).

Some years ago I was listening to a tape of a sermon on prayer. The message, which was entitled "How to Get Things from God," was preached by a pastor who has been quite influential among fundamentalists. I began listening in hopes that the content would be different from what the title implied. I was wrong. The preacher's basic prem-

ise was that if you want God to give you something or do something
for you, you must first tell Him how great He is. He explained that if
you lay on enough praise, God will decide you must be a pretty good
person if you think so highly of Him, and He will be softened up to
do for you what you want. This preacher based his conclusion partly
on a misinterpretation of Genesis 18:20-33 in which Abraham made
intercession for the Sodomites, and partly on his belief that God
would behave that way "because that's how I would be if I were
God." This is a *blasphemous* misrepresentation of both God and
praise that debases God's majesty and denies His sovereignty. First,
God is *not* susceptible to flattery and manipulation, as men are.
Second, the purpose of praise is *not* to remind God how great He is,
but is to make *us* focus on the reality of God's sovereign majesty. But
even if we set aside the sacrilege, there remains a gross distortion of
God's purposes in prayer.

Most people seem to believe that the reason we pray is either "to get
stuff from God" or "to talk God into doing something." Sermons like
the one I heard have given many people the impression that God is
either some kind of cosmic Santa Claus who doles out treats and presents to good boys and girls, or a benevolent genie who grants the
wishes of those who manage to invoke the mystic secrets of the lamp.
Unfortunately, many of God's people have been badly misled by such
erroneous teaching on the nature and purposes of prayer.

Why Should We Pray?
The name-it-and-claim-it theology of those who teach a "prosperity
gospel" says that God is obligated to give us whatever we want. They
reduce praying "in Jesus' name" to nothing more than a spiritual
equivalent of *abracadabra*, a mystical incantation that works the
magic of fulfilling our every desire when appended to the end of a
prayer. There are two important points they have missed.

First, God's promise to "give thee the desires of thine heart" (Ps.
37:4) is *not* a guarantee that He will give you whatever you desire.
Rather, God promised that if you will "trust in the LORD" (37:3),
"delight...in the LORD" (37:4), "commit thy way unto the LORD"
(37:5), and "rest in the LORD" (37:7), you will desire what God
desires.

Second, Jesus' promise to the disciples that "Whatsoever ye shall ask the Father in my name, he will give it you" (John 16:23) is *not* a promise that God is obligated to fulfill your every wish if you merely add "in Jesus' name" to your prayer. Jesus told His disciples that He was leaving them, but they would still have access to Him and to the Father through the Holy Spirit who would come. He charged them with continuing the ministry He had begun, and they were fearful that they would not be able to do it without Him. He then promised that God would give them whatever they needed for the task if they would but ask *as if they were Jesus Himself.* Far from being a promise that God will give us whatever we want to make us happy or comfortable, Jesus promised that God will give us whatever we *need* to accomplish the work God has given us to do. James' statement that "ye have not because ye ask not" (James 4:2) must be tempered with "Ye ask, and receive not, because ye ask amiss, that ye may consume *it* upon your lusts" (James 4:3).

For us to understand God's purposes in prayer, we must first understand something about God's sovereign will. For centuries now, theologians have debated the fine points of this aspect of God's nature. Some Augustinians (Calvinists) are guilty of placing such emphasis on the sovereignty of God's will that they are in danger of denying man's responsibility. But semi-Pelagians (Arminians) often so emphasize man's responsibility that they deny the sovereignty of God and end up implying that man is sovereign. Neither extreme is acceptable. Without wanting to stir up too much controversy in this context, it seems safe to conclude that God's sovereign will includes both His *intended ends* and His *appointed means.*

We know that God's intended ends are working toward both His glory and our good. "And we know that all things work together for good to them that love God, to them who are the called according to *his* purpose" (Rom. 8:28). But this does not necessarily mean that if we claim this promise we will feel better in a couple of days. Our *good* is not synonymous with our *comfort.* God is often pleased to make us comfortable in this world, but He is not obligated to do so. The context of Romans 8 indicates that our ultimate good, to which God is directing, is that we be with Him in glory (8:18-39). Therefore, this is not a promise that God will make us *comfortable,* but that God will make us *glorious* in conformity to the image of His

Son. Actually, becoming glorious may involve a great deal of hardship and discomfort. God's promise to work all things for our good
means He is working all things to bring us into conformity to the
image of Christ in this life and to glorify us with Christ in eternity.
This is a far greater promise than temporal comfort. And the reason
God does this for us is, "that he might make known the riches of his
glory on the vessels of mercy, which he had afore prepared unto
glory" (Rom. 9:23). God has determined to glorify us as one of the
means of bringing glory to Himself. Our benefit is secondary to
God's glory. It is essential that we understand this if we are to learn
to pray properly. Most people's prayer is consumed with asking God
to do things for us to make us more comfortable—more money or
material goods, better health, better relationships. We tend to be more
motivated by our desires than by God's.

Besides His *intended ends*, God's sovereign will also includes the
employment of His *appointed means*. God's sovereign will in election may have been *determined* from before the foundation of the
world (Eph. 1:4), but it is not *applied* until the lost sinner believes
(Eph. 1:13). His sovereign will includes both His intended ends (election) and His appointed means (faith). Just so, God's plan for your
life includes a program of what He intends to do in and for you to
bring you to glory, but also includes prayer as a means to that end.
This is the paradox: God will do what He intends to do, but we must
ask Him to do it in prayer.

In all of our praying, we must remember that God is the benefactor
and we are the beneficiaries. That is, our prayer does nothing for
God's benefit, but for our own. With that in mind, we must recognize
at least four things our prayer cannot do.

> 1. *Our prayer cannot enhance God's glory.* He whose glory is
>   absolute and is set "above the heavens" (Ps. 8:1) cannot be
>   made more glorious by anything you or I can do.
> 2. *Our prayer cannot increase God's knowledge.* He knows all
>   things. "[A]ll things *are* naked and opened unto the eyes of
>   him with whom we have to do" (Heb. 4:13). Therefore, His
>   knowledge cannot be increased by anything we tell Him in
>   prayer.

3. *Our prayer cannot correct His program.* He "who worketh all things after the counsel of his own will" (Eph. 1:11) is incapable of being wrong. His program needs no correction. It is not the potter, but the clay that needs shaping (Rom. 9:20-21). His program cannot be perfected or improved upon by the things we ask of Him in prayer.

4. *Our prayer cannot change His mind.* God says, "I am the LORD, I change not" (Mal. 3:6). Even the most celebrated passages in which it seems God changed His mind should be understood differently. For instance, in Genesis 18 Abraham pleads for God to spare the Sodomites ("for the sake of fifty righteous...for the sake of ten.") Two questions are often overlooked in this passage. First, why did Abraham intercede for the Sodomites? Because God prompted him to pray by specifically indicating His interest in them. Second, what did God finally do? He destroyed the Sodomites for whom Abraham had prayed. Abraham did not change God's mind, but God changed Abraham's. God did exactly what He intended to do all along, and Abraham learned to pray for others. In fact, it is likely that Abraham perceived this prayer to have been unanswered when Sodom was destroyed, not knowing what God had done with Lot in Genesis 19, and this lack of faith led directly to his lapse of obedience in Genesis 20. Another significant passage involves Jonah and the Ninevites. When the Ninevites repented at Jonah's warning, did God change His mind and withhold judgment? No. Who sent Jonah to preach and to what purpose? God went to a great deal of trouble to get this message to the Ninevites, because He intended to bring them to repentance. Even Jonah acknowledged that he was certain that was God's intention (Jonah 4:2). Then, did God lie when He said He would judge their sin? Again, no. God's wrath was still poured out on their sin. Their repentance merely delayed it. The wrath of God, which the Ninevites deserved, was poured out on Jesus Christ centuries later when He died for their sins. It was not God's mind that changed in this incident; it was Jonah's and the Ninevites'.

Then, why pray? If prayer cannot enhance God's glory, increase His knowledge, correct His program, or change His mind, what is the point? The point is that *we* are the beneficiaries when we pray. Prayer focuses our thoughts upward toward God, prayer forces us to acknowledge our need for God, and prayer fosters our dependence upon God. *God is not bent to our will; we are bent to His.* When we pray, we learn more of who He is and what He wants to accomplish in and through us.

We must also consider James' statement, "The effectual fervent prayer of a righteous man availeth much" (James 5:16b). Many take this to mean that if you will only be persistent enough in your prayer, God will eventually do whatever you demand. Not so. First, look at the three conditions for powerful prayer. It must be *effectual*, meaning, "that which works." Jesus said in John 16:23-24 that the only prayer that "works" is that which is in accord with His will. The Father is under no obligation to do what we want, and He is incapable of doing anything contrary to His own will. Therefore, for prayer to be effectual in availing much, it must first be according to the will of God.

A second condition for powerful prayer is that it be *fervent*, or "sincere and serious." Many of the things we ask God to do are things we ought to be doing ourselves. James mentions the hypocrisy of praying for people's needs to be met, yet not meeting the needs ourselves: "If a brother or sister be naked, and destitute of daily food, And one of you say unto them, Depart in peace, be *ye* warmed and filled, notwithstanding ye give them not those things which are needful to the body; what *doth it* profit?" (James 2:15-16). We might also ask if you could be considered "sincere and serious" in your prayers for your neighbor's salvation if you are unwilling to share the Gospel with him and live the Gospel before him.

A third condition for powerful prayer is that it be offered by a "righteous man." Do you qualify? *Righteousness* is that which is consistent with God's will, obedient to Him. It does not mean *sinlessness*, but it requires genuine penitence and faith when sin is recognized (1 John 1:8-10). Many people who expect their prayers to avail much are neither effectual, nor fervent, nor righteous in their praying.

But if those three conditions are met, what is promised? That your prayer will "avail much." The results promised for powerful prayer include the forgiveness of sins (James 5:16; 1 John 1:9) and the satisfaction of God's discipline (James 5:13-15; Heb. 12:5-11). Further, you become more intimately acquainted with God (Phil. 1:9-11; 3:8-10), and you will be strengthened in your spiritual warfare (Eph. 6:10-18; Mark 14:38; Luke 22:46; 2 Cor. 13:7).

Yet we complain, because we think "availing much" means "fixing my personal problems." We misidentify our real needs. Poor health and financial hardship are inconvenient and uncomfortable, but they are not our real difficulties. We don't really need better health or more money, even if our health is so poor or our money so scarce that it leads to death. We are too shortsighted. It is far more important to have our sins forgiven and God's discipline satisfied, to become intimately acquainted with God, and to be strengthened in our spiritual conflict than that we recover from poverty or illness. So, when God says that the "effectual fervent prayer of a righteous man availeth much," He means it. The problem may be that we are trying to avail the wrong things.

For What Should We Pray?

It is sometimes hard to say just what our prayer requests should be. We need to admit the truth of Paul's assertion, "for we know not what we should pray for as we ought" (Rom. 8:26). It is certainly acceptable to ask God to be merciful to the sick and grant recovery, to be merciful to the oppressed and grant deliverance, to be merciful to the traveler and grant safety, or to be merciful to the poor and grant provision. But such requests should be tempered with the qualification, "not my will, but thine be done," since God has not revealed His will in any of these matters.

Of course, there are some things we can ask God with great confidence, because He has revealed His will on many matters. Jesus taught His disciples to pray, "Give us this day our daily bread." When we pray for provision, remember that God has promised to supply. But he promised "this day" to give us our "daily bread." He did not promise to give us today our provision for tomorrow, and He never promised our daily coffee and donuts, much less our daily steak

and lobster. We must refrain from demanding more than God has
promised. We can also confidently ask God for things like victory
over temptation, wisdom to make godly choices, spiritual enlightenment that we may better understand His Word and more consistently
obey, and boldness to witness to the truth of the Gospel to the saving
of the lost.

It seems, though, that often our public prayer requests amount to little more than asking God to intervene in those circumstances of life
that cause us fear. When the early church was persecuted, they immediately went to prayer. But they did not pray for deliverance from the
persecution. They asked, instead, for boldness to preach the Gospel in
spite of persecution (Acts 4:29). We ought not to pray so much for
deliverance from circumstances as for victory over circumstances. We
hide our deepest needs in the secret places of our hearts, rarely mentioning them to God and never to one another. It may be because our
perception of church is skewed. All too often we see the gathered
believers as a sort of showplace for perfection, where we model our
spiritual strengths, when what we really need is a hospital for the
binding of wounds, where we admit our spiritual needs and find help
and solace and strength.

Who Should Pray?

Every Christian should include prayer as an integral part of his regularly scheduled personal devotions, and Christian families should pray
together daily. But churches need to pray together, as well. In the
first chapter of Acts we find the first official assembly of that group of
believers who would become the church when the Holy Spirit was
given at Pentecost. And that first meeting was a prayer meeting.
There were 120 people gathered there to pray. The variety of people
involved is important. This group was made up of both men and
women (Acts 1:14; see also Luke 8:1-3). It included both mature
Christians (the Apostles) and new converts (Jesus' brothers, cf. John
7:5). It included the known and the unknown, the respected and the
obscure. Matthew, the former Roman sympathizer and tax collector,
was there. So was Simon Zelotes, member of a band of insurrection-
ists looking to overthrow the Roman government.[1] This diverse
group was bound together by their mutual faith in Christ and the exercise of prayer. This unity was not due to a pastor, or a church pro-

gram, or the budget, or a building, or a denominational organization. They were unified in their concerted prayer that God would provide for them whatever they would need to accomplish the work Christ had entrusted to them. Not only do you need personal time in prayer, every Christian belongs in a local church, as a member, becoming personally involved in its fellowship of prayer. Your work schedule may prevent you from attending every prayer meeting, but you must not use that as an excuse to keep from being involved in the prayer ministry of your church.

Some years ago I was preaching a series of messages on the importance of prayer, and I ended up preaching myself under conviction. While I was trying to convince my congregation of the importance of personal and corporate prayer, I continued to use the mid-week service as a Bible study/preaching service. I realized that in the normal calendar of church events, we allowed only a few minutes in each service for someone to lead the congregation in prayer. We called our Wednesday evening service "Prayer Meeting," but very little time or energy was given to prayer. That has since changed. Now, we spend thirty minutes to an hour in prayer in the mid-week service. Of course, if your idea of a church service requires thirty to forty-five minutes of preaching, this kind of prayer emphasis will be hard to accept. Christians who prefer to do nothing at church but sit and listen might find this to be a lot of work. But it is vital for your growth in Christ. The church needs a regularly designated time to gather for the express purpose of praying together.

Is It Ever Wrong to Pray?

By this point I hope you agree that prayer is vital to the Christian life and to the life and ministry of the church. It is more important than almost anything else we can do. But there are times when prayer might be inappropriate or even wrong. When seeking God's will about a matter, there comes a point where His will should be clear and praying about it is at least pointless, and perhaps sin. There are three events in the life of Joshua that illustrate how our praying could become an act of disobedience.

First, *it is wrong to pray when God's instructions are clear.* In Joshua 3:7-17 we find the account of Israel's entrance into the

Promised Land by crossing the Jordan River. First, God spoke to Joshua and told him exactly what to do and how to do it. He told Joshua to have the priests take the Ark of the Covenant upon their shoulders and walk into the Jordan River. The rest of Israel was to follow at a distance of about a half-mile. When the priests reached the middle of the river they were to "stand still in Jordan" and Israel was to cross on the riverbed. As improbable as those instructions sounded, Joshua communicated to Israel what God had said, and Israel obeyed. They did not call a prayer meeting. Prayer for faith to obey might have been appropriate, but prayer about what to do would have amounted to unbelief, since God had already told them what to do. They did not need prayer, they needed action. As the priests entered Jordan, the waters were cut off about forty miles upstream, meaning that the water merely receded as they waded in its edge. They walked by faith, and not by sight, in the edge of the water, all the way to the middle of the river. The priests may have been praying as they walked, but the only appropriate prayer would have been for greater confidence, and forgiveness for doubting. Praying for God's protection on dry ground was unnecessary. He was doing that already. That kind of praying, when God has clearly told you what to do, only indicates doubt that God can or will keep His word. The clear commands of Scripture are to be *obeyed*, not "prayed about." It is disobedient and hypocritical to pray for "God's leading" in matters on which God's will is clear if we will but study Scripture and take Him at His word—which is precisely why He gave us His Word.

Second, *it is wrong to pray when my responsibility is known*. When Joshua was first appointed to leadership of Israel (1:1-9) God gave him some general instructions. He told Joshua that it was his responsibility to lead Israel into Canaan and to conquer the land. He told him to be guided by "this book of the Law," the Pentateuch. As far as Joshua knew, this was the final word from God on the conquest of Canaan. Joshua expected no further instructions, so he started making plans. He started Israel moving toward the river, and then God told him how to cross. After they crossed Jordan, Joshua got them settled into camp and rose early the next morning to scout Jericho, the first city they would encounter, in order to plan a strategy for attack. It was while Joshua was out scouting the city that God gave him further instructions (5:13-6:20). Had Joshua been back at camp in his tent

praying for guidance, he would not have met the Lord. The Lord
appeared on the hill overlooking Jericho. He was waiting for Joshua
where he should have been if he were doing the job the Lord had
assigned him. Joshua was obeying what he knew to do, and was
therefore ready to receive and obey further instructions. Then Joshua
and Israel obeyed the additional instructions God gave, as outlandish
as they seemed (basically, "march around the city until the walls fall
down.") The principle here is that *God will never give you further
guidance if you are not obeying what you already know to do.*

So you say, "Okay, what about chapter seven? Joshua didn't wait;
he didn't pray; he just acted, and he was defeated." In Joshua 7:1-9
we have the story of Achan's sin and Israel's defeat. When Jericho
fell, Israel was to destroy everything but the gold and silver, which
were to be turned over to the priests. But Achan took some of the loot
for himself. Achan's successful theft indicated that Joshua had failed
to supervise adequately. Without checking the camp to be sure that
no-one had broken God's command, Joshua sent the army against Ai.
Some have criticized his strategy, saying he should have sent the
entire army instead of arrogantly sending only 3000 men. But might
he not have been demonstrating confidence in God and concern for
the well-being of his men? They had just spent all day marching
around Jericho, then climbing over rubble and doing hand-to-hand
combat with the enemy. This was their first real activity since their
circumcision, and they were exhausted. Others have claimed Joshua
should have asked God for instructions instead of relying on his
scouts. But God had told him to conquer the land and expected him
to use his ingenuity, guided by the Law, to do that. Praying for
instruction when God had told him what to do would have been shirk-
ing his responsibilities.

The real problem was that Joshua tried to obey in one area while
neglecting another, and the army was defeated at the cost of thirty-six
lives. At that point, Joshua fell upon his face before God, accusing
God of failing to keep His word (7:6-9). God's response is instructive. He said, "Get thee up, wherefore liest thou thus upon thy face?
Israel hath sinned...Up, sanctify the people" (7:10-13). God rebuked
Joshua for praying when he should have been obeying. Joshua should
have been dealing with Israel's sin instead of whining to God. Had
Joshua obeyed in Jericho, *any* battle plan would have succeeded

against Ai. But since he disobeyed in Jericho, *no* battle plan could succeed, and God would have given no instructions other than to cleanse Israel. God's response to Joshua's prayer illustrates that *it is wrong to pray when prayer is a substitute for obedience.*

   To summarize, there are three parts to an answer to the question "Why pray?" First, God ordained prayer as a means to help us grow in Him (Col. 1:9; 2 Thes. 1:11-12). Second, God commands prayer to help us communicate with Him (1 Thes. 5:17; 1 Tim. 2:8). Third, God uses prayer to help us depend upon Him (Luke 18:1-8; John 14:13-14; 2 Thes. 3:1). Thus, we learn to pray for those things God intends to give as our wills are bent to His. And we must all pray. Our personal prayer should be a constant, daily communication with and dependence upon God. We must also pray with our families and with our churches. Corporate prayer may be the single most important activity of any body of believers. But there are also at least three circumstances in which prayer may be wrong. First, prayer is wrong if we ask God to make an exception to His clear instructions. Second, prayer is wrong if we ask God for guidance while failing to obey. Third, prayer is wrong if we blame God for our problems while tolerating sin in our lives or in the lives of those for whom we are responsible.

---

[1] It is entirely possible that this is the group to which Barabbas belonged, since his crime was "insurrection" (Mark 15:7).

CHAPTER 10
THE INSTRUCTION OF YOUR CHILDREN

The date was Saturday, August 8, 1992. The place was Barcelona, Spain. The event was the men's 4 x 100 relay in the Olympic Games. The US men's team had just set a new world-record of 37.40 seconds—an incredible average of 9.35 seconds per 100-meter leg. But the key to winning a relay is not just speed. Carl Lewis, the star US runner, knew this. Before the race, he told a reporter, "We have always had the most speed. Our problem has been that *we haven't had a consistent concept of how to pass the baton properly.*" He was only describing a foot race. But he might just as well have been talking about Christianity.

What will your children and mine learn from us that will be passed on to their children and grandchildren? Psalm 78:1-7 says,

> Give ear, O my people, *to* my law: incline your ears to the words of my mouth. I will open my mouth in a parable: I will utter dark sayings of old: Which we have heard and known, and our fathers have told us. We will not hide *them* from their children, showing to the generation to come the praises of the LORD, and his strength, and his wonderful works that he hath done. For he established a testimony in Jacob, and appointed a law in Israel, which he commanded our fathers, that they should make them known to their children: That the generation to come might know

them, even the children *which* should be born; *who* should arise
and declare *them* to their children: That they might set their hope
in God, and not forget the works of God, but keep his commandments.

We must be convinced of the truth of the Word of God and of its relevance to our own lives. Then we must instill in our children the
same knowledge of, reverence for, and understanding of the Word of
God. If we want the generations to come to "set their hope in God,
and not forget the works of God, but keep his commandments," we
must take care to pass the baton properly.

In educating our children in the Word of God, we need to avoid two
extreme attitudes. Scripture teaches that parents are to "train up a
child in the way that he should go" (Prov. 22:6) and to "bring them up
in the nurture and admonition of the Lord" (Eph. 6:4). Many teachers
today interpret these verses through their deterministic philosophy,
saying that whatever the children do or become was *caused* by the
parents, thereby placing *all* of the responsibility on the parents.
Others go to the opposite extreme, using a *laissez-faire* approach to
child rearing similar to the teaching of Dr. Benjamin Spock. These
insist that children will do what they will do regardless of the parents'
influence, since the Scriptures teach that each individual is responsible for his own choices and their consequences, placing *none* of the
responsibility on the parents. The truth is a balance between these
extremes. Each of us, including our children and grandchildren, will
answer for our own choices (Ezekiel 18:1-20), and parents will
answer for their influence on their children and grandchildren.
Parents and grandparents have a responsibility to make their influence
a powerful and godly one, and to do their best to guard their children
from ungodly influences. The challenge is to learn how to educate
our children in the Word of God without encouraging them to become
either self-righteous legalists or rebellious hedonists.

Producing Obedience from a Submissive Heart

Dr. Jim Binney, an experienced pastor and Christian counselor,
describes a process of producing obedience from a submissive heart.
Paul told the believers in Rome that, "ye were the servants of sin, but
ye have obeyed from the heart that form of doctrine which was deliv-

ered you" (Rom. 6:17). In this verse, we have the process stated in reverse order. *Sound doctrine* affects the *heart* producing *obedience*. That is, right choices will be made from the heart on the basis of sound doctrine. Dr. Binney explains an alphabetical sequence leading to either obedience or disobedience.

1. Activating Event (life's circumstances). Something happens that requires a choice.
2. Belief System (doctrinal framework). Interprets the event, decides its meaning, and recommends a response.
3. Consequential Feelings (heart response). Chooses a response based upon prioritizing beliefs.
4. Decisive Behavior (obedience or disobedience). Acts on the choice made. Will be obedient if the belief system is sound *and* the heart is submissive. Will be disobedient if the belief system is wrong *or* the heart is unsubmissive.

Practical application of the principles can be made almost without limit. For instance, say a teenager is out with friends and is presented with temptation to be sexually immoral. The confrontation with the temptation is the "activating event." Whether or not his response to the temptation ("decisive behavior") will be obedient to the instruction of the Word of God will depend upon both his "belief system" and his "consequential feelings." If his belief system is biblical, he knows such behavior is sinful, and the recommended responses might include various ways to remove himself from the temptation and avoid the sin. But he also believes he will get some pleasure from the sin. He must then decide which belief is more important to him at the moment: pleasing God or pleasing himself. If he decides it is most important that he please God, he will choose to obey and disengage from the tempting situation. If he decides he prefers to please himself, he will then decide from a subset of choices. He may give in. Or he may refrain because he fears the consequences of his behavior: the wrath of some authority, potential pregnancy, potential contact with infectious diseases, etc. In that case, his choice may be the same as the one who obeyed, but is not really *obedience*. It is still self-centeredness in the form of self-preservation. If the cause of fear is removed (i.e., using contraceptives), he may choose otherwise next time, because either his belief system is weak or his heart response is rebellious.

But teenagers are not the only ones confronted with "activating events." Medical researchers have recently begun to predict that a cure for Parkinson's disease may be on the horizon. The tests that are so promising come from stem cell research, and the projected cure will probably involve use of tissues cultured from stem cells. Let's say, for the sake of argument, that such predictions prove true and a cure is produced. Then you, or someone you love, is diagnosed with Parkinson's disease. The doctor offers to prescribe the new treatment. Do you choose to take the treatment or accept the likelihood of long-term illness and eventual death from Parkinson's? The answer may seem obvious until you learn that stem cell research and treatment requires tissue harvested from aborted fetuses. What you decide may depend upon the depth of your conviction that abortion is murder. Other aspects of your doctrinal framework also affect your decision. Is God really good? Is heaven real? Is longer life and recovery from this disease necessarily a blessing? Is it ever acceptable to cause one person's death so another may benefit?

The moral dilemmas in such choices are very real. The importance of the study of the Word of God, prayer, and the support of a good local church is evident. It is vital that we have a solid doctrinal framework through which to interpret life's circumstances, hearts that are submissive to God, and an appreciation of the urgency of transfer-ring both to the generations to come.

All disobedience is rooted in that which Hebrews 3:12 calls "an evil heart of unbelief in departing from the living God." You may protest that *your* disobedience was not motivated by an evil heart of unbelief, but you have been fooled by "the deceitfulness of sin" (Heb. 3:13). Anytime you or I choose to do wrong, in any circumstance, it is because we decided to disbelieve God. We may have decided that God did not really mean it when He said "thou shalt" or "thou shalt not." Or we may have decided that God either cannot or will not do anything about it. Or we may have decided that whatever God choos-es to do about our violation is worth it for the pleasure we get from disobeying. Any way you slice it, disobedience indicates that our belief system is wrong. *Our creed may sound orthodox, but if we can ignore what we say we believe and act contrary to that creed, we do not really believe it.* If we want to influence our children to live holy lives, it is important that we address at the foundation their belief system, that we educate our children in the Word of God.

At the same time, if we bypass the heart, we will encourage conformity without comprehension, which produces legalistic hardness. Matthew 13:18-23 illustrates various responses to the Word as it is sown.

> Hear ye therefore the parable of the sower. When any one heareth the word of the kingdom, and understandeth *it* not, then cometh the wicked *one*, and catcheth away that which was sown in his heart. This is he which received seed by the way side. But he that received the seed into stony places, the same is he that heareth the word, and anon with joy receiveth it; Yet hath he not root in himself, but dureth for a while: for when tribulation or persecution ariseth because of the word, by and by he is offended. He also that received seed among the thorns is he that heareth the word; and the care of this world, and the deceitfulness of riches, choke the word, and he becometh unfruitful. But he that received seed into the good ground is he that heareth the word, and understandeth *it*; which also beareth fruit, and bringeth forth, some a hundredfold, some sixty, some thirty.

Some choose to ignore the Word altogether, because the soil of their hearts is hard. Others respond superficially, giving outward evidence of acceptance, but dying off because they never understood that pleasing God was something they could not do on their own. Having tried to grow by their own strength, with no root in good soil, the stress of it all caused them to wither and die. They were *legalists*, trying to make it to God on their own, and were never saved. Still others give outward evidence of acceptance, but they have not understood that salvation is for the purpose of pleasing God, not themselves. Since they are only looking for what they can get out of salvation, and the Christian life is not bringing them all the pleasures they expected, and being distracted by other things that seem more attractive now, they wither and die. They were *hedonists*, interested in God only for what He would do for them, and were never saved. The only ones who grow and produce fruit are those whose hearts have been broken up

by the plow, cleared of thorns and stones, and can therefore understand what God will do in producing fruit in and through them. They
have believed the Word and allowed it to change their heart so they
can produce the fruit of obedience through the power of God in their
lives. They are the only ones in the parable who are *truly saved.*

Many church members and other professing Christians made profes-
sions of faith years ago based on a faulty belief system. Some trust
their own righteousness to please God, and some serve only for what
they think God will do for them. These are not truly saved. Others
have given up trying to obey consistently because they found they
cannot, or it just doesn't seem worth the effort, since they haven't got-
ten everything out of it that they expected. These may not be truly
saved, or their hearts may have been "hardened by the deceitfulness of
sin." So how do we instill the Word of God in the lives of our children without hardening their hearts?

Training Your Children without Hardening Their Hearts

First and foremost, the teacher must have the right attitude. Before
commanding the people of Israel to teach the Word of God to their
children, Moses told them that the words "shall be in thine heart"
(Deut. 6:6). Before Ezra could "teach in Israel statutes and judgments," he first "prepared his heart to seek the law of the LORD, and
to do it" (Ezra 7:10). Children will never learn to respond properly to
the circumstances of life from a teacher who does not respond properly from a heart in submission to God's will. This has enormous
implications in choosing a school for your children and a staff for
your Sunday School. It also means that Mom and Dad have a very
grave responsibility to set the right example and to be prepared to
teach their children. This idea of "do as I say, not as I do" only teaches children that hypocrisy is acceptable. It is true that some children
have hypocritical parents and/or ungodly teachers, and still choose to
do right. That can happen when, by God's grace, they manage to
keep their eyes on the Master Teacher, and are not greatly influenced
by those who fail to be the good influence they should be. This is the
exception, not the rule. It is incredibly foolish and presumptuous to
assume that God will overrule the quality of teaching and teachers
you provide your children, hoping they will choose to serve God in
spite of you.

The active presentation of the material is also important. After telling Israel that these words "shall be in thine heart," Moses added, "and thou shalt teach them diligently unto thy children" (Deut 6:7). The Hebrew word translated "teach" means "to whet or sharpen with a predetermined purpose in mind, with a concentrated effort." It is an intensely purposeful presentation. Verses 7-9 go on to describe the saturation method of presentation discussed in Chapter Eight. It includes formal instruction in the Word and the comprehensive informal demonstration of the life-application of the Word: sitting at home or going somewhere, getting up or going to bed, whatever you do or wherever you look, whether you are coming in or going out.

The practical application of the truth is also vital. When Ezra stood to instruct the people of Israel, he "read in the book in the law of God distinctly, and gave the sense, and caused *them* to understand the reading" (Neh. 8:8). When educating our children in the Word of God it is not enough to have them hear and even memorize the text. They must understand how to relate God's Word to their lives. We must be sensitive to their personal needs in specific situations and times. We must teach them what they need so they will be ready when they need it. James 1:22-25 speaks of the focus of becoming a doer of the Word, not just a hearer. Learning the Word is not the final objective. Learning how to apply and live by the Word is the goal.

Also important to this whole process is conversation with the student. Moses said "and thou shalt talk of them…" (Deut. 6:7b). The education process must go beyond lecture, beyond making children listen in church and Sunday School. It includes real conversation about real situations that your kids face with real answers based on real truth—God's Word. The goal is not just the transfer of information, but *transformation*. The teacher has a predetermined purpose, a concentrated effort, applying specific truths to specific needs to produce power for a specific change.

These principles have implications for families and church ministries alike. Teachers should be the right kind of people, or they should not be teachers. Sunday School teachers who are not faithfully teaching and living the Word of God ought to be rebuked and instructed. If a resistant spirit is demonstrated, and change is not evident, they should be removed from their classes. If you don't have enough

spiritually qualified teachers, change the program, not the standard.
Churches must commit themselves to refusing to "do ministry" by
planning programs then scrounging for people to implement them.
Rather, we must plan programs as we have qualified people to do
them.

None of the children in our homes or churches is the sinless Son of
God. Each has a sin nature all his own. But children will be influenced by their parents, being more likely to adopt the principles you
live by than the principles you teach. What you are at home or in private is what you are. Years of trying to tell your child how important
it is to live honestly will be ignored the first time you go into a restaurant that gives a discount for children ten and under and you tell the
waiter that your eleven-year-old is only ten. You just sold your values
for a couple of dollars. May God save us from nominal Christians
who believe they only have to act like Christ and talk like Christ when
they are at church or with other Christians. Our children must see
parents and Christian leaders who combine the humility to admit their
own failings with the character to rely on the Holy Spirit's power to
apply the Word of God to their lives to help overcome those failings
in an ongoing attempt to be consistently Christ-like.

CHAPTER 11
THE COMMITMENT OF FINANCIAL RESOURCES

The pastor of a moderate sized country church decided that it was time to replace the church's old upright piano with a baby-grand. The primary obstacle was money—or, rather, the lack of it. The church had no financial reserves in the bank, and their weekly offerings were barely maintaining staff salaries and operating expenses, so borrowing the money was not an option. What were they to do? Someone suggested that they hold a public auction. But what would they sell? They decided to solicit donations from area businesses. The pastor, staff, and church volunteers spent several weeks canvassing, requesting gifts of goods and/or services to be sold at their auction. They collected quite an assortment of items: clothing, small appliances, sporting goods, building materials, toys, furniture, gift certificates, and so on. The immediate results of the auction seemed advantageous to everyone. Donors received tax-deductible receipts. Buyers purchased things they wanted or needed and had the satisfaction of "helping a good cause." And the church got its new piano. But had their fund-raising methods been *right*? Rather than the church having extended charity to those in need in the community, it had placed itself in the community's debt by having requested charity from their neighbors. It is difficult to witness effectively of God's gracious provision of salvation to unbelievers who see themselves as having been your provider.

This, and other stories like it, point up an important question: "How is the ministry of the church to be financed?" Methods practiced by churches today present an amazing array of options. Some claim that it is appropriate to raise money for the church by hosting weekly bingo games or occasional lotteries. Most would object, though, on the ground that those activities involve gambling. Others, like the church described above, decide to host a fair, a craft show, a yard sale, an auction, or a car wash. Those may be acceptable activities and honorable ways to make money, but are they legitimate ways of raising funds for the *church*?

Our attitude toward money and our use of our financial resources and possessions are important to God. The Lord Jesus had a lot to say about money. Of the thirty-eight parables, sixteen were concerned with the handling of money and possessions. One of ten verses in the Gospels, 288 in all, deals directly with the subject of money. While the Bible provides about 500 verses on prayer, and a few less than 500 verses on faith, there are more than 2,000 verses on money and possessions. What has God said concerning His plan for financing His church? Over and over again, we find that God intends for His ministry to be financed *through the giving of His people.*

The Biblical Plan for Giving

The Apostle Paul presents an extended discussion on the biblical plan for giving in 2 Corinthians 9:1-15.

For as touching the ministering to the saints, it is superfluous for me to write to you: For I know the forwardness of your mind, for which I boast of you to them of Macedonia, that Achaia was ready a year ago; and your zeal hath provoked very many. Yet have I sent the brethren, lest our boasting of you should be in vain in this behalf; that, as I said, ye may be ready: Lest haply if they of Macedonia come with me, and find you unprepared, we (that we say not, ye) should be ashamed in this same confident boasting. Therefore I thought it necessary to exhort the brethren, that they would go before unto you, and make up beforehand your bounty, whereof ye had notice before, that the same might be ready, as *a matter of* bounty, and not as *of* covetousness. But this *I say*, He which soweth sparingly shall reap also sparingly; and he which soweth bountifully shall reap also bountifully. Every man according as he purposeth in his heart, *so let him give*; not grudgingly, or of necessity: for God loveth a cheerful giver. And God *is* able to make all grace abound toward you; that ye, always having all sufficiency in all *things*, may abound to every good work: (As it is written, He hath dispersed abroad; he hath given to the poor: his righteousness remaineth for ever. Now he that ministereth seed to the sower both minister bread for *your* food, and multiply your seed sown, and increase the fruits of your righteousness;) Being enriched in every thing to all bountifulness, which causeth through us thanksgiving to God. For the administration of this service not only supplieth the want of the saints, but is abundant also by many thanksgivings unto God; Whiles by the experiment of this ministration they glorify God for your professed subjection unto the gospel of Christ, and for *your* liberal distribution unto them, and unto all *men*; And by their prayer for you, which long after you for the exceeding grace of God in you. Thanks *be* unto God for his unspeakable gift.

It is significant that these instructions are not limited to this particular congregation, since Paul is merely telling them the same thing he has told other churches. Also notice that Paul did not simply suggest that they consider doing this. No, he commands, "I have given order...even so do ye." While this particular passage may have specific application to giving for missions work or disaster relief, it has general application to all of our giving. Paul describes here both the proper *manner* of our giving and the proper *motive* for our giving.

In the first seven verses, Paul discusses the *manner* of their giving, revealing four characteristics of the acceptable offering. First, each believer is to give *systematically*. The believer should have a plan for giving, and should practice it regularly on "the first day of the week." Notice the care Paul took concerning this collection. He sent an advance reminder of the need with encouragement to be continually faithful. He had written to this same congregation earlier with specific commands regarding their giving. In 1 Cor. 9:6-14, Paul explained that the minister of the Gospel is to be supported by the giving of God's people. "Do ye not know that they which minister about holy things live *of the things* of the temple? And they which wait at the altar are partakers with the altar? Even so hath the Lord ordained that they which preach the gospel should live of the gospel" (9:13-14). In 1 Cor. 16:1-2, he describes a system for giving in which "every one of you" should contribute funds weekly on the basis of the measure of God's material blessing. "Now concerning the collection for the saints, as I have given order to the churches of Galatia, even so do ye. Upon the first *day* of the week let every one of you lay by him in store, as *God* hath prospered him."

Besides giving systematically, the believer is expected to give *bountifully*. Failure to do so is equated with sin, particularly the sin of covetousness (2 Cor. 9:5-6). This is a consistent principle throughout Scripture.

Honor the Lord with thy substance [what you have], and with the firstfruits of all thine increase [what you gain in income, interest, produce, etc.]: So shall thy barns be filled with plenty, and thy presses shall burst out with new wine (Prov. 3:9-10).

There is that scattereth, and yet increaseth; and *there is* that withholdeth more than is meet, but it *tendeth* to poverty. The liberal [generous, unselfish] soul shall be made fat [prosperous]: and he that watereth shall be watered also himself (Prov. 11:24-25).

He that giveth unto the poor shall not lack: but he that hideth his eyes [ignores the need] shall have many a curse (Prov. 28:27).

Will a man rob God? Yet ye have robbed me. But ye say, Wherein have we robbed thee? In tithes and offerings. Ye *are* cursed with a curse: for ye have robbed me, *even* this whole nation. Bring ye all the tithes into the storehouse, that there may be meat in mine house, and prove me now herewith, [put me to the test—give as you should and see what I do] saith the LORD of hosts, if I will not open you the windows of heaven, and pour you out a blessing, that *there shall* not *be room* enough *to receive it*. And I will rebuke the devourer for your sakes [stay healthier, things last longer, dollars go farther, etc.], and he shall not destroy the fruits of your ground; neither shall your vine cast her fruit before the time in the field, saith the LORD of hosts (Malachi 3:8-11).

Give, and it shall be given unto you; good measure, pressed
down, and shaken together, and running over, shall men give into
your bosom. For with the same measure that ye mete withal it
shall be measured to you again (Luke 6:38).

Repeatedly, we see that God has stated a sowing-and-reaping principle in which He promises to bless His people in the same measure of
our confidence in Him demonstrated by our giving. If our giving is
stingy, His blessing will be meager. If our giving is bountiful, His
blessing will be abundant.

Some contend that the tithe is an Old Testament legal requirement,
and the New Testament economy sets us free from such strictures.
But they misunderstand. First, tithing was introduced *before* the law.
Abraham paid tithes to Melchizedek in Genesis 14:20, and Jacob
promised a tithe to God in Genesis 28:22. Later, tithing continued
under the law as a minimum. And with the special gifts the Israelites
were required to present on holy days, and other provisions in the law,
estimates of total *required* giving range from about 19% to 32% of
total income. The people were also challenged to bring "free-will
offerings" beyond the minimum required, and Malachi said that they
had robbed God in tithes *and* offerings. God expected much more
than 10% under the Old Testament system.

Even in the New Testament, the Lord Jesus commended giving the
tithe. "Woe unto you, scribes and Pharisees, hypocrites! For ye pay
tithe of mint and anise and cummin, and have omitted the weightier
matters of the law, judgment, mercy, and faith: these ought ye to have
done, and not to leave the other undone" (Matt. 23:23). The Pharisees
were so scrupulous in their tithing that they even gave of the plants in
their herb gardens, which were not intended for income but for personal use. And Jesus commended them for it. Further, we must not
forget that the spiritual blessings that are ours in the New Testament
economy are *far greater* than those enjoyed by the Old Testament
saints. Our level of consecration and gratitude should exceed that
which God demanded of the believers of the Old Testament. Various
polls indicate that among those who consider themselves evangelical
Christians a mere 4% claim to tithe systematically. If accurate, that
means that according to Malachi, 96% of us are systematically rob-
bing God! Is it possible to seek first the Kingdom of God, and rob

from the Kingdom at the same time? Somehow, I do not believe God is pleased when we try to defend our covetous avoidance of tithing on the ground that we consider that legalism.

A third characteristic of proper giving is that it should be *purposeful* or *deliberate*. Our giving is not to be haphazard, putting a few dollars in the plate once in a while. Each of us must determine how much we ought to give, and then commit to give it off the top, so that nothing will stop us. Of the 4% of us who do tithe, too many carefully calculate how much we *must* give to be tithing. We tend to be more generous and give a higher percentage when leaving a tip for a waitress than when the offering plate is passed. What we *can* give or *should* give in our offerings may well exceed the tithe. Everyone has unexpected expenses and other uses for the money we ought to give to God. But we must determine never to be guilty of fearing the consequences of tithing more than we fear the consequences of disobeying and distrusting God.

Fourth, Paul says that our giving ought to be *cheerful*. Not only does he say we have to give, he says we have to *enjoy* it. We are not supposed to give just because we are supposed to give. Nor are we to resent giving or think we put God in our debt because we give. God wants us to give because we love Him. Actually, the Greek word translated *cheerful* (2 Cor. 9:7) is the source of our English word *hilarious*. The implication is that our giving should be motivated out of a childlike glee—that we should be so excited about being able to give to God that we can hardly wait for the opportunity and can barely refrain from joyous laughter.

Our giving should be systematic, bountiful, purposeful, and cheerful. Taken together, these characteristics demonstrate confident trust in God, which is the most basic attitude God demands of us. When we give this way, we prove that we are not relying upon our financial resources for our security, but we believe God can and will take care of us on what we have left after we give generously to His work. Failing to give in this manner demonstrates a misplaced confidence, trusting money rather than God. God promises to bless those who trust Him, but when we trust ourselves or our money, He cannot bless.

Paul has also described the proper *motive* for giving. That motive is actually three-fold. It involves *loving as God loves, following God's example*, and *showing gratitude to God*. All of these center on the Person and work of the Lord Jesus. First, God loved us so much that He gave His "unspeakable gift," His Son, Jesus (John 3:16). We demonstrate God's love in us by our own sacrificial giving. Second, God showed us how to give when He gave His Son, and if we would be imitators of God (Eph. 5:1), we, too, must give. Finally, if we have any grasp of the significance of God's great gift of salvation in Christ, we cannot help but show our gratitude to God by giving to Him. He has purchased us with the blood of His Son. We are not doing God a favor by giving to Him something that is ours. Rather, everything we have is His and comes as a gift from Him. We are merely to return part of it to Him as a pledge that we will use all of it for His glory.

The Biblical Promises for Giving

Once we understand God's plan for giving, we can gain a better comprehension of what the Bible promises concerning giving. In 2 Cor. 9:1-15, Paul speaks of two categories of promises developed in other Scriptures: promises to the disobedient who give sparingly and promises to the obedient who give according to God's plan.

Promises to the disobedient are mentioned in verse 6, "He which soweth sparingly shall reap also sparingly." If you put out little seed, you will reap a meager harvest. Just so, if you give little, your reward will be equivalent. Other passages develop this theme. Proverbs 11:24 indicates that inadequate giving tends toward poverty—"There is that scattereth, and yet increaseth; and *there is* that withholdeth more than is meet, but *it tendeth* to poverty." Malachi 3:9 states unequivocally that inadequate giving brings the curse of God—"Ye *are* cursed with a curse; for ye have robbed me, *even* this whole nation." Paul indicates that inadequate giving brings forth all manner of evil.

But they that will be rich [whose will is set on riches] fall into temptation and a snare, and *into* many foolish and hurtful lusts, which drown men in destruction and perdition. For the love of money is the root of all [not every instance of, but every type of] evil: which while some coveted after, they have erred from the faith, and pierced themselves through with many sorrows (1 Tim. 6:9-10).

A believer who fails to give according to God's plan risks poverty, the curse of God, falling into temptation, becoming controlled by harmful desires, and being "pierced...through with many sorrows." The believer cannot afford *not* to give.

There are also promises to the believer who gives obediently. There are actually two categories of benefits promised: benefits for the giver and benefits for the recipient of the gift. The giver receives blessings from both God and man. First, God loves, or "takes delight in," the cheerful giver. It is a great blessing for God to delight in you. Further, God makes "all grace abound toward you," making sure you "always having all sufficiency in all"—that is, you will have enough of everything in every way at all times. While we need to be willing to do without some things we *want* in order to be able to give generously to God, He has promised that we will never lack anything we *need* to do His will. God has also promised to "increase the fruits of your righteousness" (9:10). Disciplined giving opens the door to further spiritual growth. Not giving faithfully hinders spiritual growth. Finally, God promises the giver that he will be "enriched in every thing to all bountifulness [generosity]" (9:11). This does not mean that He will make you abundantly rich. Paul promises that God will enrich the one who gives faithfully in every way so that he can be generous on every occasion. God wants us to so manage our personal finances that we can give generously. He has promised that if we do that, He will make sure we can continue to be generous whenever and wherever we encounter needs. Besides all these blessings from God, the giver also receives the benefit of the recipient's prayers and love (9:14)

A second category of promises refers to blessings for the recipient of our offerings. First, their needs are supplied (9:12). God has promised to supply their needs, but God does not manufacture money for ministry. His chosen method is often to provide other believers that which is needed so they can in turn give to meet the need. He blesses His faithful people so that by pooling our resources we can get His work done. General ministry needs, as well as specific relief needs, are met when God's people give. Second, those whose needs are met overflow with thanksgiving to God. They learn gratitude in the midst of need by having others give to meet that need, and God is glorified (9:12-13).

Paul says in Philippians 4:19, "But my God shall supply all your need according to his riches in glory by Christ Jesus." This verse is often lifted from its context to try to comfort a believer facing hardship. However, the context of Philippians 4:14-19 indicates that this promise is specifically limited to those who give according to God's plan. One who does not give, or who gives inadequately or begrudgingly, has no claim on this promise. Other passages already cited promise not just *adequate* supply, but *abundance* (see Mal. 3:10-11, Prov. 3:9-10; 11:25; 28:27; and Luke 6:38).

God has promised rich blessings for his people if we will give according to His plan. But if we give to accumulate personal wealth or achieve personal comfort, our motives are wrong. We must remember that heavenly treasure is worth far more than earthly wealth. We are told that the streets of heaven are paved with gold. It is unlikely that the reason for that is simply to provide a gaudy display of heaven's opulence. Rather, it serves to illustrate the truth that the substance we value most on this earth is of so little value in heaven as to find its primary usefulness as pavement, something to be trodden under foot. We must break free from the enchantment of earthly wealth. God's people possess the resources to finance God's work if we would just give according to His plan. The following words come from Isaac Watts' "When I Survey the Wondrous Cross":

> Were the whole realm of nature mine,
>   That were a present far too small;
> Love, so amazing, so divine,
>   Demands my soul, my life, my all.

God does not need your fundraising efforts, gimmicks, marketing techniques, or emotional pleas. He wants your soul, your life, your all.

CHAPTER 12
THE MINISTRY OF
EVANGELISTIC OUTREACH[1]

When I was in my teens I heard an evangelist boast, "Give me five minutes alone with anybody, and I'll lead him to Christ." At the time, I assumed he knew something I didn't know, because I had never been that successful in my own evangelistic efforts. I had witnessed to several co-workers at the fast-food restaurant where I worked, and only knew of one who had expressed repentance of sin and faith in Christ. I concluded that I needed to try harder, or needed to be more forceful, or needed to be more winsome, or needed a better technique. Still, real conversions were few and far between. Even today, most people with whom I share the Gospel do not believe. Over time, I've come to realize that the evangelist who bragged that he could lead anyone to Christ was either deliberately lying, or he was getting people to respond to his pitch without really making converts to Christ.

One of the responsibilities to which we pledge ourselves in our church's membership covenant is "to seek the salvation of our kindred and acquaintances." This is an important obligation shared by all believers. But in our evangelistic efforts we find that, by-and-large, the world is not particularly receptive to the message of the Gospel. We may be tempted to become forceful or manipulative, like the evangelist I heard. Or we might be tempted to change the message to make it more acceptable to the unbelieving world. Or we may be tempted to just give up.

The aftermath of the terrorist attacks on the World Trade Center in New York and on the Pentagon has presented Christians with both an opportunity and a challenge. The opportunity is seen in the fact that at least for a while even politicians and news casters have been seen praying and talking about God in public. People are giving more thought to their vulnerability, their mortality, and their destiny. But, in an effort to forestall retribution against American Muslims, many American politicians and religious leaders have adopted an official position of defense of and dialogue with Islam. Instead of challenging the American people to turn to Christ, people have been told they should pray to whatever god they revere. We have been encouraged to take comfort in our faith, assuming that any old faith will do.

The fact is, genuine Christianity is still neither popular nor socially acceptable. It is difficult to market the church to a world that doesn't like your message and actively hates you for what you believe. What is the appropriate attitude and practice for God's people in the evangelization of the lost? We need to stop looking for marketing techniques that work and start proclaiming the truth with boldness.

Our Authority

Shortly before His ascension, Jesus announced to His disciples their Great Commission.

> All power [authority] is given unto me in heaven and in earth.
> Go ye therefore, and teach all nations, baptizing them in the name
> of the Father, and of the Son, and of the Holy Ghost: Teaching
> them to observe all things whatsoever I have commanded you:
> and, lo, I am with you alway, *even* unto the end of the world
> (Matthew 28:18-20).

Notice that the Commission is issued on the *authority* of the universe's Creator and Sovereign, the Lord Jesus Christ. A few years later, Paul wrote to the believers in Rome saying, "For I am not ashamed of the gospel of Christ: for it is the power of God unto salvation to every one that believeth; to the Jew first, and also to the Greek" (Romans 1:16). The Apostles understood the authority of

their message. It is when we begin to question the truth of the Word
of God that we begin to sell out, looking for other ways of doing ministry. There are at least four reasons why we can be just as confident
in the same authority.

First, *the Gospel of Jesus Christ is still true.* Jesus Christ died to
pay the penalty for our sins, and He rose from the dead to offer us
eternal life in Him (1 Cor. 15:3-8). For a person to be saved from his
sin, he must recognize that he is guilty under the law and accept
God's offer of forgiveness by faith in Christ. The Gospel answers the
bad news of man's sinfulness with the good news of God's forgiveness. We proclaim this message on the basis of the absolute authority
of Christ and the Word of God. A large part of the problem with the
church's efforts at evangelism today is that we are unwilling to tell
people the *bad* news of their condition in their sin, so the *good* news
of salvation in Christ makes no sense.

A second reason for our confidence in our authority is *the Gospel of
Jesus Christ is still relevant.* For all our technological progress, every
individual is still a sinner (Rom. 3:23) and the penalty for sin is still
death (Rom. 6:23). We have more food, more free time, and more fun
than any generation before us. But those things only distract from the
spiritual famine in which most live. It is popular to assert that each
individual creates his own reality (I won't deal with the absurdity of
such a notion in this context). Foreshadowing the shift into post-
modernity, the slogan "God said it; I believe it; that settles it for me,"
became popular among Christians in the 1970s. It would have been
better to insist "God said it; that settles it; so I believe it." If God says
something, it is true, whether or not you or I believe it. Many people
talk about "making the church relevant." It is not always clear what
they mean by that. Generally, it seems that they want their church to
look and act like the world. That is not *relevance*; that is *compromise*.
The world deludes itself into believing that mankind is a law unto
himself and that there will be no accountability before God. The truth
is, we will not be evaluated on the basis of community consensus, but
by the unchanging law of God. And we will all be judged guilty
under that law. The message of the Gospel confronts every person in
every era and every culture with his most basic need of forgiveness of
sin and reconciliation to God. It is *always* relevant.

Third, *the Gospel of Jesus Christ is still effective.* The recent trend in the churches in America is to change methods and alter the message in an attempt to find something that works better. Rather than presenting the unadulterated gospel of Jesus Christ, many have begun to grasp at other things without substance. Some will *substitute talent for the truth*, thinking that if they put enough talent on display, people will come to Christ. They replace presentation of the truth of the gospel with performances by celebrity musicians, dramatic actors, and even comedians. Others *substitute gimmicks for the gospel*, thinking that if they hype their services with something strange or offer prizes for bringing visitors, applying marketing tricks to make the church grow, people will come to Christ. Still others substitute *programs for preaching*, replacing the preaching of the Gospel with the latest fads in church ministry planning. By forsaking our authority in the preaching of the Gospel, we have encouraged a shopping mall approach to Christianity, using a church marketing methodology that sees the congregation as consumers and merely tries to attract a clientele. God does not need showy talent, catchy gimmicks, or trendy programs to bring people to Christ. He wants us to preach the Gospel of salvation. People do not need to be entertained, or even happy. They need to be saved. We must reestablish our confidence in our authority to proclaim the truth, even if the world rejects both the authority and the message.

Our Audience

It is possible to be absolutely confident in our authority, and still not reach the world with the Gospel. On the basis of the authority of Christ's commission and the Word of God, someone could decide to try to evangelize a university by putting loudspeakers on the roof of his car and driving around campus shouting, "YOU ARE GOING TO HELL IF YOU DON'T GET SAVED!" It would be possible, but it would not be advisable. The Gospel itself is offensive enough; we need not be offensive in the way we present it.

We see this illustrated in the ministry of the Lord Jesus. He dealt with people honestly and directly, with authority, but always with compassion. The only folks with whom He was harsh were the religious hypocrites who gave God a bad reputation by their misrepresentation of Him. Furthermore, Jesus personalized His methods of presentation. When dealing with Nicodemus, a well-schooled Pharisee who knew and practiced the Law, Jesus told him he needed more. He needed to be born again. When dealing with the immoral Samaritan woman by the well at Sychar, Jesus confronted her with her sin, and offered her "living water." The central message was the same—confess your sin and turn to Christ for salvation. The figures used to communicate the message varied according to the setting. He met them where they were, and talked to them on their level, in their vocabulary and according to their frame of reference. But He did not leave them where He found them.

We also see this illustrated in Paul's ministry. He said, "I am made all things to all *men* that I might by all means save some" (1 Cor. 9:22). He did not mean that in order to reach an alcoholic he would drink with him. He meant that he would do as Jesus had done, without modifying his theology or compromising his testimony. His integrity depended on a consistent theology. His credibility depended on a consistent testimony. We must never sacrifice either. Jesus was known as the *"friend* of sinners," but He was not known as a *sinner*. No man could condemn Him of wrong. He did not "hang out" with sinners, but He went to where they were to tell them what was wrong. And when He got there, they knew what was wrong. They could see the difference between themselves and Christ. Why should anyone believe us when we claim to preach on the authority of the Word of God, but behave in a way that conflicts with God's Word? Our commission is to witness to the power of God to change the world, not to be changed by the world.

Paul tells us that "we are ambassadors for Christ" (2 Cor. 5:20). A good ambassador needs two essential qualities. He must properly represent the country of his citizenship, and he must thoroughly understand the country of his residence.   An ambassador is sent to a foreign land to represent his homeland, a sort of stand-in for his own nation's head of state. That is his sole responsibility. As ambassadors of Christ, we must properly represent the Lord and His kingdom to the world in which we live.

At the same time, we must thoroughly understand the people to whom we are sent as witnesses. That is not to say that we must become conversant with their vices, but that we know something of

their language. The world does not understand the language of
Christianity. Terms like *salvation, justification, redemption,* and *propitiation,* are foreign to most people. It is the believer's responsibility
to translate and interpret these biblical concepts for them. The duty of
any translator is to balance the need for being true to the original language while at the same time reaching the target people. To do that,
we have to know our own language and also to know theirs. Without
accepting or adopting the vulgarity of the world's patterns of speech,
we do need to know something of how unbelievers think and communicate. We have to *know* the culture without being *characterized* by
it—to be *in* the world without being *of* the world.

We must also present a gospel that is both confrontational and relational. You will never lead anybody to Christ just by being his friend.
He has to hear the truth of who he is and how he must respond to
Christ. On the other hand, you will rarely lead someone to accept the
truth of the Gospel if you are not at least friendly in the way you present it. People need to be able to see the truth of the Gospel fleshed
out in you. We will be most effective in "seeking the salvation of our
kindred and acquaintances" rather than those people we have never
met before and will never see again. To reach them, we must be relational. But we must also confront them with their soul's real need.

It is sometimes much easier to knock on the door of a stranger and
tell him that if he doesn't repent of his sin and accept the Lord Jesus
Christ he is on his way to eternal damnation in hell than it is to contact someone we know well. The stranger has no idea whether or not
you really believe or understand what you are saying to him. He has
no way to know if this truth has made any difference in your life. So
it is very difficult to reach someone that way. It is not impossible; it
can be done. But our best contacts are our kindred and acquaintances.
And that means we must not just tell the message, we must live it. If
we are not careful we will develop the mindset that knocking on doors
is the only way to do evangelistic work. We begin to think that telling
it is enough; living it doesn't matter. But we really need both.

Our Attitude
If we would be successful in evangelizing our kindred and acquaintances, the third, and most personal of the challenges we face is our

attitude. Evangelizing the lost is something God has told us we *must* do. Dr. Charles Ryrie points out, "In only two instances does the New Testament pronounce a curse on Christians for failure to do something. One is not loving the Lord (1 Cor. 16:22), and the other is not preaching the Gospel of grace (Gal. 1:6-9)."[2] We need to have a balance between zeal for the truth and compassion for the lost. "If we loose the truth, we've lost the message. If we loose our heart, we've lost our ministry."[3] Gene Edward Veith makes the important observation that if we want to be relevant in the postmodern world, "the church must simply proclaim the truth of God's word, the validity of God's law, and the sufficiency of the Gospel of Jesus Christ."[4] We are not called to *prove* it, but to *proclaim* it. Paul did not say, "For I am not ashamed of the Gospel of Christ: for **I am** the power of God unto salvation." He said, "...for **it is** the power" (Rom. 1:16). Salvation comes by the power of the Gospel.

Most of us would shout a hearty "Amen" to a message on taking the Gospel to the lost—seeking the salvation of our kindred and acquaintances. But if your pastor got up and declared that he does *not* believe that soul winning is important, that he is canceling all church-sponsored evangelistic efforts and forbidding church members to share the Gospel with the lost, most church members would be at least disturbed, perhaps even outraged. And rightly so. But if that happened, in most cases not much would change. In actual practice, most people in most churches rarely if ever tell anyone else how to have their sins forgiven by trusting Christ's sacrifice in their place. They are unsubmitted in their attitude, and are unwilling to witness.

Our Aim

One of the most important ministries of the church is its evangelistic outreach. We *must* "seek the salvation of our kindred and acquaintances." To do that, we must faithfully proclaim the truth of the Gospel to those who need to hear it. The New Testament record does not give evidence of the church body *assembling* for the purpose of evangelism. Believers gathered for worship, praise, and instruction; then they *scattered* to evangelize. The Apostles preached to crowds of unbelievers in the Temple (Acts 3:1-4:1), in the streets (Acts 5:15-16), and in the synagogues (Acts 13:14-16). Those who fled Jerusalem due to persecution preached the Gospel wherever they went, leading many to Christ (Acts 11:19-21). People were converted by the power of God through the public and private confrontation of the lost with the truth of their condition and the message of the Gospel. Preaching evangelistic messages to an already converted congregation may be the right message but the wrong audience.

But if we want those who need the message to actually heed the message, we must also demonstrate the effect the Gospel has had on our lives by presenting a picture of Christ in the way we think, speak, and act. To declare that the Gospel is "the power of God unto salvation," then live as if it has no power to change us, is to make God a liar. Such a witness amounts to taking God's name in vain. That is precisely why Paul advised Timothy to "Take heed unto thyself, and unto the doctrine; continue in them: for in doing this thou shalt both save thyself, and them that hear thee" (1 Tim. 4:16).

Unbelieving "kindred and acquaintances" must be challenged to admit their own sinfulness (Rom. 3:10, 23). They must recognize their own helplessness (Rom. 6:23). They must believe that the Lord Jesus Christ is the Son of God, that He died to pay the penalty for their sins, and that He rose again to offer eternal life (Rom. 5:8; John 3:16; 1 Cor. 15:2-4). They must ask God to forgive their sins, placing their total confidence of salvation in what the Lord Jesus has already done and forsaking any confidence in what anyone else can do for them (Rom. 10:9-10; Eph. 2:8-9). Then they should look for evidence of spiritual growth that will demonstrate the genuineness of their profession of faith (2 Pet. 1:5-10; Heb. 12:5-11). One's salvation is a matter of his heart attitude of belief, not his actions. But when someone truly believes, he will be changed as he becomes more like Christ in his thoughts, words, and actions. The inner working of the Holy Spirit guarantees such a change.

The Gospel promises to make new creations out of old creatures (2 Cor. 5:17), to give life to those who are dead (Eph. 2:1). The lost need to hear the truth of the Gospel message and see the change in a godly messenger. Both are vital for the church to fulfill its evangelistic commission.

---

[1] Much of the material in this chapter is adapted from "Reaching a Reluctant World," a message preached by Dr. Matthew R. Olson, pastor

of Tri-City Baptist Church, Westminster, Colorado, (Lansdale, PA: National Leadership Conference, February 27, 1996). Used by permission.

[2] Ryrie, *Basic Theology*, (Victor Books, [Wheaton, Ill.]), 1986, p. 278.

[3] Olson, "Reaching a Reluctant World."

[4] Gene Edward Veith, Jr., *POSTMODERN TIMES: A Christian Guide to Contemporary Thought and Culture*, (Crossway Books, [Wheaton, Ill.]), 1994, p. 210.

CHAPTER 13
THE SUPPORT OF MISSIONS OUTREACH

Back in 1996, on the evening of November 5, I was sitting up watching the Presidential election returns and reflecting on the character of our nation. For all the public protest over the various scandals attached to the Clinton presidency, more Americans who bothered to cast a ballot still voted for Bill Clinton over any other candidate. When it became obvious that the incumbent was going to be re-elected, the winners began their acceptance speeches. It was interesting to hear Vice-president Al Gore quote Scripture, and the passage he chose to quote struck me as more than a little ironic. Speaking in praise of President Clinton, he said, "by their fruits ye shall know them" (Matthew 7:20). He claimed that checking the fruit in the life of President Clinton reveals that he is a man of great wisdom, integrity, and character. While I might well have applied the same verse to the situation, I would have drawn a radically different conclusion. I couldn't help but be thankful that Mr. Gore did not shop for my produce, since it is obvious he is not much of a fruit inspector.

However, Mr. Gore was correct in noting that one's actions reveal one's beliefs. When a man says he believes in family values, yet cheats on his wife and supports the murder of the pre-born, then I know he does not believe in the same family values I do. Furthermore, as the Clinton-Gore ticket won re-election, a great deal was revealed about what Americans *really* value. While they feigned outrage over the President's behavior, people were more concerned with economic prosperity than public morality.

The previous chapter discussed our responsibility to "seek the salvation of our kindred and acquaintances." But going beyond that relatively small circle of contacts, our church members also promise "to contribute cheerfully and regularly to the spread of the Gospel throughout all nations." The Apostle Paul praised the believers in Philippi for their faithful support of his missions work.

> For even in Thessalonica ye sent once and again unto my necessity. Not because I desire a gift: but I desire fruit that may abound to your account. But I have all, and abound: I am full, having received of Epaphroditus the things *which were sent* from you, an odor of a sweet smell, a sacrifice acceptable, well-pleasing to God. But my God shall supply all your need according to his riches in glory by Christ Jesus (Phil. 4:16-19).

Although it is the rare Christian who would admit to having no interest in the spread of the Gospel, relatively few actually commit their resources to its support, or they do so only half-heartedly. They want the promise of God's abundant supply without the accompanying responsibility to use that supply to help spread the Gospel to all nations. They need to consider what *not* giving to missions reveals about what they *really believe.*

What Those Who Do Not Give to Missions *Really* Believe

If you are not giving regularly and generously to the support of missions, you may be indicating by your actions that you believe that *people do not need to hear the Gospel to be saved.* Perhaps you think that Romans 10:13-17 is not true. Paul tells us plainly that "faith cometh by hearing, and hearing by the word of God." Paul adds that they cannot hear without a preacher, and the preacher cannot preach without being sent. For people to come to Christ the church must send messengers to take the good news to the lost so they can hear the truth and come to faith. The formula is: Messengers + Providers = Missions. If you are neither a missionary messenger nor a missions provider, you must not believe this.

Or perhaps your failure to give to missions reveals that you believe that *God's resources are limited.* Maybe the church building needs a new roof, the parking lot needs resurfaced, or the office needs some new equipment. You rationalize that surely God would want you to maintain the church property, so you won't be able to afford to give so much to missions until you take care of some of these things. As Jesus said to the Pharisees in another context, "these ought ye to have done, and not to leave the other undone" (Matt. 23:23). We tend to forget that God has declared, "The earth *is* the LORD's and the fullness thereof; the world, and they that dwell therein" (Ps. 24:1). In 2 Corinthians 9:10-15, Paul reminds the church that as God gives both seed to the sower and bread for his food, He will "multiply your seed sown, and increase the fruits of your righteousness." If God has given us a job to do, He will provide the resources to get the job done.

But if people must hear, and God's resources are unlimited, and you still don't have the resources to give, it must be God's fault. Maybe *God does not want to provide for world evangelism.* He must not have meant it when He said, "Go ye therefore, and teach all nations" (Matt. 28:19), or "ye shall be witnesses unto me both in Jerusalem, and in all Judaea, and in Samaria, and unto the uttermost part of the earth" (Acts 1:8). If God really wanted to provide for missions, He would have provided you with greater resources for you to contribute.

Of course, there are many who would never deny that people must hear the Gospel to be saved, that God's resources are unlimited, and that God wants to provide for world evangelism, yet they see no connection of these truths to themselves. Their position is theologically orthodox, but they have concluded, *"God does not expect me to use what He gave me to benefit others."* Surely what He gave me He expects me to use for myself. Isn't God wise enough to know where resources are most needed and see to it that people get what they need? We tend to think that if God will send me a more bountiful harvest, I will have the ability to sow more. But we have the equation backwards. "But this *I say*, He which soweth sparingly shall reap also sparingly; and he which soweth bountifully shall reap also bountifully" (2 Cor. 9:6). James asks, "If a brother or sister be naked, and destitute of daily food, and one of you say unto them, 'Depart in peace, be *ye* warmed and filled,' notwithstanding ye give them not those things which are needful to the body; what *doth it* profit?"

(James 2:15-16). It would be hypocritical to claim that God wants His people to provide the resources to send messengers of the Gospel to the world, but that God does not expect you to give.

Yet some are still fearful. Recognizing their own responsibility to give, they are reluctant to commit to missions funds they expect to need themselves. They are saying, in effect, that *if I commit what I have, God cannot supply what I need.* They ignore the promise that Paul made in 2 Cor. 9:8, "And God is able to make all grace abound toward you; that ye, always having all sufficiency in all *things*, may abound to every good work." Another promise, cited earlier, says, "My God shall supply all your need according to His riches in glory by Christ Jesus' (Phil 4:19). Most Christians try to claim these verses, but few qualify. Both promises are given specifically to the believers in the churches in Corinth and in Philippi for their faithful support of Paul's missionary endeavors. The promise of God is to supply the need of those who use what they have to the glory of God, giving abundantly for the support of missions.

What Every Believer Should Determine

Each of us must be prepared to acknowledge that people must hear the Gospel in order to be saved, that God's resources are unlimited, that God wants to provide for world evangelism, He expects us to use what He gives us to benefit others, and that if we commit what we have He can supply what we need. Then we must determine to be used of God. Matthew recounts an incident in the ministry of Jesus and His disciples that illustrates this truth.

And Jesus went forth, and saw a great multitude, and was moved with compassion toward them, and he healed their sick. And when it was evening, his disciples came to him, saying, This is a desert place, and the time is now past; send the multitude away, that they may go into the villages, and buy themselves victuals. But Jesus said unto them, They need not depart; give ye them to eat. And they say unto him, We have here but five loaves, and two fishes. He said, Bring them hither to me. And he command- ed the multitude to sit down on the grass, and took the five loaves, and the two fishes, and looking up to heaven, he blessed, and broke, and gave the loaves to *his* disciples, and the disciples to the multitude. And they did all eat, and were filled: and they took up of the fragments that remained twelve baskets full. And they that had eaten were about five thousand men, beside women and children (Matt. 14:14-21).

Most Bible story books and Sunday School quarterlies, and most preachers who grew up under that instruction, emphasize one small detail found only in John's account of the event. They bring to it assumptions that are not found in the text itself and end up missing the point of the story. According to John, the food brought for distribution was in the possession of a young boy. The common assumption is that he was one of the travelers who had come to hear Jesus teach that day and had come to volunteer his personal dinner to help feed the multitude. But that is not stated anywhere in the Biblical account. It is possible to draw that conclusion if you read only John's account, but there are other details that indicate something else.

Jesus was a traveling teacher, a rabbi whose disciples followed Him from place to place as He instructed them. Because we are given the names of a specific group of twelve followers, called Apostles, we often assume that they were the entire group who traveled with Jesus. But that is not true all of the time. At one point, no more than a few weeks after this event, Jesus sent out seventy of His disciples in pairs. It would not be unreasonable to suppose that such a group would need substantial food supplies as they go from place to place. We know that on one occasion the disciples misunderstood a comment of Jesus', thinking He was rebuking them for having forgotten to bring food on that day (Matt. 16:6-8). So as a general rule, they must have carried their own stores with them. We also know that on at least one occasion Jesus made a point by calling a child from among the group to come to Him, so it is entirely possible that some of the band of disciples traveling with Jesus might have their sons with them. It is also possible that during such an assembly as this, a boy might have been given responsibility for the supplies.

It is much more likely that the "lad" in John 6:8-9 is a son of one of the disciples responsible for carrying the food than that he was one of the travelers who happened to know what the disciples were discussing and volunteered his supper. Such a boy would not be traveling alone, and such a provision would have been unlikely. Barley loaves were the poorest of breads, yet there were five of them. If one could afford to pack such an extravagant amount for one boy's meal, it would have been more likely a smaller portion of better fare. But if it were for the disciples themselves, this basket of food would have been both meager and poor, which is consistent with what we know of their typical situation.

It is also significant that when Jesus sent His disciples out in pairs shortly after this event, He did so to teach them something about ministering in His absence. Before they could be ready for the kind of ministry ahead of them, they had to be taught some important lessons about Christ's ability to meet their needs when they would take no provisions for themselves, and about His intention to use their own abilities to meet the needs of others. They would be facing multitudes of people who were shepherdless sheep and were spiritually starved. It would be their responsibility to "give them something to eat." They would not have the ability in themselves to meet the great spiritual need of the people, but if they would give what they have to the Lord, He would take it and multiply it, using the disciples to minister to the multitudes. Further, while the Lord Jesus would be using the disciples to minister to others, He would meet the needs of the disciples themselves. That is why, when evening came and the disciples suggested that Jesus send the multitude away in time to find supper, Jesus told them, "They need not depart; you give them something to eat" (Mt. 14:16). The disciples said, "we only have five loaves and two fish." We barely have enough for our own needs, we can't possibly feed the multitude, too. So Jesus said, "Give me what you have." He then took the food intended for their own supper, blessed it, and distributed it to the crowd. After they had all eaten their fill, the disciples collected twelve baskets full of the fragments for their own provision, which was much more than they would have had for themselves had they kept what they started with. This lesson was vital to their preparation for going out on their own.

The application to our support of missions by giving of our finances should be obvious. The believer must determine, *"I will use all I have for God's glory."* Jesus Christ is no longer physically present, and He has charged us with the responsibility to preach the truth of the Word to satisfy the world's spiritual hunger. We need a personal desire to meet the needs of others. We also need to be willing to do without, gladly surrendering what He has given us to His control. Believers who spend more money each week on candy, ice cream, soft drinks, and coffee than they give to the spread of the Gospel throughout all nations have a serious problem with priorities. Likewise, those who spend more for cable television than they give to missions should be ashamed. They show by their actions what they *really* believe to be important. We must not squander what God gives us on frivolous indulgence with little or no regard for His work or His glory.

Further, the believer must determine, *"I will trust the Lord to use what I give."* God can make what you give *effective* to meet the need and *sufficient* for the need. However meager it may seem in comparison to the need, God can use it to accomplish His purposes and to be enough. And if you will trust Him with what you have, He will also provide for your needs. That is precisely the point of the feeding of the five thousand. Jesus could take five barley loaves and two fish, barely enough for a bite for Jesus and His disciples, and make it satisfy the hunger of the multitude and sufficient for the hungry disciples.

You have no right to expect the missionary, evangelist, or minister of the Gospel to make greater "sacrifices" than you are willing to make, to live by greater faith than you are willing to exercise. If they are supposed to *go* and trust God to provide, you must be ready to *give* and trust God to provide. Neither have you any right to expect God to evangelize the world without your participation—to assume that it is the responsibility of other Christians, but not yours. You must admit that it is not appropriate for a Christian to wonder, "Does God want me to give for missions?" Rather, the Christian should only ask, *"How much does God want to give to missions through me?"*

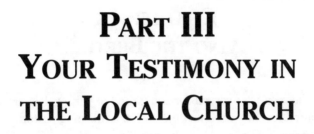

PART III
YOUR TESTIMONY IN
THE LOCAL CHURCH

Chapter 14
Loving the Brethren

One of the men who served for some time in various leadership roles in our church recently accepted the call to a full-time pastorate. During the years prior to God's leading him to his own church, he had occasionally filled in for me and had done some pulpit-supply preaching elsewhere. During one six-month stretch, he served as interim pastor for a church in a neighboring town. That congregation was a particularly quarrelsome bunch, each one seeming to be more concerned with getting his own way than anything else. Upon his return from his months with that church, he said, "I've decided that the hardest thing about pastoral ministry is having to be nice to mean people." I knew what he meant. Professing Christians often treat each other abominably. One church member can be hateful to or gossip about another, but let the one they've mistreated be the least bit ungracious in expressing their objection, and suddenly he is condemned for being "unloving."

Another aspect of our church covenant is the pledge "to walk together in Christian love." The Lord Jesus told His followers, "By this shall all men know that ye are my disciples, if ye have love one to another" (John 13:35). One of the most important evidences of our relationship with Jesus Christ is to be our love for one another. His emphasis was on the *unity* that genuine Christian love produces. To have unity in our

walk, while being distinct in personalities and abilities, we must
demonstrate the love of Christ toward one another.

If you, as a church member, would contribute to this loving unity
within your congregation, there are some important lessons to learn
from 1 Peter 1:22-2:3.

Seeing ye have purified your souls in obeying the truth through the
Spirit unto unfeigned love of the brethren, *see that ye* love one
another with a pure heart fervently: Being born again, not of corruptible seed, but of incorruptible, by the word of God, which liveth
and abideth for ever. For all flesh *is* as grass, and all the glory of
man as the flower of grass. The grass withereth, and the flower
thereof falleth away: But the word of the Lord endureth for ever.
And this is the word which by the gospel is preached unto you.
Wherefore laying aside all malice, and all guile, and hypocrisies,
and envies, and all evil speakings, As newborn babes, desire the
sincere milk of the word, that ye may grow thereby: If so be ye
have tasted that the Lord *is* gracious.

In this passage we are given a command to love one another, we are
shown the source of our capacity for love, and we are presented with
the challenge of love.

The Command to Love

In verse twenty-two we find what at first glance seems to be a contradiction. Peter *commends* his audience for their obedience to the truth
through the Spirit in their unfeigned love of the brethren, then turns
around and *commands* them to love one another with a pure heart fervently. Or perhaps Peter is just being redundant, saying in effect, "You
are doing a good job—keep it up." But there are different Greek words
for categories, types, or levels of love. The two words most commonly
occurring in the New Testament are *phileo* and *agapao*, or one of their
derivatives. Both of these words are used in 1 Peter 1:22.

The first of these, *phileo*, describes a "brotherly affection." What
Peter has actually said is, "Seeing ye have purified your souls in obeying the truth through the Spirit unto unfeigned *philadelphia*...." Peter
commends these believers for the genuineness of their affection for
each other. This quality of love is usually evidenced simply through

mutual acts of kindness, like being courteous to one another, greeting one another with a warm handshake and a smile, enjoying a time of fellowship with one another, helping one another in times of distress, and so on. However, it is usually pretty easy to be nice to someone who is nice to you. Even the unsaved recognize the rudeness of someone who is ungracious to a person who has shown him a kindness.

Having commended these believers for their *philadelphia*, Peter goes on to challenge them to demonstrate *agapao*, a deeper level of love. This is a sacrificial love—the love God shows toward us. It could be defined as "a selfless joy in another through determination to benefit another." There is an important contrast between this kind of love and that brotherly love that is based upon shared interests. This is a love in which the one who loves determines to do that which is needful for the one who is the object of his love. It really has nothing to do with anything they have in common. The truth is, you and God have very little in common, but God chose to love you anyway, not because of what you are, but because of who He is. That is *agape* love.

We are tempted to protest that it is hard to love someone who does not share our interests. It is at precisely this point that we need the aid of the Holy Spirit. It takes the power of God for you to love someone who does not love you in return. When the church covenants together "by the aid of the Holy Spirit, to walk together in Christian love," we expect everyone to keep his word. But what you must understand is that when you make such a pledge in obedience to God's command, you are committed to keep your word even if nobody else does. The command of God is not conditioned upon love being reciprocal. We are commanded to love on the basis of the Holy Spirit's presence within us, not on the basis of how we feel or how others respond. This level of love is not "warm fuzzies;" it is a fervent act of the will. This kind of love is demonstrated by doing for the loved one what he needs, not necessarily what he desires. In *phileo* love, we try to *please* the one we love. But in *agape* love our goal is to *help* the ones we love, and that is not always the same thing.

The Apostle John, in his first epistle, reiterates Peter's command.

Beloved, let us love one another: for love is of God; and every one that loveth is born of God, and knoweth God. He that loveth not

knoweth not God; for God is love. In this was manifested the love
of God toward us, because that God sent his only begotten Son into
the world, that we might live through him. Herein is love, not that
we loved God, but that he loved us, and sent his Son *to be* the propitiation for our sins. Beloved, if God so loved us, we ought also to
love one another (1 John 4:7-11).

Having begun with a command, followed by the explanation, John
concludes that we have an obligation to love one another sacrificially.
His final statement here almost has the force of a challenge: "How dare
you not love [*agapao*] one another!"

The Capacity for Love

Peter told us that we gain the capacity for *agape* love through the aid
of the Holy Spirit, given at the New Birth. One of the ways in which
Christianity is fundamentally different from all other religions is that in
Christianity our salvation is the starting point. In all other religions,
one's salvation is the goal. Whether you examine Buddhism,
Hinduism, Islam, or even some perverted forms of "Christianity" (e.g.,
Roman Catholicism), salvation is the end, not the beginning. Followers
of other religions strive to attain unto salvation, but the believer in
Christ obtains salvation as a free gift. And from the moment of his salvation, the believer has the capacity to develop a sacrificial love for others. John even insists that those who do not demonstrate this level of
love are not really saved. "We know that we have passed from death
unto life, because we love the brethren. He that loveth not *his* brother
abideth in death" (1 John 3:14).

The Lord Jesus said, "Greater love hath no man than this, that man
lay down his life for his friends" (John 15:13). That level of love is
also described by Paul in Romans 5:7—"For scarcely for a righteous
man will one die: yet peradventure for a good man some would even
dare to die." But Paul goes on to make the point that Jesus Christ loved
us more than we love others. He loved us so much that He gave
Himself to die for our sins. "But God commendeth his love toward us,
in that, while we were yet sinners, Christ died for us" (Rom. 5:8).
Christ died for us when we hated Him. He died for us even though we
were His enemies. That goes well beyond a brotherly affection. It is

that level of love to which Peter challenges the church to "love one another with a pure heart, fervently."

Christ loves all of us. His love does not depend upon what or who we are. For God to love you or me, it had to be unconditional, for we could never deserve His love. But we must not make the mistake of miss-defining unconditional love. God *loves* us unconditionally, but *accepts* us only on His terms. *Love* and *acceptance* are two different concepts, but the distinction between them is often blurred in this discussion. God loves us without our having to qualify for it. His love is based upon His own will, not our loveliness, so His *love is unconditional*. But God only accepts us on the basis of faith in the shed blood of Christ and His resurrection from the dead (Rom. 10:9-10), so His *acceptance is conditional*. He loves the world, but will accept only those who trust Christ's sacrifice for their salvation. While it will grieve God to cast multitudes that He loves into the lake of fire, He will do so because His *acceptance* is conditioned upon faith in His Son. Likewise, our loving people unconditionally does not mean that we accept them just the way they are. It means we love them in spite of their imperfections. We want to benefit them even though we may have to reject their behavior and refrain from fellowship.

If we are not careful in making this distinction clear, we are prone to numerous errors. It will affect, for instance, one's attitude toward discipline. Because we love unconditionally does *not* mean that we ought to tolerate the bad behavior of a rebellious teenager or an unruly church member, any more than Christ puts up with it. Hebrews 12:6 tells us, "For whom the Lord loveth he chasteneth, and scourgeth every son whom he receiveth." The Apostle Paul wrote to the church at Corinth and sternly rebuked them for tolerating known sin in the life of a church member (1 Cor. 5). He told them that if they truly loved that man, they would do for him what he needed, and put him out of the church until such time as repentance was evidenced. Actually, failure to discipline is evidence of hatred, not love, while enforcing discipline is often the only loving thing to do.[1] If we jettison the concept of punishment for wrongdoing because we are supposed to love, we destroy the concept of true, biblical love.

Suppose that your six-year-old son comes in from playing outside, and he has a board with an old rusty nail in it. He has stepped on the

130

nail and punctured the sole of his foot. In trying to comfort him, you say to him, "I'm sorry you hurt yourself. I don't want you to experience any more pain, so I'll go to the doctor and get your tetanus shot for you." That is not love; it is stupid. You are not the one with the injury that needs the injection; he is. A tetanus shot may be unpleasant, but a tetanus infection is deadly. Because you know he needs it, even though he has already been hurt by the nail, he needs to be hurt again by the needle, so he can be protected from the potentially destructive infection that the nail introduced into his system.

Another factor in our capacity for this *agape* love involves the Word of God. Consider again what Peter wrote in 1 Peter 1:23—"Being born again, not of corruptible seed, but of incorruptible, by the word of God, which liveth and abideth forever." Peter is saying that since we come to faith by the prompting of the Holy Spirit through the Word of God, we can be sure that our salvation is eternal because the Word that gave us life continues to live in us. In contrast to corruptible seed, that must "fall into the ground and die" (John 12:24) in order to produce life, the Word of God in us does not die. Its incorruptibility is one of the bases of our assurance that we are secure. It is the working of the Word of God in one's heart that brings him to the place of repentance and faith. Paul tells us in 2 Timothy 3:16 that "all Scripture is given by inspiration of God and is profitable…." We are also to master the Word of God and allow it to master us. We learn by the revelation of God's Word, and we grow by the power of God's Word. Peter goes on to explain in the opening verses of 1 Peter 2 that if we want to conquer all the wicked attitudes listed in verse one, we need to yearn for "the sincere milk of the word, that ye may grow thereby." We need that compelling longing for God's Word. As we learn His Word, and grow by it, we increase our capacity for the *agapao* we are to demonstrate toward one another.

Have you ever been responsible for feeding a newborn baby? Do you remember what it was like? When the baby is hungry, he will latch on to his mother's breast or the bottle with something approaching desperation. The baby knows there is nourishment there. You can stick a pacifier in the baby's mouth, and that may quiet him for a moment. But it doesn't take the baby long to realize that he is getting nothing from the pacifier. He will not be satisfied. When a baby is hungry, he wants to eat, and that can sometimes be a lot more often than you are ready to feed him, giving you very little rest between feedings. It is that level of desire for "the sincere milk of the word" that God expects us to demonstrate. How well do you think that baby would do if he were fed no more often or with no greater regularity than you attend church services? He would starve. Is it any wonder that so many Christians are spiritually weak and sickly?

So, to walk together in Christian love, we must first of all be born again, and we must be instructed in God's Word. It must follow, then, that if we *fail* to walk in Christian love, we either are not truly born again or we are disobedient to God's Word. This brings us to consider the challenge of love.

The Challenge of Love

In 1 Peter 2:1 God provides a list of several sinful attitudes and actions that must be laid aside: malice, guile, hypocrisy, envies, and evil speakings. Since Peter is addressing believers, and commanding that they "lay aside" these attitudes, he must have had reason to think the believers to whom he wrote were guilty of them. If a person has been saved by the power and grace of God, how can he get to the point that he bears malice, plots manipulations, behaves hypocritically, envies, or speaks evil of another believer? It happens when he fails in the challenge of love.

The first aspect of that challenge is that we must learn to *appreciate differences*. That is not to say that we "celebrate diversity" as it has come to be defined in our present cultural milieu, which uses the phrase as a euphemism for encouraging immorality. However, there are differences in the body of Christ, and we must recognize legitimate diversity within God's will. In 1 Corinthians, Paul addresses this idea. The church in Corinth was congratulating themselves for their generosity in tolerating the wicked life of one of their members (1 Cor. 5:1-2). As we've already seen, Paul rebuked them for that, saying that they should have put that person out of the church (5:4-7). But the church was also having all sorts of disputations on other issues. What Paul tells them in 4:7 and 15:41 is that they need to begin by accepting God's design. "For who maketh thee to differ *from another*? And what hast thou that thou didst not receive? Now if thou didst receive *it*, why doest thou glory, as if thou hadst not received *it*?" (4:7). No two believers are identical, but we have a natural tendency to think that everyone else ought to be more like ourselves. What arrogance! It was God who made us distinct. Of course, if you were the designer, you might have designed yourself a little differently. We need to learn to accept God's design in others and in ourselves, and to thank Him for the fact that He is the Designer. Don't expect everyone to think and act alike, or to have the same gifts, abilities, or calling. God's plans for each individual are distinct and personal.

Paul also said that *"One* star differeth from *another* star in glory" (15:41). His original audience had a more limited understanding of the analogy than we have today. They could tell that some stars were brighter than others, or more helpful for navigation than others. They even recognized some differences in color. But we know today that there are enormous differences among the stars. Surface temperatures alone are estimated to vary by as much as hundreds of thousands of degrees. Differences in diameter are estimated to vary by millions of miles. It is difficult to appreciate those differences from our distant perspective, but we must admit that the differences between one star and another are far greater than the differences between any two believers in the church. And that is all part of God's design.

Once we accept differences that are by God's design, we must also fulfill God's plan. He created each of us for distinct purposes, and has gifted each of us for particular service. There is really little to be gained by envying someone who you think sings better than you do, or looks prettier than you do, or plays tennis better than you do, or makes crafts nicer than you can, or whatever it may be that tempts you to envy. In 1 Corinthians 12:4-6 Paul tells us that there are differences in *gifts* (gracious endowments), *administrations* (offices within the church), and *operations* (powers of influence exerted on others). Individually, we need to be fulfilling God's purposes for our lives. If we do not appreciate the differences within the family of God by accepting God's design and fulfilling God's purposes, we will fail in the challenge of our love. We will love those who are more like ourselves and grow to despise those who are not. We will not demonstrate the loving unity God demands.

A second aspect of the challenge of our love is that we must *avoid divisions.* Divisions come when, instead of accepting God's design and fulfilling His purposes, we *resent* God's design and *resist* His purposes. In 1 Corinthians 1:10, Paul told the church that there were to "be no divisions among you; but *that* ye be joined together in the same mind and in the same judgment." In Chapter 12 (vv. 4-22 and 27-30) Paul gives additional instructions to the church that they not resist God's purpose by all desiring the same gift. We frustrate God's design when we allow the variety of ministry abilities and interests to cause division among us. We sin when we allow differences to cause contention among God's people. Essentially, the challenge of our love is to be different without being divided.

God provides for us an historical illustration of this kind of division of responsibility with mutual support in 1 Chronicles 19:9-13. It occurred during the reign of David, at a time when David decided to send a gift to the prince of the Ammonites because his father had died. This prince's father had done David a good turn, so upon his death David sent messengers with a special gift. But the prince misconstrued David's intentions. The advisors to the prince said, "Don't trust David. He's just sent these men in to spy out our land and discover our weaknesses." So they humiliated David's messengers by shaving off their beards and cutting off their garments just below their buttocks, sending them back as a rebuke to David. Anticipating that David would be angered by this treatment of his men, the Ammonites proceeded to prepare the army for war, planning a pre-emptive strike on the army of Israel. They even recruited the Syrian army to assist them. The Ammonites and the Syrians marched to war against Israel, all because they chose to misinterpret David's gesture of kindness. The Ammonites planned to crush the Israelite army by approaching from one direction while the Syrians attacked from another. By the time Joab, captain of David's army, got word of the plan, they were already surrounded and badly outnumbered. Rather than surrendering, Joab separated his troops into two divisions, taking personal command of one half while his brother Abishai commanded the other. These two divisions were then arranged back-to-back in the valley while they watched the two enemy armies descending upon them from opposite directions.

> Now when Joab saw that the battle was set against him before and behind, he chose out of all the choice of Israel, and put *them* in array against the Syrians. And the rest of the people he delivered unto the hand of Abishai his brother, and they set *themselves* in

array against the children of Ammon. And he said, If the Syrians be too strong for me, then thou shalt help me: but if the children of Ammon be too strong for thee, then I will help thee. Be of good courage, and let us behave ourselves valiantly for our people, and for the cities of our God: and let the LORD do *that which is* good in his sight (1 Chronicles 19:10-13).

Joab had assumed half of the responsibility—defense against the Syrian attack. Abishai had been assigned the other half—defense against the Ammonite attack. But they also pledged mutual support. Each was expected to fulfill his own responsibilities, but if either enemy army began to overrun the Israelite defenders, the other division of the army of Israel would come to their aid. That is what Paul meant when he wrote to the churches of Galatia and told them that each man was responsible to bear his own burdens, and in the same context commanded, "bear ye one another's burdens" (Galatians 6:2-5). He did not contradict himself. We each have our own God-given responsibilities to fulfill, but we also have an obligation to our brethren whose burdens overcome them.

The evening before His crucifixion, Jesus told His disciples, "A new commandment I give unto you, that ye love one another, as I have loved you, that ye also love one another. By this shall all *men* know that ye are my disciples, if ye have love one to another" (John 13:34-35). What is "new" about this commandment? Jesus has often taught that loving others was vital. He had pointed out on more than one occasion that the first and greatest commandment is to love God, and the second is similar, that you love your neighbor as yourself. But on this occasion, Jesus takes the command to love to a new level. No more are we to love our neighbors as ourselves. Now we must love as God loves us. "Love one another as I have loved you." That is the "new" aspect. Jesus became a man to die for us while we were still His enemies, while we still hated Him. We are to love one another to that degree. Everyone will know that we are His disciples, if we love one another.

---

[1] These ideas will be developed further in the chapters on Discipline (18) and Intervention (21).

CHAPTER 15
BEHAVING WITH INTEGRITY

A friend has served the Lord for many years in Puerto Rico. He has been instrumental in the establishing of several churches on the island and is the founder and president of a Bible college that prepares young men and women for ministry throughout the Spanish-speaking world. In September of 1999, a hurricane struck the island and caused some damage to the property of the college. One mission board associated with his ministry sent a check for $2500 to help with repairs. Wanting to do the work as economically as possible, he bought the necessary materials, and the college staff and students provided the labor. Their expenses eventually totaled just over $800. Several people made suggestions about how they could use the rest of the money, but he decided they needed to return it to the mission board. He sent the balance back, explaining that money given for disaster relief should be used for nothing else. Within days, he got a call from the office of that mission board saying that this was the first time in the history of their ministry that anyone had returned any money. The week after that call, this missionary was surprised to find in his mail an unexpected donation of $5000 from another source. God had honored his integrity by sending three times the amount they had returned.

When someone joins our church, one part of the covenant they make includes the promises, "to be just in our dealings, faithful in our engagements, and exemplary in our deportment." Since the Bible has a great deal to say about justice in our dealings, faithfulness in our engagements, and exemplary deportment, and since there are practically limitless applications for each, these subjects will not be dealt with comprehensively. Do not simply read this chapter to see if reference will be made to your particular weakness or sin. You may be tempted to assume that if yours is omitted, you must be in fine shape. Every believer should consider what these phrases mean with hearts that are open to the conviction of the Holy Spirit.

Justice in Our Dealings

Concerning Abraham, God said, "For I know him, that he will command his children and his household after him, and they shall keep the way of the LORD, to do justice and judgment; that the LORD may bring upon Abraham that which he hath spoken of him" (Genesis 18:19). Proverbs 20:7 says, "The just *man* walketh in his integrity: his children *are* blessed after him," then in next chapter adds, "To do justice and judgment *is* more acceptable to the LORD than sacrifice" (21:3). There are at least three areas of life that require that we be just in our dealings. We must demonstrate integrity in financial matters, integrity in government dealings, and integrity in social relationships.

Demonstrating *integrity in financial* matters involves both proper conduct of one's business and proper care in one's stewardship. In doing business, we are commanded to have absolute integrity—paying the agreed upon price, honoring a contract, measuring with an honest balance, paying a fair wage, and so on. There are many ways to compromise your integrity and displease the Lord without actually stealing by shoplifting, over-billing, or cheating on your taxes. Perhaps you are tempted to tell less than the whole truth about that car you are selling. Or maybe you are tempted to make misleading statements to try to drive down a price on something you are purchasing. Do you pay your bills on time, or do you make creditors send you more than one notice or call repeatedly to try to collect what you owe? Are you generous and understanding to those who are indebted to you? How do you treat the sales clerk or the waitress who serves you? Concerning your stewardship, it must be repeated that God expects absolute integrity in faithful tithing (see Chapter Eleven.) Often a believer makes a pledge to give to some special project, like missions or a building fund, over and above his tithe. Do you consider such a pledge binding, or do you believe it is acceptable to break you word to God and to your church? We expect God to take good care of us, but then many refuse to acknowledge His supply in returning even a tenth to Him.

To be just in our dealings also involves *integrity in regard to government*. This includes, but is not limited to secular government. As far as civil law is concerned, we are expected to be obedient, because "the powers that be are ordained of God" (Rom. 13:1). One indication that a person has failed to be just in his dealings is when he intentionally disobeys the law. This includes significant laws prohibiting murder, rape, and larceny, as well as less important laws prohibiting littering and unauthorized parking in a handicapped zone. Granted, the former are more destructive and have greater consequences, but we are still bound to obey the less significant regulations. It is more than a little inappropriate to try to witness of the goodness of God in setting you free from bondage to sin and putting the likeness of Christ in you when you are speaking to a police officer who just stopped you for driving 70mph in a 55mph zone. Whether your heart is so blatantly rebellions that you disregard authority by burglarizing property or your heart is only quietly rebellious in that your disregard for authority is limited to violating traffic laws, all disobedience comes from a heart attitude of rebellion.

The same respect for governmental authority should be demonstrated in every arena, including the home, the workplace, and the church. A teenager who stays out past his parents' curfew or who goes someplace his parents have not approved is unjust in his dealings. An employee who disregards the instructions of his boss at work, or gripes and complains, is unjust in his dealings. Someone who disregards the policies of a place of business or ignores the policies of the church is unjust in his dealings. It may not be evil to wear hard-soled shoes on a hardwood floor, but if the sign in the gym says "only sneakers are permitted on the basketball court," you are unjust in your dealings if you walk across it in your wing-tips or your high-heeled pumps. It may not be evil to eat a doughnut in the church auditorium, but if the church has a "no food in the sanctuary" policy, you are unjust in your dealings to do so. Our church constitution expects Sunday School teachers and junior church workers to attend all services of the church unless providentially hindered by something like an emergency, illness, work conflict, or vacation. There is no verse of Scripture that mandates that policy, but if a person agrees to teach Sunday School, he should be prepared to obey it. To fail to do so would compromise his integrity and place him in violation of his covenant with the church.

Another way to have integrity in governmental dealings involves acceptance of responsibility. American citizens are expected to vote in elections and serve when called upon for jury duty. Are you just in your dealings, or do you shirk your responsibilities? Fathers are to provide for their own families, to train them in the Word of God, to see that their children are educated, and so on. Christians are expected to be active in the ministry of their church, contributing their talents and time to the work of the Lord. If your church is congregational in polity, having periodic business meetings to plan programs and allocate funds, church members should attend and participate in those meetings. Failure to accept proper responsibility in these areas makes one unjust in his dealings.

Being just in one's dealings also involves *integrity in social relationships*. While this aspect could bear a good deal more elaboration than we will give it here, three characteristics of how we are to treat one another stand out: humility, love, and godliness. In Philippians 2:3, Paul commands, "*Let* nothing *be done* through strife or vainglory, but in lowliness of mind let each esteem other better than themselves." If we would be just in our dealings, we must learn to put the needs of others ahead of our own. As discussed in the previous chapter, Jesus said to His disciples, "By this shall all *men* know that ye are my disciples, that ye have love one for another" (John 13:35). The man with real integrity in his social relationships will so love others that he is willing to make personal sacrifices for their benefit and to see them grow in their relationship with the Lord. Paul wrote to Timothy to "exercise thyself *rather* unto godliness…[for] godliness is profitable unto all things" (1 Tim. 4:7-8). Peter also asked, "*Seeing* then *that* all these things shall be dissolved, what manner *of persons* ought ye to be in *all* holy conversation and godliness?" (2 Peter.

3:11). Too many people like the *idea* of being a Christian without the *obligations*. A man of real integrity will demonstrate godliness in all he does.

Faithfulness in Our Engagements

The word that best sums up the description of the person who is faithful in his engagements is *consistency*. He is consistent in regard to the truth and consistent in regard to commitments. *Faithfulness* is often equated with one's respect for the truth and for personal commitments and responsibilities.

Mine eyes shall be upon the faithful of the land, that they may dwell with me: he that walketh in a perfect way, he shall serve me. He that worketh deceit shall not dwell within my house: he that telleth lies shall not tarry in my sight (Psalm 101:6-7).

Most men will proclaim every one his own goodness: but a faithful man who can find? (Prov. 20:6).

Then the presidents and princes sought to find occasion against Daniel concerning the kingdom; but they could find none occasion nor fault; forasmuch as he was faithful, neither was there any error or fault found in him (Dan. 6:4).

Consistency in regard to the truth includes the twin aspects of honesty and integrity. Honesty is faithfully saying only that which is truthful. Integrity is faithfully doing that which is consistent with the truth you speak. Every believer is obligated to be so faithful that no dishonesty or lack of integrity can be attributed to him. But this also involves consistency in regard to commitments. One important characteristic of the person who is faithful in his engagements is dependability; he can be counted on to always keep his commitments. He is the kind of person who can be given a job and practically ignored. Without even having to check on his progress or the outcome, you know it will be done and will be done right. A Christian who is not the best worker he can be is not faithful in his engagements.

But that involves more than just getting the job done, and getting it done well. It also means getting it done on time. One who is faithful in all his engagements can also be counted on to be punctual. People generally fit into two categories in regard to their attitude toward others in their treatment of time: those who are usually late, and those who are usually on time. Habitual tardiness is an evidence of a supremely arrogant attitude, an attitude of self-love rather than love of others. Someone who is so careless about time commitments that he often leaves others waiting for him can be considered both a liar and a thief, because his tardiness often constitutes both a broken promise and time and energy stolen from every person who had to wait for him. Oh, they usually have an excuse. Perhaps the car wouldn't start—meaning, "it didn't fire up the first time the engine turned over." Or maybe they got caught in traffic—meaning, "there was a car in front of me driving only the speed limit." Or even the alarm didn't go off—meaning, "I forgot to set the alarm." On the other hand, people who are faithful in their engagements habitually leave enough time to allow for little delays and still keep people from waiting for them. Those times people do have to wait for them are rare and surprising.

Being faithful in our engagements is evident in how we fulfill all of our responsibilities, whether on the job, at church, or at home. If you are a contractor, you keep your promises concerning work quality, price, and completion dates. If you are an employee, you show up on time, work hard while on the clock, and don't slip out early. If you are a Sunday School teacher you prepare your lesson ahead, get to your classroom early to supervise the children, and teach your class carefully and conscientiously. If you sing in the choir, you get to practice on time, take good care of your music, pay attention without causing distractions during rehearsal, and follow the director carefully during performance. That is what it means to be "faithful in our engagements."

Blameless in Our Behavior

To be "exemplary in our deportment" is an old-fashioned way of saying we will demonstrate blameless behavior. Titus 3:8 says, "that they which have believed in God might be careful to maintain good works." In Ephesians 2:10 we are told, "For we are his workmanship, created in Christ Jesus unto good works, which God hath before ordained that we should walk in them." In 1 Timothy 4:12 Paul said, "Let no man despise thy youth; but be thou an example of the believ-

ers, in word, in conversation, in charity, in spirit, in faith, in purity."
This, too, is an area of concern that deserves more space than we can
permit it here, since *deportment* includes the way we look, the way
we act, and the way we think.

To be "exemplary in our deportment," we must be *blameless in our
appearance*. One of the most important principles of dress is *appro-
priateness*. Jeans and sweat shirts may be appropriate dress for a
football game, or working in the garage, or walking in the park, but
they are hardly appropriate attire for coming together to worship the
Lord God Creator of the Universe and Righteous Judge of our souls.
Many people would dress better for a job interview than they do for
church. If your church announced that the governor of your state, or
the Queen of England, would be present in the church service the next
time you meet, most would wear your finest clothes out of respect for
the high position held by those dignitaries. But when we just get
together with our own congregation, mostly people we know, to meet
with the Lord Jesus Christ, we seem to think it is more important to
be comfortable or fashionable than to be respectful. We ought to
dress better for worship than we do for work or play. The problem is
that too many of us worship our work, work at our play, and play at
our worship.

A second important principle of dress is *modesty*. In our society,
this is especially a problem with women's clothing. A good rule of
thumb is: "If your clothing draws attention to any part of the body
God did not intend for public display, it is immodest." While this is a
very difficult subject for a pastor to deal with tactfully, it is important.
Ladies need to be discerning. If a blouse is tight enough, sheer
enough, or cut low enough that it calls attention to her chest, it is
immodest. If her skirt is so short or so tight that it calls attention to
her legs or hips, it is immodest. If she has to keep pulling at her
clothes to feel covered, she should wear something else. Ladies, with
honest help from their husbands or fathers, should examine their
wardrobes and eliminate any questionable garments. No one ought to
be able to question your righteousness because the way you dress is
inappropriate or immodest.

To be "exemplary in our deportment," we must also be *blameless in
our activities*. No one ought to be able to question you righteousness

because activities you participate in cast doubt on your commitment
to God's kingdom. But many tend to make choices on the basis of
what they *like* to do rather than on what they *ought* to do. There are
some places Christians ought never to go to avoid putting themselves
in the place of temptation and to avoid giving the impression that they
are participating in evil. Many Christians' television and movie view-
ing habits have been compromised because their consciences have
been callused by the decadence of our culture. Content that was
shocking ten years ago is no longer so troubling because it is not that
much worse than something else you saw recently. We become less
discerning of evil and its consequences as our sensitivities are dulled
by exposure. Violent and vulgar video games, as well as state spon-
sored and private gambling opportunities provide more avenues of
temptation. Many Christians are so influenced by the popular music
industry that even much of the music that purports to *worship* is hardly exemplary or blameless. If the places you go, the movies you
watch, the games you play, or the music you use can imply a desire to
fulfill fleshly lusts rather than obedience to God's Word, you fail to be
exemplary in your deportment.

Finally, to be "exemplary in our deportment" we must be *blameless
in our attitudes*. A Christian with a critical attitude is hardly demonstrating the righteousness of Christ. A Christian with a fretful spirit is
unconvincing when testifying of a hopeful expectation for eternity
with Christ. A Christian who constantly complains is not the kind and
charitable person God commands us to be. A Christian with a proud
or haughty attitude demonstrates an anti-God state of mind. There is
no place in the church for any of these attitudes. Unfortunately, many
church members demonstrate just such attitudes every day—in their
relationships at home, dealings at work, conducting of business, or
ministering in the church. And church leaders are not immune. Some
of the most boastful, or critical, or complaining, or fretful people you
may ever meet are deacons, or elders, or pastors in their churches. It
is disgraceful to have such attitudes displayed by those in positions of
authority or influence within the church. If we would be exemplary in
our deportment, we must "let this mind be in you which was also in
Christ Jesus" (Phil. 2:5).

The prophet Micah wrote, "He hath showed thee, O man, what *is*
good; and what doth the LORD require of thee, but to do justly, and

to love mercy, and to walk humbly with thy God?" (Micah 6:8). The members of our church, as one body in Christ, have committed ourselves by solemn vow to "be just in our dealings, faithful in our engagements, and exemplary in our deportment." It behooves us to keep our promise.

CHAPTER 16
CONTROLLING YOUR TEMPER

When I was in my early teens, I attended a large Christian school that did not have an interscholastic sports program. As a sort of compensation, several of the guys would get together after school to play ball. Where we met depended on whether we were going to play basketball, baseball, or football. Even though disagreements and disputes were not uncommon, we generally got along pretty well. On one occasion, though, something happened that I did not like. I don't remember what it was that made me angry, but I was furious. I was so mad at one of my friends that I charged at him intent on … I'm not sure what—I just know I wanted to slug him. At the time, I was a slightly chubby 5'4" high school freshman. The boy I wanted to clobber was an athletic 6'2" senior. I am still grateful that he was either feeling more gracious than I or that he didn't feel particularly threatened by my attack. He let me live.

Unfortunately, the kind of boiling rage I felt that day is not confined to stupid fourteen-year-olds. Even supposedly mature men and women can behave in much the same way I did that day. If you don't believe it, just attend a few Little League Baseball or youth league soccer games and watch the parents when there is a controversial call or coaching decision. Angry behavior can even be seen in the church. Business meetings that disintegrate into brawls are pretty unusual—we at least try to express our wrath with a little more decorum than that. But angry words and vindictive spirits have damaged many churches and destroyed many individuals. The ability to control one's temper is a vital element to one's testimony in the church. Paul writes,

> Be ye angry, and sin not: let not the sun go down upon your wrath: neither give place to the devil...And grieve not the holy Spirit of God, whereby ye are sealed unto the day of redemption. Let all bitterness, and wrath, and anger, and clamor, and evil speaking, be put away from you, with all malice. And be ye kind one to another, tenderhearted, forgiving one another, even as God for Christ's sake hath forgiven you (Eph. 4:26-27, 30-32).

In the light of this instruction, we need to examine four common opinions about anger, contrasting them with biblical instructions about anger, and draw some conclusions on the limited circumstances in which an expression of anger may be acceptable.

Common Opinions about Anger

Many people approach their own anger with the assumption that "anger is acceptable as long as I don't let it out and hurt others." In defense of this view it can be noted that child abuse, spousal abuse, and murder are a few extreme examples of what can happen when an angry person vents his anger on others. In Genesis 4, it was Cain's anger that led to the murder of his brother Abel. So you should keep your anger bottled up so it won't hurt anyone else, right? Wrong! Anger bottled up is malice, hatred, and bitterness. Proverbs 10:18 says, "He that hideth hatred *with* lying lips ... *is* a fool." Hebrews 12:15 warns "lest any root of bitterness springing up trouble *you*, and thereby many be defiled." Further, it is precisely this "bottled up" anger that Paul was forbidding with the Greek word *orge* (translated "anger") in Ephesians 4:31. This word refers to a wrathful or angry state of mind, as contrasted with the angry outburst intent on revenge indicated by the Greek word *thumos* (translated "wrath").

Many others have drawn the opposite conclusion, deciding that "anger is acceptable as long as I don't keep it in and hurt myself." We have heard enough pop-psychology opinions contending for this view that many of us have come to believe it. It is argued that anger is one of the chief causes of stress, and stress is credited with causing as much as 90% of all illness. Since it is true that habitual anger can destroy your health, especially when kept bottled up inside, you should vent your anger, right? Wrong again! Proverbs 22:8 says, "He that soweth iniquity shall reap vanity: and the rod of his anger shall fail." Proverbs 19:11 says, "The discretion of a man deferreth his anger; and *it is* his glory to pass over a transgression." Solomon also adds in Ecclesiastes 7:9, "Be not hasty in thy spirit to be angry: for anger resteth in the bosom of fools." Further, if we look back at Ephesians 4:31, we find that Paul included angry outbursts in his list of actions and attitudes to be "put away" from the believer who does not want to "grieve the holy Spirit of God" and who wants to demonstrate a Christlike spirit.

If you can't let it out, and you can't keep it in, perhaps "anger is acceptable as long as I don't become *too* angry." Anger is only wrong when you lose control, right? Still wrong! Proverbs 27:4 says, "Wrath *is* cruel, and anger *is* outrageous." Psalm 37:8 says, "Cease from anger and forsake wrath: fret not thyself in any wise to do evil." Echoing his words in Ephesians 4, Paul writes in Colossians 3:8, "But now ye also put off all these; anger, wrath, malice, blasphemy, filthy communication out of your mouth." In all honesty, this is where the wording of our church covenant is somewhat unfortunate, leading to some confusion. Since we pledge to "avoid all…excessive anger," many may suppose that "anger in moderation" is acceptable. As we've seen in the passages cited, the Scriptures hold us to a stricter or higher standard than our covenant implies. There is nothing in the language of these passages that even hints that moderation in the expression of your temper is God's intent. We are simply told to "cease" and to "put off" such attitudes and actions. It would seem better to pledge to avoid "all inappropriate anger," which would include, but not be limited to "excessive anger."

A fourth wrong opinion says "anger is acceptable as long as I don't stay angry too long." People will admit that they may blow up occasionally, but defend it because they don't stay angry. This attitude seems to be defended in Ephesians 4:26, where Paul writes, "Be ye angry and sin not: let not the sun go down upon your wrath." Countless pastors and others have counseled people to "never go to bed angry" on the basis of this passage. But that is not what Paul meant. First, there is no mention of "going to bed" in this passage; it refers to "sun...down." Further, it is possible that the passage should be understood to say, "In your anger, stop sinning! Get over this habitual anger before another day passes." If so, he was chiding his readers for their anger and commanding an immediate relinquishing of their right to be angry. But Paul may well have been saying, "Be angry, but do not sin. Do not let the sun go down without dealing with the cause of your anger." If that is the case, this passage represents a kind of shorthand command for church discipline. Since Paul goes on to demand that they tolerate "no place" for the devil, and specifically commands dealing with sins like stealing, corrupt speech, bitterness, wrath, etc., he may be insisting on a righteous indignation toward sins in the church that must be disciplined.

Regardless of which interpretation we settle on for Ephesians 4:26, Paul has *not* said that believers may be angry without sinning as long as they get over it before dark. Just five verses later he says, "Let all bitterness, and wrath, and anger, and clamor, and evil speaking, be put away from you, with all malice" (4:31). Notice that Paul uses the word *all* twice in giving his absolute command to put away these six different manifestation of anger. The Scriptures *never* commend anyone for flaring up in anger quickly as long as its duration is brief. We are repeatedly told to be very slow to be roused to anger. But this does not mean you are free to brood over an offense until you explode. It means that you must exercise such mastery over your temper that you never flare up. Proverbs 15:18 says, "A wrathful man stirreth up strife: but *he that is* slow to anger appeaseth strife," and Proverbs 16:32 says, "*He that is* slow to anger *is* better than the mighty; and he that ruleth his spirit than he that taketh a city." James writes, "Wherefore, my beloved brethren, let every man be swift to hear, slow to speak, slow to wrath: For the wrath of man worketh not the righteousness of God" (James 1:19-20). As a matter of fact, Proverbs warns against even keeping company with an angry person: "Make no friendship with an angry man; and with a furious man thou shalt not go: Lest thou learn his ways, and get a snare to thy soul" (Prov. 22:24-25).

Anger that flares up in emotional turbulence is sin, being characteristic of an uncontrolled spirit, and is specifically forbidden in Ephesians 4:31. Anger that is accompanied by irritation, exasperation, or bitterness is also sin. All of these attitudes are motivated by pride

and interfere with a believer's fellowship with God and with his
Christian brethren (James 4:6; 1 Peter 5:5-6). The overwhelming
majority of times that most people are angry fall into one of these categories. Whether the anger is directed toward your spouse, your children, your parents, your employer, your employees, the clerk at the
store, or the driver who cuts you off in traffic, it can almost always be
described in these terms. We must conclude that *the only way anger
can be expressed without sin is if it is governed by the will of God.*

Acceptable Expressions of Anger

What kind of anger is not "excessive anger" and is, therefore, an
appropriate part of the Christian life? Is it possible for anger to be
experienced and expressed by a person under the control of the Holy
Spirit and in accordance with the will of God? These are the questions we must answer if we would know what constitutes a Spirit-controlled temper. It is instructive for us to consider some biblical examples.

Many Scriptures speak of the wrath of God. Since God is absolutely holy and without sin, any time He is angry it is good. When is He
angry, or toward what is His anger directed? Romans 1:18 says, "For
the wrath of God is revealed from heaven against all ungodliness and
unrighteousness of men, who hold [shackle] the truth in unrighteousness." God's anger was displayed toward unbelieving, rebellious
humanity in Genesis 6, so he destroyed all but Noah and his family
with the Flood. God was also angry with His own people. When the
Israelites complained, apparently about His choice of campsites while
in the wilderness under Moses' leadership, God sent "the fire of the
LORD" to consume them (Numbers 11:1-3). When they continued to
complain about their limited diet, wanting meat because they were
dissatisfied with the manna God had miraculously provided for them,
"the anger of the LORD was kindled greatly" (11:10). In response,
God told Moses to tell Israel that He would give them more meat than
they wanted. "Ye shall not eat one day, nor two days, nor five days,
neither ten days, nor twenty days; *But* even a whole month, until it
come out at your nostrils, and it be loathsome unto you" (11:19-20).
Even the leaders of God's people are not immune from God's wrath
when they are in the wrong. When Miriam complained about Moses'
leadership, God smote her with leprosy (Numbers 12:1-10). When

Moses interceded on her behalf, God cleansed her of her leprosy, but she remained quarantined for a week "shut out from the camp" (12:14-15). His wrath and judgment were even poured out upon His own Son when He was made sin for us (Isaiah 53: 4-5, 10-11). While believers are spared God's wrath, its having been satisfied by Jesus' death in our place, God still "chastens" and "scourges" His children to correct us when we are wrong (Hebrews 12:5-11). So we see that the wrath and judgment of a Holy God toward sin is an appropriate anger. It is not "excessive" even when the judgment seems harsh (leprosy or death) or permanent (damnation).

There are also occasions in the New Testament where we see Jesus Christ displaying anger. Since Jesus is both the Son of God and equal with the Father (John 1:1-14; 5:18; 10:30; 14:9-11), and He always did His Father's will, whenever He is angry it is good. In John 2:13-16 we have an account of Jesus' actions in reclaiming the Temple for the Father, signifying that the Temple worship would be fulfilled in Him, and the Temple sacrifices would be replaced by His sacrifice. "And when he had made a scourge of small cords, he drove them all out of the temple…and said…make not my Father's house an house of merchandise." A similar event at the close of Jesus' earthly ministry is also recorded (see Matthew 21:12-13; Luke 19:45-48). On another occasion, there was an incident in which Jesus was angry with His disciples. People "brought young children to him that he should touch them: and *his* disciples rebuked those that brought *them*. But when Jesus saw *it*, he was much displeased, and said unto them, Suffer the little children to come unto me, and forbid them not" (Mark 10:13-14). Then in Matthew 23 we read Jesus' scathing denouncement of the hypocritical religious leaders for their misrepresentation of God and misapplication of Scripture that was leading the people astray.

On the basis of the testimony of the Gospel record, we can conclude that Jesus' anger was always prompted by His zeal for allegiance to the Father. Jesus was never angry over personal inconvenience—not when the disciples forgot to bring food for a journey, not when they were too dull to understand. Also, Jesus was never angry over personal grievances or injuries—not when the people from His home synagogue in Nazareth tried to throw Him off a cliff as a false prophet, not when the Roman soldiers scourged Him and nailed Him to the cross. Jesus was only angry when the Father's reputation was at stake or when others were being deceived.

We can also learn much about anger and its consequences from two events in the life of Moses. In Exodus 32:19-32, Moses descended from Mount Sinai with the tablets of the law engraved by the very hand of God. When he came down to the camp of Israel, he found the people debauched. In his absence, they had fashioned a calf of gold, were worshipping it, and were behaving shamefully. When he grasped the situation, Moses smashed the stone tablets, destroying the only portion of Scripture ever given by the very hand of God. He went on to grind up the golden calf, mixed the powder with water, and forced the Israelites to drink it. He called upon the Levites, the only ones who would stand with him, to draw their swords and execute the rebels. Three thousand Israelites were slain that day. For this vigorous display of anger Moses was commended as a hero of the faith for his defense of God and His righteousness.

Several years later, Moses' anger was again kindled toward Israel. In Numbers 20:2-12 we are told of their complaints of thirst. This is not the first time they had so complained. Earlier, God had told Moses to strike a particular stone with his rod to bring forth water for the people. Moses had obeyed, and Israel had experienced God's miraculous supply. On this later occasion, God instructed Moses to speak to the rock. But Moses was so angry with the people that he struck the rock again. For this display of anger, God told Moses he would no longer be able to lead Israel—he would not even be allowed to enter the Promised Land. In Exodus 32 the stone tablets were broken and three thousand people died, and Moses was commended. In Numbers 20 all Moses did was hit a rock with a stick, the apparent equivalent of stomping out of a room and slamming a door, and he was condemned. What was the difference? It was the offense for which he was angry. The first time it was because the people God had redeemed would dare to forsake Him so blatantly and blasphemously. The second time it was personal frustration over being criticized for things beyond his control, and then claiming credit for taking care of the situation for such a whining group.

Taken together, the examples of God's wrath, of Jesus' anger, and the two incidents in the life of Moses vividly illustrate that anger in

God's people is only appropriate when God's word and God's will are knowingly disobeyed by God's people, or when God's enemies usurp authority beyond the scope granted them by God. In each case we must exercise caution. It is all too easy for personal exasperation, irritation, or frustration to insinuate themselves. The Bible gives us many warnings against the temptation to sin in anger. The only passage that may constitute a command to be angry is Ephesians 4:26, if it is understood as instructions to execute swift discipline in cases of sin in the church. And even that passage warns that those exercising such discipline guard their hearts and actions that they "sin not." The anger of men can only be called *righteous indignation* when it is for the protection of God's reputation or of God's people.

We must acknowledge the fact that Scripture teaches that one very important evidence of genuine Christianity is a Spirit-controlled temper. If God's people are to be known by our love for one another (John 13:35), and the presence of the Spirit is evidenced by our self-control (Galatians 5:22), we must learn to control our tempers (Ephesians 4:26-32).

CHAPTER 17
ABSTAINING FROM INTOXICANTS

The career of the famous singer/actress Lillian Roth was eventually destroyed by a long bout with drunkenness.[1] Later, after she "dried out," Ms. Roth had an opportunity to re-launch her acting career, but made an uncharacteristically wise choice instead. Rather than moving back into the life that had encouraged her drunkenness, she went public with her story in the hopes that it would help others. The Chicago American published her life story in 1955. The following is an excerpt:

You know now that alcohol creeps insidiously into your life, so insidiously you aren't aware of it until it's too late.

At first it was four or five whisky sours a night. Soon the four or five became a pint and then a fifth. And you couldn't start the morning without a drink.

Then the two-ounce bottles in your bag grew to six ounces and finally fifths...Odd. No one ever commented that you were rarely seen without those big handbags.

Soon you were on a fifth a day, taking the stuff slowly, a drink or two every four or five hours. Then every three hours. Then two hours. Finally every hour. Then a quart through the day and a quart through the night.

As the years went on something terrifying happened. You couldn't hold as much. You began to throw it up. One part of you cried: "I want it!" The other part cried: "I can't take it!"

Your body reached a point of revolt; you were sick all the time. Sometimes you vomited all morning before your stomach retained an ounce of it—the drink your body needed so desperately.

The next stage was worse. You lay in bed and drank around the clock; drank, passed out, waked, drank, vomited, drank, vomited, drank, passed out....

Then, still worse, the shakes. Only liquor could relieve it, but your body rejected liquor.

And after the shakes, the horrors, the delirium tremens, when you heard sounds that were not there and saw things that did not exist....Then the hours of pacing your room, and tearing your hair, and you have reached the worst stage of all; your medicine is your poison and there is no end but madness....

What a tragic picture! But it is a scene that has been repeated in countless lives over countless generations.

Included in our church covenant is a pledge to "abstain from the sale of, and use of, intoxicating drinks as a beverage." In some Christian circles and cultures the consumption of alcoholic beverages is more accepted than in others. However, our church takes the position that such behavior is inappropriate for a believer. In the last several years, concerned citizens of the United States have embarked upon a nation-wide campaign to eliminate drunk driving. That is good, as far as it goes. But pledging not to drink and drive is far short of what we desire of members of our church. We have taken a solemn oath before Almighty God that we will keep ourselves completely separate from both selling and using intoxicating drinks as a beverage.

Members do not violate this oath if they use alcohol in medication or as an antiseptic. But if one is taking his medicine when he is not sick, or drinking his mouthwash, he is using them as a beverage. He has violated his oath and has sinned against God. Further, if one uses an "intoxicating drink" in preparing food in such a way that the alco-

hol will evaporate during the cooking process, he has not violated his
oath or God's command. But if he tastes the cooking sherry as he
adds some to the recipe, he is using it as a beverage. He has broken
his word and sinned against God. In general, having alcoholic beverages in the house for cooking purposes may be unwise. It can be dangerous to place such temptation before you and your family.

In Paul's letter to the Church at Ephesus he charges,

And be not drunk with wine, wherein is excess; but be filled with
the Spirit; Speaking to yourselves in psalms and hymns and spiritual songs, singing and making melody in your heart to the Lord;
Giving thanks always for all things unto God and the Father in the
name of our Lord Jesus Christ; Submitting yourselves one to
another in the fear of God (Ephesians 5:18-21).

In studying this subject, we need to consider the characteristics of
intoxicating beverages and the consequences of drunkenness. We will
also examine the merits of the cases for temperance and for abstinence.

The Characteristics of Intoxicating Beverages

The Scriptures point out at least three dangerous characteristics of
intoxicating beverages and their effects on one's mind: they deceive,
they distort, and they ultimately destroy the mind and body. First,
Proverbs 20:1 says, "Wine *is* a mocker, strong drink *is* raging: and
whosoever is deceived thereby is not wise." That is, intoxicating beverages deceive you by getting your attention as a loud, clamorous
noise, then they make a fool of you. Second, Isaiah 28:7 says,

But they also have erred through wine, and through strong drink
are out of the way; the priest and the prophet have erred through
strong drink, they are swallowed up of wine, they are out of the
way through strong drink; they err in vision, they stumble *in* judgment.

Isaiah has said that intoxicating beverages *distort* the truth by making you unable to think or see straight—your judgment is impaired.
Third, Proverbs 23:29-35 gives an extended warning of alcohol's
power to *destroy* you.

Who hath woe? Who hath sorrow? Who hath contentions? Who hath babbling? Who hath wounds without cause? Who hath redness of eyes? They that tarry long at the wine; they that go to seek mixed wine. Look not thou upon the wine when it is red, when it giveth his color in the cup, *when* it moveth itself aright. At the last it biteth like a serpent, and stingeth like an adder. Thine eyes shall behold strange women, and thine heart shall utter perverse things. Yea, thou shalt be as he that lieth down in the midst of the sea, or as he that lieth upon the top of a mast. They have stricken me, *shalt thou say, and* I was not sick; they have beaten me, *and* I felt *it* not: when shall I awake? I will seek it yet again.

Solomon's point is that intoxicating beverages will abuse you, while at the same time enslaving you. Following Isaiah's denunciation of the priests in Isaiah 28:7 for having given themselves up to wine and strong drink, verse 8 reads, "For all tables are full of vomit and filthiness, so that there is no place clean." The descent into bondage described by Lillian Roth parallels the description given of the drunkard in Scripture. Alcoholic beverages are characterized by deception, distortion, and destruction.

The Consequences of Drunkenness

One may argue that an occasional drink does not make him a drunkard. But if he understands the characteristics of alcohol that we have just examined, he must admit that an occasional drink places him in peril of becoming a drunkard, with all the attendant consequences. Something so characteristically dangerous and evil will bring appropriately devastating results.

First, giving oneself to alcoholic beverages will *end in poverty.* Proverbs 21:17 says, "He that loveth pleasure shall be a poor man: he that loveth wine and oil shall not be rich." Proverbs 23:21 adds, "For the drunkard and the glutton shall come to poverty." Implied in these passages are twin financial woes of the drunkard: loss of income to his passions, and loss of initiative for work. The drunkard wastes his money on alcohol, and he wastes his life in drunkenness.

Second, drunkenness *ends in perversion.* It corrupts one's morals. Notice the warning in Proverbs 23:31-33, "Look not thou upon the wine when it is red, when it giveth his colour in the cup, *when* it moveth itself aright. At the last it biteth like a serpent, and stingeth like an adder. Thine eyes shall behold strange women, and thine heart shall utter perverse things." Alcoholic beverages reduce inhibitions, and open the door for succumbing to seduction, lust, and perversity. Drunkenness also corrupts one's message. Proverbs 31:4 and 5 warns, "*It is* not for kings, O Lemuel, *it is* not for kings to drink wine; nor for princes strong drink: Lest they drink, and forget the law, and pervert the judgment of any of the afflicted." Isaiah 5:22-23 adds, "Woe unto *them that are* mighty to drink wine, and men of strength to mingle strong drink: Which justify the wicked for reward, and take away the righteousness of the righteous from him!" Further, Isaiah 28:7-11 says,

> But they also have erred through wine, and through strong drink are out of the way; ... Whom shall he teach knowledge? and whom shall he make to understand doctrine? *them that are* weaned from the milk, *and* drawn from the breasts. For precept *must be* upon precept, precept upon precept; line upon line, line upon line; here a little, *and* there a little: For with stammering lips and another tongue will he speak to this people.

The point of these passages is that alcoholic beverages reduce one's ability to think and act rationally, consistently, or biblically. Even without moral corruption, they destroy one's testimony.

A final consequence of drunkenness is that it ultimately *ends in perdition*. The prophet Habakkuk writes,

> Woe unto him that giveth his neighbour drink, that puttest thy bottle to *him*, and makest *him* drunken also, that thou mayest look on their nakedness! Thou art filled with shame for glory: drink thou also, and let thy foreskin be uncovered: the cup of the LORD'S right hand shall be turned unto thee, and shameful spewing *shall be* on thy glory (Hab. 2:15-16).

The statement "let thy foreskin be uncovered" essentially means "let it be revealed that you are uncircumcised and, therefore, are not a part of God's people." The Apostle Paul writes in 1 Corinthians 6:9-10,

> Know ye not that the unrighteous shall not inherit the kingdom

of God? Be not deceived: neither fornicators, nor idolaters, nor adulterers, nor effeminate, nor abusers of themselves with mankind, Nor thieves, nor covetous, nor drunkards, nor revilers, nor extortioners, shall inherit the kingdom of God.

Drunkards are included in that list of sins that lead to damnation. Paul also says in Galatians 5:21, "Envyings, murders, drunkenness, revellings, and such like: of the which I tell you before, as I have also told *you* in time past, that they which do such things shall not inherit the kingdom of God."[2]

The following advertisement, which may be the benchmark for truth in advertising, was printed in the Boise [Idaho] Democrat, February 24, 1886. It was written by James M. Lawrence to announce the opening of his new bar "The Naked Truth Saloon."

> Friends and Neighbors: having just opened a commodious shop for the sale of liquid fire, I embrace this opportunity of informing you that I have commenced the business of making drunkards, paupers and beggars for the sober, industrious and respectable portion of the community to support. I shall deal in family spirits which will incite men to deeds of riots, robbery and bloodshed, and by so doing diminish the comfort, augment the expenses, and endanger the welfare of the community.

> I will on short notice, for a sum, and with great expectations, undertake to prepare victims for the asylums, poor farms, prisons and gallows.

> I will furnish an article that will increase accidents, multiply the number of distressing diseases, and render those who are harmless incurables.

> I will deal in drugs which will deprive some of life, many of reason, most of property, and all of peace, which will cause fathers to become fiends, and wives widows, and children to become orphans and all mendicants [beggars].

> I will cause many of the rising generation to grow up in ignorance and prove a burden and a nuisance to the nation. I will cause mothers to forget their offspring, and cruelty to take the

place of love.

I will sometimes corrupt the ministers of religion, defile the purity of the church, and cause temporary spiritual and eternal death,
and if any be so impertinent as to ask me why I have the audacity
to bring such accumulated misery upon the people, my honest
reply is "*Money.*" The spirit trade is lucrative and some professs-
ing Christians give their cheerful countenance.

From the U. S. government I have purchased the right to demol-
ish the character, destroy the health, and shorten the lives and ruin
the souls of those who choose to honor me with their custom.

I pledge myself to do all that I have promised. Those who wish
any of the evils before specified brought upon themselves or their
dear friends, are requested to meet me at my bar where I will for a
few cents furnish them with the certain means of doing so.

The Case for Temperance

Despite the evidence of the character of alcoholic beverages and
their consequences, some believers still argue for temperance. Since
most of the warnings deal with drunkenness, not just an occasional
drink, they interpret the body of Scripture to permit drinking of alcoholic beverages in moderation.

The first argument set forth in defense of temperance, as opposed to
abstinence, is that *wine was produced by Jesus.* The incident cited is
found in John 2:1-11. Jesus was attending a marriage feast in Cana of
Galilee and he performed His first miracle by turning water into wine.
Since the Greek word used in this account refers generally to any beverage made from the juice of the grape, it tells us nothing about
whether the juice was fresh or fermented. Arguing from silence that it
must have been fermented because it does not say it was fresh is a
weak argument indeed. But when one understands the Hebrew practice of serving wine at such a festival, the whole argument becomes
moot.

The fermentation of juice into wine was the only method of preservation available to the people of Jesus' day, and since grapes ripen
seasonally, the juice would have to be preserved if it were to be avail-

able. Also, the water supply was uncertain and often contaminated, requiring purification by the easiest method available in their day— mixture with an antiseptic. Fermented juice was the only readily available antiseptic for this purpose. So the legitimate purpose of fermentation was twofold: preservation of the juice and purification of the water. For fermented juice to be blessed for serving at a public festivity, especially one as high and holy as a wedding, Jewish law required that it be diluted with at least three parts water. This would drop its alcohol content to a maximum of about 1%, since their distillation process would only produce a vintage with 3.5-4% alcohol content. By today's standards, this would earn a classification of "non-alcoholic" because it would no longer be an intoxicating drink. The quality of a wine would be determined by how much water could be added and it still retain its flavor—the best wine being mixed with as much as ten parts water. While a chemical analysis of the mixture would reveal traces of alcohol, it would be so dilute as to make it impossible to become intoxicated. Further, wine diluted with only one part water (about 1.5-2% alcohol) was called "strong drink" and was forbidden because it could lead to drunkenness. Wine undiluted was designated "unmixed wine," even in the classic Greek writings of Homer, Pliny, Aristophenes, and others, and was considered something only a "Barbarian" or "Scythian" would drink. J. W. Shepard, in his *The Christ of the Gospels* [1892], says:

> Jesus made real wine out of the water. But there was a great difference between the Palestinian wine of that time and the alcoholic mixtures which today go under the name of wine. Their simple vintage was taken with three parts of water and would correspond more or less with our grape juice. It would be worse than blasphemy to suppose, because Jesus made wine, that he justifies the drinking usages of modern society with its bars, strong drinks, and resulting evils (p. 90).

A second argument set forth in favor of temperance is that *wine was prescribed by Paul*. In 1 Timothy 5:23, Paul advised Pastor Timothy, "Drink no longer water, but use a little wine for thy stomach's sake and thine often infirmities." The problem with using this passage to defend an occasional beer or glass of wine is that Paul's prescription was specifically limited to medicinal purposes in small doses. Timothy was to take "a little" for his "stomach's sake" and only because of his frequent illness. There is no support in this passage for "social drinking."

The Case for Abstinence

This brings us to the position we have taken in our church—that a believer should abstain from imbibing alcohol as a beverage. Besides the general warnings cited earlier, there are two additional reasons for this position: alcoholic beverages are forbidden for priests, and alcoholic beverages are forbidden for preachers.

Leviticus 10:8-11 says,

And the LORD spake unto Aaron, saying, Do not drink wine nor strong drink, thou, nor thy sons with thee, when ye go into the tabernacle of the congregation, lest ye die: *it shall be* a statute for ever throughout your generations: And that ye may put difference between holy and unholy, and between unclean and clean; And that ye may teach the children of Israel all the statutes which the LORD hath spoken unto them by the hand of Moses.

The reason for the prohibition is clear—to make a distinction between the holy and the unholy, the clean and the unclean. It was to allow the priests to serve as an example to all Israel, and to qualify them to teach the Scriptures. Admittedly, the prohibition for the priesthood is an Old Testament regulation, but many of the Old Testament regulations had purposes with a New Testament application. Significantly, 1 Peter 2:9 describes *all believers* as "a chosen generation, a royal priesthood, an holy nation, a peculiar people; that ye should show forth the praises of him who hath called you out of darkness into his marvelous light." God's purpose in forbidding the priests to drink had to do with their separation for service and the distinction between the holy and the unholy. But according to Peter, all believers of the church age are "royal priests" separated for that same service. All of us constitute a holy nation—everything about the life of the believer is to be sanctified as holy unto God. It follows, then, that there is no place for drinking of alcoholic beverages in the life of the holy believer/priest. It would profane the sanctuary of the Holy Spirit.

But alcoholic beverages were not just forbidden to the Old Testament priests. They were also forbidden to preachers. In the Old Testament, that included those appointed by God to the special calling of the Nazarite (Nu. 6:3). John the Baptist was the last of the Old Testament Nazarites (Luke 1:15).[3] Again, it is significant that all believers of the New Testament Church Age are commanded to witness to the truth of the Gospel (Mt. 28:19-20; Acts 1:8). Some have claimed that those commands were limited to the Apostles, even though there is no way to prove that the Twelve were the only ones present when the Commission was given. But no such claim can be made for Hebrews 5:12-14,

> For when for the time ye ought to be teachers, ye have need that one teach you again which *be* the first principles of the oracles of God; and are become such as have need of milk, and not of strong meat. For every one that useth milk *is* unskillful in the word of righteousness: for he is a babe. But strong meat belongeth to them that are of full age, *even* those who by reason of use have their senses exercised to discern both good and evil.

The writer is scolding his audience for not having mastered the Word of God sufficiently to teach it to others. The implication is that every believer has a responsibility to be a teacher/preacher of the truth of the Word of God. If those who were told to testify to the truth of the Gospel are to abstain from alcoholic beverages, that applies to all believers.

Rudyard Kipling was well known as a poet and novelist. He also became renowned for his drinking and his long-time advocacy for intoxicating beverages. Even though he was a British subject, he was outspoken in his opposition to prohibition in early twentieth century America. But he changed his position. In his *American Notes*, he explains why.

> The other sight of the evening was a horror. The little tragedy played itself out at a neighboring table where two very young men and two young women were sitting. It did not strike me till far into the evening that the pimply young reprobates were making the girls drunk. They gave them red wine and then white, and the voices rose slightly with the maiden cheeks' flushes. I watched, wishing to stay, and the youths drank till their speech thickened and their eyeballs grew watery. It was sickening to see, because I knew what was going to happen.

...[T]hey got indubitably drunk—here in that lovely hall, surrounded by the best of Buffalo society. One could do nothing except invoke the judgment of Heaven on the two boys, themselves half sick with liquor. At the close of the performance the quieter maiden laughed vacantly and protested she couldn't keep her feet. The four linked arms, and, staggering, flickered out into the street—drunk, gentlemen and ladies, as Davy's swine....They disappeared down a side avenue, but I could hear their laughter long after they were out of sight.

And they were all four children of sixteen and seventeen. Then, recanting previous opinions, I became a prohibitionist. Better it is that a man should go without his beer in public places, and content himself with swearing at the narrow-mindedness of the majority...than to bring temptation to the lips of young fools such as the four I had seen. I understand now why the preachers rage against drink. I have said: 'There is no harm in it, taken moderately,' and yet my own demand for beer helped directly to send those two girls reeling down the dark street to—God alone knows what end.

...It is not good that we should let it lie before the eyes of children, and I have been a fool in writing to the contrary.

"And be not drunk with wine, wherein is excess; but be filled with the Spirit" (Eph. 5:18). The influence of the Holy Spirit makes us more wise, not less. One evidence of the presence of intoxicating drinks is loss of control. One evidence of the presence of the Spirit is self-control. Anything that bypasses one's conscious mind, or inhibits one's ability to think and act rationally, is not of God. Alcohol has been for centuries the chief destroyer of homes and reputations. In today's society, with abundant pure water and easy access to other well-preserved beverages, there is simply no excuse for a believer's indulgence in consuming alcoholic beverages.

---

[1] "Drunkenness" is a better word than "alcoholism," because the latter seems to imply that the problem is not the drunkard's fault.

[2] This is not to say that any of these are "unpardonable" sins. Any and all

sin can be forgiven. Immediately following the list of sins in 1
Corinthians 6:9-10 for which none "shall inherit the kingdom of God,"
Paul adds, "And such were some of you: but ye are washed, but ye are
sanctified, but ye are justified in the name of the Lord Jesus, and by the
Spirit of our God." The passage in Galatians serves to balance the *liberty*
of the believer, which is the theme of that book, with the *duty* of the
believer to forsake the "works of the flesh" (5:16-21) and demonstrate
the "fruit of the Spirit" (5:22-25).

[3] Even though his role in history is recorded in the New Testament
Gospels, John the Baptist lived in the Old Testament economy, prior to
the death and resurrection of the Lord Jesus Christ.

CHAPTER 18
DISCIPLINING OFFENDERS

Robert Bork, whose nomination to the Supreme Court by President Reagan was defeated by the liberal jihad launched against him, has critiqued American culture in a book he entitled *Slouching Towards Gomorrah* (New York: HarperCollins Publishers Inc., 1996). During the campaign leading up to the 2000 presidential primaries, Republican candidate Alan Keyes was asked by a reporter if he agreed with Bork, that America is "Slouching Towards Gomorrah." Keyes replied, "No. I think it is quite obvious that we are *rushing headlong* towards Gomorrah." While they may disagree on the haste with which we are headed there, both of these men make the point that our culture is descending into utter decadence.

Many of us have pointed to the abominable behavior of President William Jefferson Clinton as one of the factors contributing to our cultural destruction. However, it was not so much the President's manifold sins that were the problem. What has truly hastened our destruction, and demonstrated the depths to which we have already sunk, was our inability as a nation to muster the moral courage to impose any meaningful disciplinary consequences for his sins. The United States Congress did succeed in impeaching President Clinton, but the Senate was unwilling to hold him accountable.

When the President of the United States can act with complete disregard for both the law of God and the laws of our land with virtual impunity, it is no wonder that personal integrity and basic morality are such rare commodities in our land. And the church is not immune to the problem. While sins within our congregations are rarely as spectacular as President Clinton's, they may well be quite similar in kind. Honestly, the behavior of professing believers is barely distinguishable from their unbelieving neighbors. The truth is, as long as we believers are alive on this earth we are subject to failures and to being dominated by the flesh. This is the very matter that caused the Apostle Paul to cry out in Romans 7:24, "O wretched man that I am! who shall deliver me from the body of this death?" Furthermore, as long as we have contact with other people there will be personality clashes, differences of opinion, and disagreements that can develop into problematic conflicts which must be dealt with biblically.

If any church is to survive as a visible body of Christ, biblical discipline must be sustained within that church. To know how to do that, we must first understand what the Bible teaches about church discipline. Then we must commit ourselves to maintaining it. This will require personal determination to carry out the proper procedures in the right attitude when another believer needs to be disciplined either privately or publicly. It will also require personal dedication to maintaining our own lives in such a way that we do not need to be disciplined by others.

Ultimately, discipline should be personal—each of us is to be self-disciplined, under the influence of the Holy Spirit. But the church has also been charged with the responsibility to exercise corporate discipline in cases where self-discipline has failed to adequately control an individual's behavior, passions, or attitudes. It is the latter aspect of discipline that we need to consider in this context. We must answer the question, "How should the church deal with the believer who has done something wrong, who has 'caused an offense'?" In Matthew 18:15-22, Jesus gave the disciples some instruction concerning this.

> Moreover, if thy brother shall trespass against thee, go and tell him his fault between thee and him alone: if he shall hear thee, thou hast gained thy brother. But if he will not hear *thee*, *then* take with thee one or two more, that in the mouth of two or three witnesses every word may be established. And if he shall neglect to hear them, tell it unto the church: but if he neglect to hear the

church, let him be unto thee as a heathen man and a publican.

What we often fail to notice is that in the very next verses Jesus continues by adding,

Verily I say unto you, Whatsoever ye shall bind on earth shall be bound in heaven: and whatsoever ye shall loose on earth shall be loosed in heaven. Again I say unto you, That if two of you shall agree on earth as touching any thing that they shall ask, it shall be done for them of my Father which is in heaven. For where two or three are gathered together in my name, there am I in the midst of them (Mt. 18:18-20).

God's promise to do whatever "two of you shall agree on" is given within the context of exercising church discipline—correcting a brother who has done wrong. Peter immediately asked, "Lord, how oft shall my brother sin against me, and I forgive him? Till seven times?" (18:21). Peter was actually being quite generous, so he was probably surprised when Jesus said, "I say not unto thee, Until seven times: but, Until seventy times seven" (18:22). Jesus' point is that you should not keep track. If you are keeping score that long, tallying up that many identical offenses, you have a serious problem with bitterness in your own heart. Right here in the text from which we learn how to correct a brother, to bring him to repentance by rebuking him when he has done wrong, we find both the promise that God is working through us if we will do it for His glory, and the instruction that we must be prepared to forgive (see Chapter Twenty-three).

The Biblical Purposes of Church Discipline

Much harm has been caused by misguided attempts at "discipline," often growing from misunderstanding its nature and purpose. It is helpful to realize that the concepts of *discipline* and *discipling* are identical. A disciple is a learner, one in training to become like his instructor or master. In our personal growth as disciples of Christ, we are to become increasingly accurate reflections of Jesus Himself. We should have the same goal for those we would disciple, "that the man of God may be perfect, throughly furnished unto all good works" (2 Timothy 3:17). That is accomplished through the study and application of Scripture, which is "profitable for doctrine, for reproof, for correction, for instruction in righteousness" (3:16). "Discipline," then, is not "punishment" but "doctrine, ... reproof, ... correction, ... instruction in righteousness." Paul writes, "Brethren, if a man be overtaken in a fault, ye which are spiritual, restore such a one in the spirit of meekness; considering thyself, lest thou also be tempted" (Galatians 6:1).

We ought to exercise discipline in a biblical manner simply to be obedient to God's command. This is what He told us to do, and that should be sufficient to constrain us to obey. But we can also identify at least three reasons *why* we are instructed to confront a brother who has done wrong.

First, *we must exercise discipline to maintain the purity of the local church.* This theme is developed in 1 Corinthians 5 as Paul writes to the church in Corinth to tell them how to deal with the sin in the life of one of the men in their congregation who was living immorally. He said that if they would allow this sin to go unchallenged in their church, they were prone to falling into sin themselves. A local congregation must take steps to correct those things that would breed corruption in its midst. For the good of the whole body, they have the responsibility to correct anything that might encourage rebellion or might simply encourage apathy.

Second, *we must exercise discipline to maintain the testimony of the local church.* If there is an individual in the church that we know is behaving wickedly, and we tolerate that person's behavior by allowing him to continue as a member in good standing with the church, we are endangering the good name of the church and of our Lord within the community. In recent years we have been beset by numerous highly publicized scandals involving sin in the lives of well-known television pastors and evangelists. Generally, the publicity has occurred when the congregation who had the responsibility to exercise biblical discipline failed to do so and someone else had to step in. The very people who should have been acting to protect the Lord's reputation by cleansing the sin often hurt the testimony of His people by trying to hide or excuse the sin. In such cases, we invite the reproach of the world upon us for sin in our midst, and we have provided excuses for the wickedness of the lost by our own hypocrisy.

Third, *we must exercise discipline to help individual believers live effective Christian lives.* The goal of church discipline, as it relates to the individual who has been in the wrong, is to set the erring brother back on the paths of righteousness. It is not so you can punch him in the face, knock him to the ground, and stomp him into oblivion. Neither is it so we can pat ourselves on the back for being so spiritual that "we don't do what *he* did, so we are going to take care of it." As Paul wrote, we are to "restore such a one in the spirit of meekness." The point is not destruction, but restoration. We are to be encouraging the sinner to get back to living for the Lord, while at the same time encouraging those who might contemplate straying to remain faithful to Christ.

The Biblical Principles of Church Discipline

There are three governing principles that should guide all imposed discipline, whether it be in the church congregation, a Sunday School class, your home, or any other setting. We learn these from the way God Himself disciplines His children.

First, *our discipline must be motivated by love.* Shortly before His crucifixion, knowing that the time for His departure from them was rapidly approaching, Jesus told His disciples, "By this shall all men know that ye are my disciples, if ye [cast out the sinner]." Actually, that is *not* what Jesus said; it's just what some of us seem to think He *should* have said. Jesus really said, "A new commandment I give unto you, That ye love one another; as I have loved you, that ye also love one another. By this shall all men know that ye are my disciples, if ye have love one to another." (John 13:34). But true love will exercise discipline, because genuine love seeks to *help* the individual, whether or not it *pleases* him. Sometimes the most loving thing we can do is discipline the wayward, even to the point of casting out the sinner. Hebrews 12:6 says, "whom the Lord loveth he chasteneth, and scourgeth every son whom he receiveth." But biblical discipline, including appropriate punishment for wrongdoing, must be motivated by a desire to help the one being disciplined. If it is motivated by anger, or by a vindictive spirit, it is not "discipline," but "revenge."

Second, *our discipline must be intended for reconciliation.* In the Sermon on the Mount, Jesus said, "Therefore, if thou bring thy gift to the altar, and there rememberest that thy brother hath ought against thee; Leave there thy gift before the altar, and go thy way; first be rec-

onciled to thy brother, and then come and offer thy gift" (Matthew
5:23-24). If your conscience pricks you, reminding you that you have
caused an offense against your brother, you must make it right before
offering a gift to God. Only then should you return to give your
offering to the Lord. Your offering is as unacceptable as Cain's until
you make things right with your brother. Proper discipline must be
motivated out of a desire to restore fellowship by reconciling adver-
saries.

In order to show the need for reconciliation it may sometimes be
necessary to sever a relationship, hoping that the separation will only
be temporary. To continue to accept unconditionally a brother's mis-
behavior, with no consequences within the relationship, is unbiblical.
That is why Jesus said in Matthew 18:15, "If he shall hear thee, thou
hast gained thy brother." As we read on, we find that if the one in the
wrong refused to repent and ask forgiveness, separation would eventually be necessary. But the separation is intended to bring restoration
to fellowship. We must never separate from or discipline a brother
merely so we can boast of the fact that we have distanced ourselves
from someone or something.

But some may protest, "Didn't Jesus say, though, that 'if he neglect
to hear the church, let him be unto thee as a heathen man and a publican'?" He certainly did. But what is the church's relationship with
"heathens" and "publicans" to be? Are we to congregate on Sundays
and congratulate ourselves that we are not "heathens" and "publicans"? That is Pharisaism, not Christianity. Our relationship with
unbelievers is not to be one of close fellowship, but we are to be trying to win them. We are to tell them the truth about their condition
and pray that they will respond to the truth in repentance, find forgiveness in Christ, and join our fellowship. The goal is still reconciliation.
The difference is that if the disorderly member refuses to hear the
church, we should assume he is not an erring brother who needs to be
set right, but an unbeliever who needs to be saved.

Third, *when we discipline, we must be prepared to forgive.* In Luke
17:3-4, Jesus said, "Take heed to yourselves: If thy brother trespass
against thee, rebuke him; and if he repent, forgive him. And if he
trespass against thee seven times in a day, and seven times in a day
turn again to thee, saying, I repent; thou shalt forgive him." Sadly,

many believers have taken the first part of verse three to heart, "if thy brother trespass against thee, rebuke him." They don't forgive because they are too busy enjoying the rebuking. The sense of authority, or of power, or of moral superiority can be almost intoxicating as the offender is put in his place. On the other hand, believers are often taught to leave out another part of the verse and read it as, "if thy brother trespass against thee, ... forgive him." This leaves out a necessary step. The erring brother, for his own good, must be rebuked in order to teach him the need to repent. Restoration to fellowship is inappropriate without confrontation and correction of the sin.

This is not divine sanction for you to hold a grudge, but a divine method for dealing with wrong. The Lord Jesus "is not willing that any should perish, but that all should come to repentance." Does that mean that everyone will eventually be spared? No, heaven is for those who "come to repentance," accepting Christ's sacrifice for sin. The Lord will not get any joy out of any soul in hell, but the grief it may cause Him will not permit Him to accept anyone who is unrepentant. Just so, those involved in disciplining an offender must be ready to forgive, but that forgiveness is possible only if genuine confession and repentance are demonstrated and restitution is made wherever necessary. Discipline must never serve to cause those performing the disciplinary action to feel superior for their own purity, nor should it be avoided to spare the feelings of the sinner. It must not be a tool for self-exaltation, but it must be exercised for sinner-reclamation.

The Biblical Procedures for Church Discipline

Because this is such a difficult matter to handle correctly, many churches are paralyzed by uncertainty about what to do or how to do it when faced with a situation demanding disciplinary action. The Scriptures address situations in which one believer is wronged by another—*personal offenses*, and situations in which a biblical command is clearly violated or one is known to practice something clearly condemned in Scripture—*public offenses*.

Personal Offenses

On the basis of what Jesus said in Matthew 18:15-17, the *first step* in dealing with personal offenses is for the one who has been sinned against to go to the offender and attempt reconciliation. Of course, it is better if the one in the wrong takes the initiative to seek forgiveness on the basis of the conviction of his own conscience without having needed the rebuke from the one wronged (Matthew 5:23-24). If that happens, the whole process is simple, because it is ended. But we are not always quick to realize or admit when we have caused an offense. Sometimes we need to be told we have done wrong. In that case, the one who has been offended is commanded by God to take the initiative, for the good of the offender, and go to the one who wronged him. This is not so you can "tell him off" with divine sanction, but so you can do him some good, and to gain your brother.

Involved in this step is the assumption that the one offended is ready to forgive. If you can't go to the person who wronged you with a heart that is ready to forgive, desiring to restore the fellowship that was broken by the offense, then you need to first ask God to forgive your self-righteous pride before you make matters worse. Be sure, too, that the act for which you confront your brother is really a cause for offense. It could be that the real problem is not what he did, but your own wounded pride. Would God consider what happened a trespass against you, or was it merely something you did not like? Many problems have been caused in the body of Christ by Christians who believe that God has appointed them to go from person to person pointing out every petty thing they find objectionable. If it does not involve a violation of Scripture, it should probably be overlooked in love. You may find that you need to apologize for your own bitter and vindictive spirit. But if one did not know you had ill feelings toward him, leave him in peace and just take it up with the Lord.

Also involved in this step is the necessity for the offender to be ready to make restitution where possible and to repent, forsaking his trespasses. Restitution may involve taking steps to undo problems caused by things he has said or done, or it may involve financial reparation. Of course, the offended one may voluntarily waive his right to restitution, which would be commendably merciful. But the offender must be truly willing to make restitution.[1]

However, personal confrontation of the offender with his offense sometimes fails to resolve the situation. The offender may not admit his offense, or he may not care that he has done wrong. If so, the *sec-*

ond step requires that the one offended take one or two brethren with him as witnesses to again seek reconciliation. Handling the situation this way will serve at least two purposes. First, it will help limit the knowledge of the offense. The one offended is not complaining to others, publicizing what the offender did to him. Only the offended one, the offender, and now the selected witnesses should be aware that there is a problem. If you publicize the problem at this point, you are guilty of backbiting and gossip, offenses of your own for which discipline may be necessary. Second, the witnesses can help by giving advice and observing the spirit of the two in case later testimony is needed. These are not witnesses to the offense, as if they came along to add their support to the grievance. They are there to act as mediators, and to be able to testify that the offended has followed biblical protocol in his attempts to be reconciled with his brother. It is to be hoped that by this time the offender can either satisfactorily explain his position, showing that no wrong was done, or that he will realize his sins and repent, make restitution, and be forgiven.[2]

If both steps one and two have been followed and have failed to resolve the situation, a *third step* is necessary. The offended one must tell the matter to the church and leave it to the congregation to judge.[3] The congregation should hear the testimony of all parties involved: the one bringing the charges, the one against whom the charges are brought, and the witnesses who were present in the second step. They should act as judge and jury, gathering appropriate information and questioning witnesses. If, after careful and prayerful deliberation, the one accused is vindicated, the matter is settled. Of course the attitude of the one bringing the charges may require disciplining *him*. If the accused is judged to be guilty, he should be instructed to make any necessary restitution and be reconciled with the injured party. If the guilty offender accepts and obeys the judgment of the church, he should be restored to full fellowship. If the guilty offender refuses to abide by the church's judgment, he is to be removed from membership and excluded from fellowship within the church. If a person has been so disciplined by the church body, individual members of that body are bound by that decision to cease fellowship with the one being disciplined or forfeit their own membership/fellowship within that church.

For an individual member to maintain a relationship of fellowship with the disciplined one is wrong for several reasons. First, it undermines the effectiveness of the discipline as an attempt to bring the disciplined one to repentance. Second, it provides the disciplined one with an opportunity to cause division in the church, compounding his sin and the church's problem. Third, it violates the command of God to "mark and avoid" (Rom. 16:7) those who cause strife and division in the church, to "come out from among them and be ye separate" (2 Cor. 6:17), and to "have no fellowship" (Eph. 5:11) with them that do such things. Fourth, it violates the church covenant of the one who pledged to "sustain the discipline of this church."

Public Offenses

Sometimes church members are guilty of committing offenses that are more public than personal. Their impact on the church body is greater than wounds of a more private nature. Such sins would include immorality (1 Cor. 5:1-5), teaching false doctrine (1 Tim. 1:19-20; 6:1-5; 2 Tim. 2:16-18), a "disorderly walk" or unchristlike lifestyle (2 Thes. 3:6, 14), and causing divisions (Rom. 16:17-18; Titus 3:10). Cases like these may or may not directly involve anyone else in the church. For instance, a person guilty of adultery may be entangled in an illicit relationship with someone who is not a part of the church, or a person may be living "disorderly" in that he is stealing from his employer. The church still has a responsibility to exercise discipline, even though no individual within the church may have been the direct victim of the offense.

First, in cases like these, discipline is not always initiated by the victim. Rather, the first church member with knowledge of the offense should seek out the offender and try to resolve the difficulty. What is necessary for resolution depends on the nature of the offense. Obviously, if you notice sin in the life of a fellow believer and church member, you have no way of knowing if you are the *first* one to notice. Don't ask around to find out if anyone else has noticed—that would be gossip-mongering. Just assume you are the first, and approach the sinner in a "spirit of meekness" (Gal. 6:1). If no one else has approached him, you may be able to reclaim the brother without unnecessary damage to his testimony that would result from more public knowledge. If others have already approached him, you will just be adding more weight to the rebuke and warning from his brethren.

Second, if the offender does not repent and take the initiative to undo the harm caused by his sin, the person with knowledge of the matter should consult the officers of the church and leave it with them to settle the situation. If the officers are already aware of the sin, one should wonder why nothing seems to have been done about it. Requesting anonymity at this stage would be pointless unless the accuser has failed in his biblical obligation to confront the sinner personally. Attempting to prompt disciplinary action by the church while remaining anonymous is hypocritical and self-serving. Besides, the one who brings it to the attention of the officers will almost certainly be called upon to testify before the officers, and possibly the congregation, because the accused is entitled to face his accuser and answer specific allegations.

The third step is really up to the church officers responsible for handling such disciplinary matters. They should meet to hear from both the accused and the one bringing the accusation. If the one accused disproves the charges, the matter is closed unless the officers believe the accusation to have been malicious, in which case the accuser is now in need of disciplinary action. If the one accused is determined to be guilty and he repents of the wrong, he is to be forgiven. If no one else knows of the offense, and no one else is affected by it, the matter would then be closed. The officers must decide if others must be notified of the resolution in order for reconciliation to be complete, or if any restitution is necessary and appropriate for restoration to fellowship.

A fourth step may be necessary. In some cases the matter may have to go before the entire congregation. This would generally require proper notification, a formal hearing with witnesses testifying and being cross-examined by the congregation and the accused, and a formal decision by the congregation. In a church with a congregational form of government, the accused is generally regarded as being entitled to appear before the assembly. He has a right to receive a copy of all charges being brought against him and to know who is making the charges. He has the right to answer the charges before the church. The church then would bear the responsibility to vote to convict or to acquit the accused of the charges. If he is found guilty, but refuses to repent and/or make any restitution deemed necessary, he is to be removed from membership and fellowship.

If, at any stage of the process, the wrongdoer petitions the church for forgiveness and corrects his wrongs to the satisfaction of the church, he should be reinstated to fellowship (2 Cor. 2). The cutting off from fellowship is to be in force for every member of the congregation until the disciplined one comes before the officers of the church to confess and repent, offering any appropriate restitution, and seeking restoration. Since the problem had escalated to involve the entire congregation, any time congregational discipline has been enforced the repentance must also be public. It is good for the offender to learn such humility. It is good for the congregation to witness such repentance. It will stop speculation among members, since the resolution is public and complete, permitting real reconciliation and restoration to fellowship.

Depending on the nature of the offense, and the offender's position within the church, restoration to fellowship may *not* include full restoration to former status, at least until he has adequate time to demonstrate trustworthiness. For instance, if the offense involved sexual immorality, the guilty party should not be restored to any position of authority or trust that he might hold within the church. If the youth pastor were found to have taken indecent liberties with one of the teenage girls in the youth group, he may genuinely repent and be forgiven, but still face criminal prosecution if the girl were a minor. Even if she were of legal age, he should not be allowed to continue to work with the teens. As another example, if one of the ushers were found to have been stealing from his employer, he may repent, repay that which he took, and be forgiven, but it may be unwise to put him in the way of temptation by allowing him to continue to handle the church offerings.

Church discipline should be designed and practiced to correct offenses, or remove offenders from fellowship with the hope that erring persons can be helped. The objective of discipline is to reclaim, not to punish. It should always be governed by love and grace. If individual believers who covenant together as members of one local church are to sustain the discipline of that church, they must accept what the Bible teaches about church discipline and commit themselves to practicing it. That must include personal determination to follow biblical methods when another believer needs to be disciplined, and it includes a personal commitment to maintain your own life in such a way that disciplinary action need not be brought against you.

---

[1] More will be said about the subject of forgiveness in Chapter Twenty-three.

[2] This implies another reason for taking witnesses: they will be able to help determine the legitimacy of the claim to injury. The Scriptural instructions assume that one actually sinned against another and the one offended has a valid case. But given our all-too-human tendency to over-react and misconstrue, the witnesses can sometimes help point out to the offended that the transgression was unintentional or even imaginary.

[3] Specific procedures here will vary among local churches. I've assumed the congregational form of government prevalent in Baptist churches. If the church uses a presbytery form of government, this step in the disciplinary process would generally be handled by a representative board. Even in congregational churches, established procedures often involve an intermediate step in which a representative body hears the case in hopes of settling it without going before the entire congregation. Christ's instructions pre-dated the organization of local churches, and Paul's instructions do not give details of procedure. Since church organizational forms are not clearly delineated in Scripture, considerable latitude may be found in the way local churches handle the ultimate resolution of disciplinary matters. The important point is that a church must establish a procedure that is consistent with the instructions of Scripture, whether or not it is identical with other churches' procedures.

Part IV
Your Contribution to the Local Church

CHAPTER 19
INTEREST IN OTHERS

Over the last several weeks, I've watched the news about a church not far from Atlanta. The church itself, as well as three or four leaders of the church, has been sued by a former member over an incident that occurred in 1998. The youth pastor had taken a group of thirty-two teenagers (13-17 year olds), along with eight adults, to a laser light show at Stone Mountain. He had to park the bus some distance from the seating area for the show. He instructed the kids to stay together in groups, and to return straight to the bus following the show. Apparently, one group of five teens couldn't find their way back. Thinking he knew how to find the bus, one of the boys decided to run across a busy four-lane highway, where he was struck by a car and killed. Since none of the adults were with that particular group, the parents of the boy accused the church and its leaders of negligent homicide. The church's defense has been that the fifteen-year old boy was old enough to be responsible for his own safety.[1]

Whatever the court ultimately decides in this case, and the church's legal strategy aside, the incident serves to remind us that we do, in fact, have an obligation "watch over one another in brotherly love." The duty of a baby-sitter is to "watch over" her charges and to keep them from getting into trouble or danger—to keep them safe. She is not expected to manipulate those for whom she is responsible, controlling every aspect of their activity, but she is expected to supervise

their activities to be sure they fall within acceptable guidelines. As
the children grow older, we may dispense with baby-sitters but still
enlist the aid of chaperones. When we have a church activity for the
teens we expect it to be supervised by responsible adults. If the youth
group is having dinner at a restaurant, the chaperone does *not* go to
each person and place the order for his meal, cut up his food, put each
bite in his mouth, and take the napkin and dab his lips. A person who
does that is not a chaperone, but a pest. The duty of the chaperone is
to see to it that the teenagers behave themselves according to our standards of propriety. Often, the chaperone does his job simply by his
presence, without having to say or do anything, because the teens
know they are being held accountable.

Believers go through a similar growth process. New believers are
like spiritual infants, who need a good deal of supervision and instruction. As believers mature in Christ, they progress toward greater independence and responsibility. The point of the above analogies is to
illustrate the principles of responsibility and accountability. There is a
sense in which we are to serve as one another's chaperones through
life. Before taking offense at being compared to children, remember
that Jesus Christ calls us His "little children" in the very context of
the command to love one another (John 13:33). Many of us assume
that we have outgrown any need for someone to whom we are
accountable. That is simply not true. The most self-centered and
unloving people in the church today are those who are too lazy to
accept responsibility and too proud to accept accountability.

The theme of the book of Galatians is that we are saved by grace,
not by keeping the law. Therefore, the letter speaks much of Christian
liberty. Paul insists that we have been set free from bondage to sin
and to self. It has become popular today for people to come to
Galatians seeking to find justification for fulfilling their own sinful
desires. They assume the liberty spoken of in this book means
"license to do what you want to do," and conclude that being set free
from bondage means we are no longer obligated to obey God. They
could not be more wrong. This liberty that is ours in Christ is *not*
permission from God to do what you *want* to do or be what you *want*
to be. Rather, having been set free from bondage to the law of sin
that had reigned in our hearts, we are now able to do what we *ought*
to do and be what we *ought* to be.

It is in this very epistle that we find the instruction to correct one another when we see one caught up in sin. Galatians 6:1 says, "Brethren, if a man be overtaken in a fault, ye which are spiritual, restore such an one in the spirit of meekness; considering thyself, lest thou also be tempted." We are not to assume that others have liberty to behave as they please. We are to be interested enough in their spiritual condition that we will risk their displeasure by bringing their disobedience to their attention. Our responsibility for one another, and for our own local church, includes demonstration of a love so deep that we desire restoration to fellowship when one falls into sin. As we said in the last chapter, church discipline must be motivated by love.

Restoration to Fellowship

In pointing out the need to restore one another to a place of fellowship when one is found to have done wrong, the first thing Paul did was to remind us that we are related as family. Before he ever told the Galatian believers to help each other with their faults, he called them "brethren." It is not by accident that Paul begins this statement with that word. He did the same when he addressed the Thessalonian believers about the same matter. "But ye, brethren, be not weary in well doing. And if any man obey not our word by this epistle, note that man, and have no company with him, that he may be ashamed. Yet count *him* not as an enemy, but admonish *him* as a brother" (2 Thes. 3:13-15). This familial relationship involves mutual love and mutual accountability.

Not only has Paul pointed out our relationship as family, he has indicated our responsibility to restore those with "faults." The word translated *faults* in Galatians 6:1 refers to an "unplanned mistake, giving in to a sudden temptation." It is not a rebellious, hard hearted desire to follow after one's own will, nor is it a fractious and divisive attitude that intentionally stirs up strife within the church (cf. Romans 16:17-18). It describes a temporary condition arising from the weakness of the flesh succumbing to the temptation of the moment, sin that may even be unconscious. But in 2 Thessalonians 3, Paul is talking about a more serious offense, involving deliberate disobedience and/or false teaching. In those cases, the offender is to be treated more severely, being put out of fellowship until repentance is made.

But even in such cases, the loving relationship of family is emphasized.

Paul's instruction to *restore* those with faults is also important. The
same Greek word shows up in Matthew 4:18-22, but is translated differently. Following a catch of fish so great that the net broke (Luke
5:1-11), Jesus came upon James and John as they were *mending* their
net. In its tangled or torn condition the net was no good for catching
fish, which was its purpose. The fisherman had to untangle and mend
the net to restore it to usefulness. You don't mend a net with a chain
saw or a sledgehammer. The process was deliberate and painstaking.
They may have to splice cords and retie knots. It takes a firm but
gentle hand to restore the net without doing further harm. Keeping
the nets in good repair also required both *careful craftsmanship* and
constant attention. Daily attention to small problems with the nets
keeps them from becoming badly damaged or destroyed and main-
tains them in a constant state of soundness and usefulness.

The goal of dealing with the faults is restoration to usefulness. You
must not approach a brother about sin in his life simply to make him
feel useless. It must be done to bring him back to a condition of usefulness. However, it must also be noted that the net, in its damaged
condition, was *not* useable. Psychologists often want us to believe
that the problem with guilt is that we feel it. They try to coach people
on how to deal with guilt *feelings* rather than dealing with the sin that
caused the guilt in the first place. Denying real guilt doesn't help.
The only solution for real guilt is to admit our sin and ask for forgiveness. Denying that the nets are torn will not catch fish. But the tears
in the nets must be dealt with in such a way that the end result is a
useful net.

By now you may already have in mind someone whose faults you
are eager to correct, someone whose usefulness you are more than
ready to restore. Take care. It is very easy for the restorer to become
nothing more than a busybody and a pest. Like the chaperone with a
napkin dabbing up every little dribble, he criticizes every pointless little thing. There are at least three important differences between a
restorer and a busybody. First, a restorer talks *to* the person with the
problem, while the busybody talks *about* him. Second, the restorer
views the problem as a *wound* to be bound up, while the busybody

views it as *news* to be broadcast. Third, the restorer is genuinely motivated by a loving desire to have both himself and the one being helped become more like *Christ*, while the busybody acts out of a selfish desire to make the other more like *himself*.

So, when attempting to restore a brother, be sure to do so "in a spirit of meekness, considering thyself, lest thou also be tempted." There are at least two types of temptation you must beware. First, you might be tempted to participate in the sin. The closer you get to it, the more attractive or acceptable it can appear. You might listen to the excuses of the brother who stumbled, and in your compassion be moved to think his actions not so bad. You must remember that you are no less prone to sin than is the person you are trying to help. Second, you might be tempted to indulge in pride. You may adopt a condescending attitude of spiritual superiority, exalting yourself as some spiritual giant that God has placed in the church to correct everyone else's spiritual errors. You are just as much a sinner as the one you desire to help. He may well have seen in you weaknesses similar to those you are pointing out to him. According to Philippians 2:3-4, even the one you are correcting must be esteemed better than yourself. We would all do well to remember that it is only by the grace and mercy of God that any of us are saved. But we must also remember that God has given us a responsibility to "watch over one another in brotherly love."

Support in Weakness

Immediately after commanding that we confront and restore a brother "overtaken in a fault," Paul commands, "Bear ye one another's burdens, and so fulfill the law of Christ" (Gal. 6:2). There are some burdens that are too great to bear alone. We who have been set free from the burden of sin ought to understand that better than anyone else. But we are quick to forget that there are times in each of our lives that we endure difficulties we cannot bear in our own strength. One reason God has given the believer a fellowship in the church family is for mutual support in time of need. These difficulties come in many forms, but Paul is speaking here of spiritual struggles. We are obligated to help each other in times of spiritual weakness. It may be through a word of rebuke when someone is straying, or it may be through a word of encouragement when someone is downhearted.

Some have protested, "Christians should not get discouraged." In a sense they are correct. Discouragement tends to strike when the circumstances of life weigh heavily upon us, and our joy is not supposed to depend upon circumstances. The fact that we have been saved by grace should help us transcend circumstances. But the truth is, we often do get our eyes off of eternity and become discouraged by difficulties. We need to be sensitive to the fact that the person who is struggling may not need a sermon right now. What he may need is somebody to lean on, to hold his hand, to sit and "weep with those who weep."

Sarah was a five-year-old who used to spend hours with the Roberts, an elderly couple who lived next door. She would often be at their home "helping" in the garden, or sharing some new discovery or talent. The day came when Mr. Roberts died, leaving Mrs. Roberts alone. The day after the funeral, Sarah's mother noticed that Sarah spent an especially long time with Mrs. Roberts in the glider swing on her back porch. When she finally returned home, Sarah's mother asked, "What were you and Mrs. Roberts talking about for so long?" Sarah said, "Oh, we weren't really talking; I was just helping Mrs. Roberts cry." Sarah knew something intuitively about bearing one another's burdens.

The point is that we need one another's help. Paul provides an extended discussion of our mutual reliance upon one another in 1 Corinthians 12:12-27 by describing the church as a body made up of many different parts, each of which has its own contribution to make to the whole. We need to realize that within the church no one is so important that he need not help others, or that he needs no one else's help. We must also see that no one is so unimportant the he has nothing to contribute, or that he is unworthy of your help. Genuine Christian love *works*, it doesn't just talk about it (James 2:14-26). There are diversities of gifts in the church, and the church needs each of us to contribute that which God has enabled us to provide. The various parts of the body each have their own functions, yet they are interdependent and supportive of one another. We, too, as a church, must interact in that manner. "Whether one member suffer, all the members suffer with it" (1 Cor. 12:26). To see this illustrated, all you need to do is smash you finger with a hammer. Your reflexes will cause you to immediately rush to support the injured finger by grasping it with the uninjured hand. In the same way, we need to support one another within the church by having that kind of loving interest in one another.

But at the same time, we must take personal responsibility. Galatians 6:5 says, "For every man shall bear his own burden." While in the King James English verse five seems to contradict verse two, an examination of the original language indicates that two different words are translated *burden*. In verse two the word is for an unspecified great weight that someone may need assistance in bearing. In verse five we find the word for a soldier's pack containing everything he must have for the march and the battle. It would be irresponsible to shift that burden to someone else, who has his own pack to carry. You have no right to expect someone else to do your Bible study, prayer, witnessing, and obeying for you. Each of us is personally responsible for his own faithfulness and growth. Further, the emphasis throughout the Scriptures is on your responsibility to others, not on their responsibility to you. It is on duties, not entitlements. You are to be ready to help others with the burdens that seem too heavy to bear, without necessarily expecting help with your own burdens. When you give an account to Christ one day, you will not be able to protest, "It's not my fault. No one was there to help me." That will not be an acceptable excuse, because Jesus Christ said, "My grace is sufficient for thee: for my strength is made perfect in weakness" (2 Cor. 12:9). However, God may also say, "There are those you could have helped, but you didn't offer; you failed in your responsibility to your brethren" (see 2 Cor. 1:4). Taken together, Galatians 6:2 and 5 teach that *every believer is responsible for assisting others in their trials and tests, and every believer must accept responsibility for his own faithfulness.*

Perhaps we can best summarize what it means to watch over one another in brotherly love by quoting the words of the Apostle Paul.

> So then every one of us shall give account of himself to God. Let us not therefore judge one another any more: but judge this rather, that no man put a stumbling block or an occasion to fall in *his* brother's way…. Let us therefore follow after the things which make for peace, and things wherewith one may edify another…. We then that are strong ought to bear the infirmities of the weak,

and not to please ourselves. Let every one of us please *his* neighbor for *his* good to edification. For even Christ pleased not himself: but, as it is written, The reproaches of them that reproached thee fell on me. For whatsoever things were written aforetime were written for our learning, that we through patience and comfort of the Scriptures might have hope. Now the God of patience and consolation grant you to be likeminded one toward another according to Christ Jesus: That ye may with one mind *and* one mouth glorify God, even the Father of our Lord Jesus Christ (Romans 14:12, 13, 19; 15:1-6).

---

[1] The judge recently declared a mistrial. The jury, unable to reach a unanimous decision, was deadlocked 10-2 in favor of the church. The counsel for the plaintiffs has announced their intention to re-try the case with a new jury as soon as possible.

CHAPTER 20
INTERCESSION FOR OTHERS

Jan was a long-time friend of our family and the wife of a pastor who had been very influential in my life, particularly during my collegiate years. A few years ago, I received word that she was very sick. A little over five years before, she had undergone surgery to remove a malignancy. She had follow-up radiation and chemotherapy regimens, and regular check-ups revealed no signs of problems. When she went in for her fifth annual post-cancer examination, expecting an "all clear" pronouncement, the doctor discovered that the cancer had returned. More surgery and other treatments followed, but there was no sign of improvement.

Jan's children had an especially hard time watching their mother's condition deteriorate. At one point, her teenage daughter said, "Mom, I know you always say that we are supposed to accept God's will for our lives. But if you could change this, you would, wouldn't you?" But Jan answered, "Well, it is no fun being sick, and I would love to be here to see you graduate from high school. But I can tell you honestly that I am perfectly content with God's will. I wouldn't change a thing." In the weeks that followed, hundreds of church members, friends, and acquaintances joined this family in praying diligently for her recovery. Yet the Lord took her home. She was forty-six years old.

After her death, many people expressed gratitude for the impact this godly lady had on their lives. But some spoke of their frustration and confusion over what seemed an untimely death. All of the prayers for her recovery had gone unanswered. It looked as if the weeks of intercession on her behalf had been in vain. But that was not true. For one thing, Jan and her family had been greatly encouraged by the knowledge that so many cared enough to pray. Besides that, those who prayed learned some important lessons about intercession for one another. First, we learned something about our relationship to one another in Christ. Christians who had never met one another joined together in prayer for this one who was their "sister." Second, we learned to pray diligently for the needs of someone other than ourselves. As Jan was dying and her family was in distress, others learned to care. Third, we learned something about praying for God's will, not our own. While many prayed for Jan's healing, that was never her prayer. At her funeral, her husband read a prayer that Jan had copied into the flyleaf of her Bible. It was written by Ruth Harm Calkins, but had been Jan's daily prayer for years.

> Change me, God. Please change me. Though I cringe, kick,
> resist and resent, pay no attention to me whatever. When I run to
> hide, drag me out of my safe shelter. Change me totally.
> Whatever it takes. However long You must work at the job.
> Change me—and save me from spiritual self-destruction.

In our church covenant, we promise "to remember each other in prayer." Praying for one another is one of the most important things we can do for each other as brothers and sisters in Christ. Those for whom we pray will benefit from our intercession on their behalf. And when we pray, we also benefit through our communication with the Lord and our focus on the needs of others. But how should we pray? Unfortunately, we often undermine our own prayers. There are at least three attitudes that can hinder our prayer for one another: a spirit of independence, a spirit of self-interest, and a spirit of superficiality.

Weakened by a Spirit of Independence.

For years, American culture has emphasized individual liberty at the expense of personal responsibility. This has led to a social climate dominated not by loving concern for one another, but by envy of one another and enmity toward one another. It has been interesting to see how quickly much of that self-centered attitude has been replaced with a helpful spirit. All it took was a moment, as we absorbed the information that our nation had been attacked by terrorists and thousands had died. As we watched people fleeing the destruction in New York City, and saw massive rescue and recovery operations begin, Americans experienced an attitude adjustment. Our newly discovered vulnerability has, at least for a while, encouraged an *esprit de corps* that has been largely absent from American culture for some time.

While I would certainly hope this resurgent spirit of charity and patriotism would endure, it has till now stopped well short of the spiritual revival America needs. Even in our churches, there remains much of the old competitive spirit of self-exaltation, and those of us who are independent of denominational oversight are especially susceptible. In our view that the local church is to be governed by Christ as its head, independent of human authority outside our local assembly, we are in danger of forgetting the measure of dependence that really exists among believers within the church and between the church and Christ. But this can be true in any church, regardless of polity. That proprietary spirit that insists "this is *my* class," or "this is *my* responsibility," or "this is *my* turf" to be defended from those who might do things a little differently, puts self ahead of the body and denies our need for one another.

Paul writes in Ephesians 3:14-15, "For this cause I bow my knees unto the Father of our Lord Jesus Christ, Of whom the whole family in heaven and earth is named." When Paul prayed, he prayed for that which would benefit the whole family of believers, not merely for that which would benefit him. We must learn to do likewise. When Jesus taught His disciples to pray, He started His model prayer by addressing "**Our** Father" (Matthew 6:9).

When you and I pray, we must include each other in the equation. We tend to pray to "*my* Father," emphasizing our personal relationship with the Lord, and forgetting our familial relationship with one another "of whom the whole family in heaven and earth is named." God is not more your Father than your neighbor's. He is the Father of all who have trusted Christ Jesus to forgive their sins. When we forget our complete dependence upon God and our need for one another, we may begin to ask God to help us at another's expense. If you truly love your brother, you could never ask for something that might hurt him, but will always pray for that which would benefit him. If there is conflict in the relationship between you and your brother, it is difficult to pray properly to Him who is the Father of you both.

Defeated by a Spirit of Self-interest

Paul's prayer for the believers in Ephesus continues with some specific requests in Ephesians 3:16-19. But before examining those requests, we need to consider the attitude brethren need to have toward one another to be able to pray for each other as Paul prayed for these believers. If we would avoid a spirit of self-interest that would defeat our prayers, there are at least five characteristics of the attitude we should demonstrate.

First, we need a *forgiving spirit*. The disciples had asked Jesus to teach them to pray, and the Lord had replied with His a model prayer usually referred to as the Lord's Prayer. But immediately following that prayer, the Lord Jesus explained something important. He said, "For if ye forgive men their trespasses, your heavenly Father will also forgive you: But if ye forgive not men their trespasses, neither will your Father forgive your trespasses" (Matthew 6:14-15). He left little room for doubt or misunderstanding. If you want to have your sins forgiven, you forgive; if you are not forgiving, you will not be forgiven. In Mark 11:25, the Lord also said, "When ye stand praying, forgive." If you are going to be able to communicate with your Father, you had better be ready to forgive.

An important part of what Jesus is teaching is that in our work with one another within the church it is inevitable that disputes and offenses will arise. We are all fallen creatures and will do offensive things, and we all have our own ego problems that make us easily offended. This was illustrated dramatically in the case of Job. He had suffered much inexplicable sorrow and loss. His friends had accused him of great sin, hypocrisy, and unbelief. But even after God addressed Job from the whirlwind and told Job's friends, "ye have not spoken of me *the thing that is* right, as my servant Job *hath*" (Job 42:7), Job remained in bondage to Satan. It is following all this that we are told, "the Lord turned the captivity of Job when he prayed for his friends" (Job 42:10). Job must have had a very forgiving heart.

Have you seen some of your prayers go unanswered? One reason may be an unforgiving spirit. *God is under no obligation to answer the prayers of one who is unwilling to forgive his brother.* For us to "remember each other in prayer," we must first be practicing forgiveness among the brethren. You cannot honestly pray "**our** Father" when you know that there is a problem between you and another believer that you have been unwilling to forgive (see Chapter Twenty-three).

A second characteristic of a proper attitude in prayer is that we need a *humble spirit.* The Lord Jesus provided an illustration in Luke 18:9-12.

And he spake this parable unto certain which trusted in themselves that they were righteous, and despised others: Two men went up into the temple to pray; the one a Pharisee, and the other a publican. The Pharisee stood and prayed thus with himself, God, I thank thee, that I am not as other men are, extortioners, unjust, adulterers, or even as this publican. I fast twice in the week, I give tithes of all that I possess.

This Pharisee was a very good man, to all outward appearances. His problem was not what he did, but his pride in what he did. I suspect that there are some people in every church who are much like the people in Jesus' audience. Most of us, and sometimes all of us, believe deep inside that God is satisfied with the level of righteousness we have attained. We think this way, largely because we know other believers whom we consider less righteous than we are. That amounts to trusting in ourselves that we are righteous, and despising others. Let's not read this and say, "I thank thee God that I am not like that Pharisee," lest we become the new Pharisees. When you are tempted to think, "I thank thee that I am not as other men are," you are not likely to be able to pray "**our** Father." For us to remember each other in prayer, we must be willing to forget ourselves, and pray for the Lord to help others even at our own expense.

Third, we need a *spirit of unity.* In 1 Timothy 2:8, we are told to "pray everywhere...without wrath and doubting." Literally, this says

that we are to pray "without anger and disputing." To "remember
each other in prayer" we need a unity of spirit, not ill feelings and dis-
putation. Paul begs the church to "walk worthy of the vocation
wherewith ye are called, with all lowliness and meekness, with longsuffering, forbearing one another in love, endeavoring to keep the
unity of the spirit in the bond of peace" (Ephesians 4:1-3). One of the
best ways to do that is to meet with other believers with the express
purpose of spending time in prayer. Churches whose mid-week
prayer meeting has become simply a mid-week preaching service may
have forfeited a valuable opportunity to help the church grow in unity
through corporate prayer. By the same token, there are many believers who could participate in those prayer meetings but fail to do so
because other concerns seem more important. That spirit of self-interest interferes in the fulfilling of our obligation to remember one
another in prayer.

Fourth, we need a *selfless spirit*. James 4:1-3 says,

From whence *come* wars and fightings among you? *Come they*
not hence, *even* of your lusts that war in your members? Ye lust,
and have not: ye kill, and desire to have, and cannot obtain: ye
fight and war, yet ye have not because ye ask not. Ye ask, and
receive not, because ye ask amiss, that ye may consume *it* upon
your lusts.

The word *lusts* is not limited to inordinate sexual desires, but refers
to any strong yearning. People lust for many things. Some lust for
possessions, others for power or prestige. The warning from James is
that we are prone to ask for things in prayer that are motivated by our
own desires, not by a desire to see the will of God fulfilled. Such
selfishness in our praying is destructive. Some seem determined to
make sure their interests are mentioned whenever public requests are
being offered. Don't misunderstand—there is nothing wrong with
mentioning a need publicly. But mentioning one's requests just to
make sure your needs do not go unnoticed when others are being recognized is indicative of carnality, not spirituality. Others pray for
every request mentioned publicly, as if they feared that God may not
listen to someone else's prayer in regard to those requests. Again,
there is nothing wrong with that *per se*, but let's be careful not to give
the impression that we think we are the only ones God ever hears. To

remember each other in prayer involves praying that God will do for each other what He deems best, whether or not it makes either one of us happier or more comfortable.

Finally, we need a *loving spirit*. This one summarizes all the others. There is a warning issued in 1 Peter 3:1-7 "that your prayers be not hindered [cut down]." This passage is specifically addressed to husbands and wives, whose relationship should epitomize human love. But since we are to love one another as Christ has loved us (John 13:34), and Christ loves the church as a husband his wife (Ephesians 5:25), the application of this warning to the church at large seems appropriate. The form of the verb *hindered* in this verse indicates that this is the purposeful action of God in response to improper behavior on the part of the believer. The implication is that if we are not loving one another, genuinely having one another's best interests at heart, God will not hear; He will not answer our prayers.

Frustrated by a Spirit of Superficiality

We must have a good relationship with one another, with a spirit of forgiveness, humility, unity, unselfishness, and love, if we expect to be able to pray "**our** Father." But besides a spirit of independence and a spirit of self-interest, there is a third attitude that will hinder our prayers for one another: a spirit of superficiality which concerns itself primarily with temporal needs.

Our prayers for one another tend to focus on the outer man, the physical and material needs, not the inner man and the spiritual needs. Now, there is nothing wrong with trying to meet one another's physical and material needs (see Chapter Twenty-one), nor is there anything inappropriate with asking God to help with physical and material needs. However, a lot of those needs are not as important as we sometimes think they are. It is unfortunate that we get so distracted by the material and temporal that we forget to pray for the eternal. Perhaps we stick to the superficial needs because we fear we will be too intrusive or meddlesome. But it may also be that we only pray for one another's superficial needs because we are focused on our own superficial needs and avoid thinking about our spiritual needs. We may see nothing but the temporal, failing to even recognize the spiritual.

When Paul prays for the Ephesian believers, the kind of requests we usually make for one another are conspicuously absent. He doesn't pray that they will make more money or get better jobs or become more comfortable or enjoy good health or long life. Those are the very things that our unsaved neighbors want out of life. Is it possible that we are guilty of assigning life's highest values to things of little or no eternal significance? When we stand before the Lord's Judgment Throne, I do not think the most important factors in our eternal rewards are going to have anything to do with our annual salary, the kind of car we drive, the neighborhood in which we live, our physical fitness, or how long we lived. In the final analysis, the Lord is going to pay more attention to the kind of things Paul prayed that these Ephesian believers might have. This prayer reveals three categories of concern, having to do with one's personal relationship with the Holy Spirit, the Lord Jesus Christ, and God the Father.

First, we see that we need to pray for one another to have *the Holy Spirit's power*—"That he [God] would grant you, according to the riches of his glory, to be strengthened with might by his Spirit in the inner man" (Ephesians 3:16). When was the last time you prayed for other members of your local church congregation by name that they live each day in the Spirit's power, have victory over sin and temptation, experience fullness of joy and contentment, and overcome the discouragement of life's circumstances? We are more likely to pray that they will not experience difficult circumstances than we are to ask that they will triumph through them. If each of us is living by the Spirit's power, we will live according to God's will and walk obediently in His way. Perhaps we do not pray for others to live in the Spirit's power because we are not living in the Spirit's power. Maybe we do not pray for ourselves to live in the power of the Holy Spirit because we know that to do so we would have to change. We may be unwilling to quit living in our religious ruts and become truly *Christian*, or Christ-like. It is less threatening to our apathetic state to pray for others on the same superficial level we pray for ourselves, rather than to pray that we might be "strengthened with might by his Spirit...according to the riches of his glory." Our interest in superficial concerns frustrates our prayer for one another to have spiritual power.

A second category of requests in Paul's prayer indicates the need to pray for one another to have *the Son's companionship*. "That Christ may dwell in your hearts by faith; that ye, being rooted and grounded in love, May be able to comprehend with all saints what *is* the breadth, and length, and depth, and height; And to know the love of Christ, which passeth knowledge…" (Ephesians 3:17-19a). When Paul prayed "that Christ may dwell in your hearts by faith," he was not praying for their salvation, for they were already believers who had been blessed "with all spiritual blessings in heavenly *places* in Christ" (Ephesians 1:3). The Greek word translated *dwell* (3:17) is a compound word that literally means "to settle down and be at home." It describes a permanent residence in and possession of one's heart. It involves having free and easy access to all, as the homeowner, as opposed to the restricted access of a house guest. We need to pray for one another to have such fullness of Christ's dwelling within that He may have complete access to and control over our lives. We also need to pray for a fullness of trust in Christ, that complete lack of worry that comes only from absolute confidence.

Paul also prayed that the Ephesian believers would be "rooted and grounded in love,"—to be well anchored and securely founded upon the love of Christ. The love of Christ is the soil from which spiritual fruit can grow. This is a love that does for us what we *need*, not necessarily what we *desire*. Paul also speaks of "comprehending" and "knowing" this love, which is to grasp Christ's love in its completeness and to know Christ's love by personal experience. This is contrasted with a superficial knowledge that "passes." So, when we remember one another in prayer, we need to pray that Christ will have complete access and control of our lives, that we will have complete confidence in Christ, that we may become ever more securely anchored and firmly established in the love of Christ, and that we will both comprehend and experience the rich fullness of His love. Is that what we pray for ourselves and for others in the church?

The final category of requests Paul makes for the believer in Ephesus is that they have *the Father's fullness*—"…that ye might be filled with all the fullness of God" (Ephesians 3:19b). That is a brief statement; but, O, what a challenging one! Few Christians would claim that "being filled with all the fullness of God" accurately describes their present condition, let alone the condition of every

member of their church. We need to pray more diligently for one
another to become godly unto the measure of His fullness in us.
Although we will never be equal with God, we can reflect His moral
attributes. As the Holy Spirit strengthens us in the inner man, and we
mature in Christ, cultivating His companionship and experiencing His
love, we can begin to manifest God's love, mercy, compassion, forbearance, righteousness, and holiness. This is what has been called
"maturing in Christ," and it can be a lifelong process of bringing us,
by the power of the Spirit of God, into conformity with Christ.

Whatever your vocation, whether you are a doctor or a mechanic, a
manager or a maintenance worker, a farmer or a grocer, God expects
you to demonstrate the fullness of God in all you do. You come into
contact with a certain circle of acquaintances on a regular basis, and
you may well be the best representation of God they will ever see. If
their opinion of God is based on what they see in you, what do you
suppose they think of God? That is a sobering question. You will
never succeed in being an effective "follower [imitator] of God"
(Ephesians 5:1) without Divine assistance. You need to have your
Christian brethren praying for you, just as they need to have you praying for them.

Do you really think it is sufficient to pray that the guy across the
aisle from you will feel better or have more money or goods? It is
even more important for you to pray for him to live in the power of
the Holy Spirit, to experience and understand the fullness of Christ's
love and companionship, and to mature to the measure of the fullness
of God. When we remember one another in prayer, let's remember to
pray for what we need most. We must lay aside any spirit of independence, self-interest, or superficiality. Then we can with confidence echo the ending of Paul's prayer:

> Now unto him that is able to do exceeding abundantly above all
> that we ask or think, according to the power that worketh in us,
> Unto him *be* glory in the church by Christ Jesus throughout all
> ages, world without end. Amen (Ephesians 3:20-21).

As we lift these words to God, we must remember that this is not a
statement of confidence in what God will do for *me* through prayer,
but what God can do for *others* through my prayers.

CHAPTER 21
INTERVENTION FOR OTHERS

In the aftermath of the terrorist attacks of September 11, 2001, we have witnessed a resurgence of selfless intervention for one another. It has, in some cases, even risen to the level of heroism. We will not soon forget the selflessness of the firefighters and police officers who rushed *into* the burning World Trade Center, heading toward their own deaths in order to help others escape. Nor can we forget the courage of those who brought their plane down in a field in western Pennsylvania rather than let the terrorists crash it into another strategic target at the cost of many more lives. Countless others gave of their time and resources to aid in the rescue and recovery efforts in New York and Washington. Still more have given to help those widowed and orphaned by the attacks.

But what about situations in which the loss is not so spectacular and the need is not so immense? One of the most vivid evidences of true friendship is one's presence and assistance when you are sick or distressed. Many times people have said, "I always thought (so-and-so) was my friend, but while I was in the hospital he (or she) never came to see me and never even called." Most of us can think of a time when we were sick or in some sort of trouble and someone in particular disappointed us by not coming to us in our need. But most of us can also think of someone who was a special blessing to us by simply being there and offering love and help. On the other hand, there have probably been times in most of our lives when a friend, or neighbor, or brother in Christ needed companionship and comfort and we did not go to them. But we may have a hard time thinking of a time when we failed to go to a friend in need. If we were so self-absorbed at the time of their need that we did not think to go to them, it is unlikely that we will recall that they needed us.

The Epistle of James is a practical treatise on how to demonstrate our Christian faith in our daily lives. The theme of the book is that faith without outward demonstration is worthless. To say that you believe and then to act as if you don't makes you a hypocrite. In James 1:27, we are told, "Pure religion and undefiled before God and the Father is this, To visit the fatherless and widows in their affliction, *and* to keep himself unspotted from the world." Many of us work very hard at keeping ourselves unspotted from the world, or at least we put on an outward show of doing so. Whether we *really* do it or not is open to debate. But we sometimes miss the first part of this statement—to visit the fatherless and widows in their affliction.

There are people in every church who have never visited anyone in need that was not a relative or their closest friend. It is usually a very small minority who make a regular practice of visiting the sick or distressed. Few of us trouble ourselves to spend any time with someone with whom we do not have an especially close relationship. Yet we all pledge to "aid each other in sickness and distress." Granted, our covenant says "aid," not "visit," but we all know that sometimes the most important "aid" you can give others is simply your presence and an encouraging word when they are feeling afflicted.

Of course, if you can do more for their assistance, and all you do is visit, you have not done enough. James 2:14-17 says,

> What *doth it* profit, my brethren, though a man say he hath faith, and have not works? Can faith save him? If a brother or sister be naked, and destitute of daily food, And one of you say unto them, Depart in peace, be *ye* warmed and filled; notwithstanding ye give them not those things which are needful to the body; what *doth it* profit? Even so faith, if it hath not works, is dead, being alone.

Here, James has pointed out the hypocrisy of saying you will pray for someone's needs to be met while withholding the needed aid that was within your power to provide. What good is your claim to faith if you will pray for someone but not help them? You should do both—believe God will help, and believe God can use you to provide the help needed.

The natural question to ask, then, is "For whom am I responsible?" Jesus was once asked a similar question.

And, behold, a certain lawyer stood up, and tempted him, saying, Master, what shall I do to inherit eternal life? He said unto him, What is written in the law? how readest thou? And he answering said, Thou shalt love the Lord thy God with all thy heart, and with all thy soul, and with all thy strength, and with all thy mind; and thy neighbour as thyself. And he said unto him, Thou hast answered right: this do, and thou shalt live. But he, willing to justify himself, said unto Jesus, And who is my neighbour? And Jesus answering said, A certain *man* went down from Jerusalem to Jericho, and fell among thieves, which stripped him of his raiment, and wounded *him,* and departed, leaving *him* half dead. And by chance there came down a certain priest that way: and when he saw him, he passed by on the other side. And likewise a Levite, when he was at the place, came and looked *on him,* and passed by on the other side. But a certain Samaritan, as he journeyed, came where he was: and when he saw him, he had compassion *on him,* And went to *him,* and bound up his wounds, pouring in oil and wine, and set him on his own beast, and brought him to an inn, and took care of him. And on the morrow when he departed, he took out two pence, and gave *them* to the host, and said unto him, Take care of him; and whatsoever thou spendest more, when I come again, I will repay thee. Which now of these three, thinkest thou, was neighbour unto him that fell among the thieves? And he said, He that showed mercy on him. Then said Jesus unto him, Go, and do thou likewise (Luke 10:25-37).

This is a very familiar story, even among unbelievers. Legislatures all over the United States have established legal protection from liability for those who offer emergency assistance in good faith. Those statutes are generally called "Good Samaritan laws" even by people who either do not know or refuse to acknowledge the source to which such a reference alludes. Even the secular world has recognized that there is much that we can learn about aiding one another in sickness and distress from the example of the Good Samaritan.

Loving Intervention Given by Practical Help

In the previous chapter we considered the need to look beyond one another's superficial needs and pray for our deeper, spiritual needs. However, while we are to pray for spiritual growth, we are also to pray for and *deal with* the practical needs of life. In the story Jesus told, it was only the Good Samaritan who demonstrated true neighborliness. Others in the story—the priest and the Levite—were the spiritual leaders of the people. Perhaps when they saw the wounded man they determined to pray for him, feeling justified in doing nothing more. Their artificial piety allowed them to claim concern for deeper, spiritual matters as their excuse for ignoring the immediate practical needs of the injured traveler. Only the Samaritan bothered to stop and help. Jesus is teaching the same thing James said. A practical demonstration of love by assisting someone in distress is a demonstration of true faith and righteousness. In examining the actions of the Samaritan, we find that he gave practical assistance to the victim of the thieves in three ways or at three levels. He helped by providing silver, by providing sustenance, and by providing shelter.

Practical help includes *giving silver*—providing money to help bear a financial burden. The Good Samaritan helped by spending his own money. For the good of this injured man, whom he did not even know except as a fellow traveler, he took some of the financial resources that he had brought along on his journey to pay for his own needs. He did not worry about the fact that what he spent on this fellow may have left him without enough funds for dinner, or so short of funds he might have to cut his own trip short. We do not know anything about this Samaritan's personal wealth, but it is likely that the priest and the Levite who failed to help possessed greater means than he did. Still, the Samaritan gave what was needed.

Practical help also includes *giving sustenance*—providing clothing, medicine, or food to help meet physical needs. The Good Samaritan also helped this man by giving his own medicine and clothing. The oil and wine that he used to cleanse and medicate the wounds of this

unknown fellow-traveler were part of the provisions he had brought
along on his journey to meet his own needs. He was not traveling
with a personal caravan, nor was he hauling a wagon loaded with possessions. Travelers today tend to pack more clothing for a weekend
trip than this Samaritan would have owned. Yet when he saw another
in more immediate need than himself, he freely gave what he had to
meet those needs. What did he use to bind up the injured man's
wounds? I doubt if he just happened to have packed a bag of worthless rags to take on his trip. The man he was helping was naked, so
he couldn't very well tear strips from that man's clothing to use as
bandages. He must have used something from his own stores. We
have no idea the value of the garment, or cloak, or blanket that the
Samaritan might have torn into strips to use to bind up the wounds of
this man, but whatever he used was worth enough to him to have provided it for his own use on this trip. It was his loving compassion for
the injured man that made him decide his provisions had a greater
value as bandages for the wounded traveler than they were worth to
him whole. Further, while the story does not specifically say so, he
probably did not take the man to the inn naked. If not, the garments
with which he clothed the man before loading him on his donkey
were not likely to have been extra clothing he packed just in case he
came across someone in need. But he saw a man who needed what
he had more than he did, so he gave what he had.

Third, practical help includes *giving shelter*—provision of trans-
portation and a place to stay while recovering from injuries. Once he
found the man, cleansed his wounds, bound them up, and dressed the
man, the Good Samaritan did not leave him sitting beside the road.
He also gave this stranger whom he found "in sickness and distress"
the shelter he needed when he loaded him on his own donkey and
took him to an inn. That means the Samaritan had to walk the rest of
the way into town, and it is doubtful that the bandits had robbed this
man at the very gates of the city. Besides paying for the man's provision and care for the days the Samaritan stayed in Jericho, he left the
equivalent of two-day's pay to help cover additional costs of his con-
valescence and committed himself to reimburse the innkeeper for
"whatsoever thou spendest more." He did not even know this man,
and he had no idea that anything he spent would ever be repaid. Yet
he gave him silver, sustenance, and shelter.

It ought to shame us when we come back to the instruction given by James: "If a brother or sister be naked, and destitute of daily food, And one of you say unto them, Depart in peace, be *ye* warmed and filled; notwithstanding ye give them not those things which are needful to the body; what doth it profit?" We are not always as generous toward the needs of a brother or sister as this Samaritan was toward a man he did not even know. Further, notice that James did *not* say "as long as it does not inconvenience you too greatly, or leave you a little short financially." We may well be willing to provide the type of assistance offered by the Good Samaritan as long as it does not diminish our own comfort significantly. But there is not much blessing in giving something that represents little or no sacrifice on our part.

Loving Intervention Given by Personal Involvement

It is apparent that the Good Samaritan was *unconcerned about the cost.* He told the innkeeper to take care of the man and he would repay him whatever it cost to do so. His help was generous and selfless. He pledged more than he had on his person. He committed himself to go into debt, at least temporarily, to help this man. He did not consider himself to have fulfilled his obligation to this wounded traveler simply by taking him to town. He was committed to seeing to it that the man fully recovered. That goes beyond practical help to actually becoming personally involved.

Further, the Good Samaritan was *unconcerned about convenience.* We are not told his purpose in traveling from Jerusalem to Jericho, but it is unlikely that he was a resident of either city, or he would not have been called a Samaritan. While he may have made this journey often, it was not a daily commute. Whatever his purpose, he had to change his plans at least a little to help this man. He risked personal injury, not knowing that the thieves were gone. He gave this stranger some of what he had provided for himself on his trip, and committed more as needed. He made at least three unplanned stops in order to help: first, at the roadside to offer assistance; second, at the inn to drop him off for care; and third, when he committed to come back and check on the man on his way back through town.

In my own travels, whether local errands and visits or out of town trips like this Samaritan was making, the three things most likely to irritate me are unscheduled stops, slow moving traffic, and unplanned expenses. This Samaritan willingly accepted all three for the good of a man he didn't even know. But perhaps the most remarkable aspect to this whole story is that the Samaritan was *unconcerned about con-gratulation* for his aid. Who were the Samaritans? They were despised as half-breeds and apostates. They lived in a region between Galilee (to the north) and Judea (to the South) that most devout Jews would avoid like the plague. When traveling between Galilee and Judea, Israelites would usually cross to the east side of Jordan, travel-ing several miles out of their way, just to by-pass Samaria. They wanted nothing to do with Samaria or Samaritans. This Good Samaritan had every reason to expect that the inured man would actu-ally *resent* having been helped by a despised Samaritan. The innkeep-er, who would gladly take his money, would despise the man who gave it and think him a fool. Given the Jewish attitude toward Samaritans, it is even possible that the innkeeper did not allow the Samaritan to stay in the inn where the injured traveler was to be housed. But we remember the Samaritan as the *Good* Samaritan at least in part because he was not concerned about his reputation or social station. He did not care about being properly appreciated. He did what he could to help, expecting not even thanks in return. That is precisely the spirit we should exemplify as we "aid each other in sick-ness and distress."

You may think you have done your duty when you drop twenty dol-lars in the offering for the church benevolence fund, but that is just a starting point. We must each learn real selflessness and develop a willingness to sacrifice for the good of others. That is going to require providing practical help for those in need and becoming per-sonally involved in the lives of the afflicted. You may need to con-quer a tendency to be more critical than helpful. You may have to spend less time and effort praying for what you want God to do for you and more time and effort seeking God's help for your neighbor. If you are like most people, you have probably been less than gener-ous or less than cheerful in the aid you have offered those in sickness and distress, because it might cost you, inconvenience you, or you might not be properly appreciated. But learning to meet the needs of others is part of the obligation we have for one another in the church.

CHAPTER 22
SENSITIVITY[1] TOWARD OTHERS

A young mother was seated near the back of the church auditorium with a fussy baby. As the service progressed, the noise became increasingly distracting for those near them, making it difficult to concentrate on what was going on in the worship service. After a few minutes, the mother heard someone say, "I wish she'd keep that baby quiet! I can't hear a thing." Shortly after that, the mother left with her baby. She has yet to return. It is impossible to know how many times a similar scenario has been played out in our churches.

The truth is, I would be both sympathetic toward and frustrated with both adults involved in such a situation. Several things ought to have happened if the congregation were showing Christian sensitivity. If the young mother had been sympathetic toward those seated near her, she should have recognized that her child was disrupting their worship and should have taken the child out. However, if those sitting near the young mother had been sympathetic toward her, they should have considered that she might have been struggling with this child for some time and may have needed a break. She may have needed the worship service more than they did. A sympathetic believer might have offered to take the child to the nursery or some other designated area, so the mother could remain in the service. Unfortunately, in this case the young mother was so distracted by the child's behavior that she did not notice the discomfort of those around her. Those seated near her were also only thinking about themselves, so they offered no help. Of course, if someone had offered to help, the young mother might have become defensive, thinking, "How dare you criticize me and my baby!"

Because of our sin-natures, when we are in a stressful situation we are likely to say or do the wrong thing. That is why cultivating Christian sympathy in feeling and Christian courtesy in speech is both so important and so difficult. Our Christian sensitivity involves both our inner feelings and our outward expression of them. Truly sympathetic feelings should be expressed in courteous speech. Discourteous speech, on the other hand, indicates unsympathetic feelings. Whether one's speech is intentionally malicious or merely ignorantly thoughtless, it indicates an unawareness of the feelings of another that is based in unconcern for that other person. The problem is that we are quick to recognize when someone has been unsympathetic toward our own feelings, yet slow to see that we have been unsympathetic toward theirs. Without realizing how self-centered we are, we usually spend more time thinking about our own needs and desires than those of others.

You can be sure that in any congregation on any given occasion on which they are assembled, there are some who are at least a little concerned about what others think of them. Some may worry that someone sitting near them might think their hair looks a little odd that day, or that no one will notice their new clothes, or that someone might notice that their colors don't match as well as they thought they did when they dressed. Others refuse to sing above a barely audible mumble because they fear someone might hear them sing a sour note. What they fail to realize is that few, if any, will even notice. Almost everyone else is just as self-absorbed as they are, worrying about what others think of them. On any given Sunday, the person across the aisle from, or in back of, or in front of you is no more likely to be trying to think of something to compliment about you than you are trying to think of something to compliment about him. Church members spend more time trying to impress one another (and "trying not to embarrass myself" is the same thing), than really fellowshipping with one another with Christian sensitivity. Believers need to develop genuinely sympathetic feelings and truly courteous speech.

Sympathy in Feeling

Paul writes that believers are to "rejoice with them that do rejoice, and weep with them that weep. *Be* of the same mind one toward another. Mind not high things, but condescend to men of low estate. Be not wise in your own conceits" (Romans 12:15-16). This passage indicates that there are four aspects to sympathetic feelings that believers, particularly those from the same congregation, are to share. They are to share the same joys, the same sorrows, the same mind, and the same humility.

Sharing the same joy means to rejoice when others are blessed, without a twinge of envy over someone's receiving some blessing you may wish you had received. *Sharing the same sorrows* involves grieving with a brother or sister without even a trace of relief that what happened to them did not happen to you. In 1 Corinthians 12:26, Paul says, "And whether one member suffer, all the members suffer with it; or one member be honored, all the members rejoice with it." He has simply taken the admonition of Romans 12:15 and reversed the order.

Sharing the same mind requires a unity of mind that is only going to be accomplished properly when all parties involved are thinking like Christ. In Romans 12:2, Paul writes, "And be not conformed to this world: but be ye transformed by the renewing of your mind, that ye may prove what is that good, and acceptable, and perfect, will of God." In Philippians 2:5, he says, "Let this mind be in you, which was also in Christ Jesus." One of the results of sharing the mind of Christ will be that you are able to really see an issue from another's point of view. But that is also going to require *sharing the same humility*. Romans 12:10 admonishes believers to "*be* kindly affectioned one to another with brotherly love; in honor preferring one another." Philippians 2:3 says that we must "*let* nothing *be done* through strife or vainglory; but in lowliness of mind let each esteem other better than themselves." That describes a humility that truly puts the needs and interests of others ahead of your own.

Think for a moment about how it is possible for you to hear someone speak. You are not connected by anything other than the air between you. What are the physics involved in the transmission of sound through the air? Pressure produced by the speaker's diaphragm and other muscles forces air from his lungs through his vocal cords to produce tones of varying pitches, depending on the tension of the vocal cords. The speaker shapes those tones into vowel sounds by varying the size and contour of his mouth and changing the position of his tongue. Then those sounds are punctuated with consonant sounds by the action of his tongue, jaw, and lips. All of this produces sound waves that are transmitted by the vibration of the air, and those vibrations eventually impact your eardrums and cause them to vibrate. This causes further vibrations in the structure of your inner ear, which your brain then interprets as speech patterns that you recognize as words. For you to understand a speaker at all, the most basic thing that must happen is for your eardrums to vibrate *in sympathy with* his voice. Those vibrations are actually called *sympathetic vibrations*. Now, if you put on headphones and listened to the radio while the same person was speaking to you, the sound of his voice would not reach your ears. Your eardrums would be vibrating *in sympathy with* another source of sound, making them *unsympathetic* to the voice of the speaker. Similarly, to be sympathetic in our *feelings* toward one another, we need to be attentive to others' feelings and internalize them as our own. This involves letting their feelings override our own or those from other sources, causing us to truly feel as they do. This should, in turn, evoke a response based upon having really understood and internalized their feelings.

Perhaps you have witnessed a demonstration of a goblet being shattered by someone singing a high note. To break the goblet, the singer has to match the pitch of the goblet. If you flick the edge of the goblet, you will hear a ringing tone. If the singer can match the tone exactly, and sustain the tone long enough and with enough force, the goblet will begin to vibrate in sympathy with the singer's voice. And, because the goblet is both rigid and fragile, too much sympathetic vibration will cause it to shatter. Sometimes we may be afraid that if we are too sympathetic with someone else's feelings, we might be damaged like the goblet. But most of the time we are so intent on either expressing or hiding our own feelings that we are not even aware of others'. We ought to be more like an eardrum—flexible to interpret sound and to vibrate in sympathy with a variety of sounds—than like the goblet—rigid and tuned only to a single pitch, responding only when its own tone is sounded. Developing sensitivity toward others involves sympathy toward a wide range of feelings and requires that we cultivate the ability to share the same joys, the same sorrows, the same mind, and the same humility.

Courtesy in Speech

If we are genuinely sympathetic in our feelings toward one another, we will also be courteous in our speech. Related to "cultivating courtesy in speech," our covenant also enjoins us to "avoid all tattling, backbiting, and excessive anger." This means that we have pledged that we will never be guilty of any form of destructive talk or anger toward one another, nor will we listen to others who express such speech.

It has been said that no one has a finer command of language than the person who can keep his mouth shut. Peter writes, "For he that will love life, and see good days, let him refrain his tongue from evil, and his lips that they speak no guile" (1 Peter 3:10). Matthew adds, "But I say unto you, That every idle word that men shall speak, they shall give account thereof in the day of judgment" (Matthew 12:36). If our speech is going to be courteous and godly, we will have to apply two general principles to the words we speak. We will have to shun evil words and speak good words.

When you stand before God on the day of judgment, if this were the only issue for which you are called to account, what do you think God will have to say to you? You may be thinking, "I wish that *were* the only thing for which I would be held accountable. That is such a minor thing." Unfortunately, God does not consider such matters minor infractions. Paul wrote the following in Romans 1:28-32.

And even as they did not like to retain God in *their* knowledge, God gave them over to a reprobate mind, to do those things which are not convenient; Being filled with all unrighteousness, fornication, wickedness, covetousness, maliciousness; full of envy, murder, debate, deceit, malignity; whisperers, Backbiters, haters of God, despiteful, proud, boasters, inventors of evil things, disobedient to parents, Without understanding, covenant breakers, without natural affection, implacable, unmerciful: who knowing the judgment of God, that they which commit such things are worthy of death, not only do the same, but have pleasure in them that do them.

Of the twenty-two sins listed here as being the products of a reprobate mind, at least fourteen of them have to do with attitudes and/or
speech that impact interpersonal relationships. God has ranked such
sins as whispering and backbiting along side sins we tend to consider
much more evil, like fornication, homosexuality, and murder. We
must remember that *any* sin in the life of the believer is high treason
against the King.

The Epistle of James has a great deal to say about the characteristics
of the tongue. Consider James 3:2-12.

> For in many things we offend all. If any man offend not in word,
> the same is a perfect man, *and* able also to bridle the whole body.
> Behold, we put bits in the horses' mouths, that they may obey us;
> and we turn about their whole body. Behold also the ships, which
> though *they be* so great, and *are* driven of fierce winds, yet are
> they turned about with a very small helm, whithersoever the gov-
> ernor listeth. Even so the tongue is a little member, and boasteth
> great things. Behold, how great a matter a little fire kindleth!
> And the tongue *is* a fire, a world of iniquity; so is the tongue
> among our members, that it defileth the whole body, and setteth
> on fire the course of nature; and it is set on fire of hell. For every
> kind of beasts, and of birds, and of serpents, and of things in the
> sea, is tamed, and hath been tamed of mankind: But the tongue
> can no man tame; *it is* an unruly evil, full of deadly poison.
> Therewith bless we God, even the Father; and therewith curse we
> men, which are made after the similitude of God. Out of the
> same mouth proceedeth blessing and cursing. My brethren, these
> things ought not so to be. Doth a fountain send forth at the same
> place sweet *water* and bitter? Can the fig tree, my brethren, bear
> olive berries? Either a vine, figs? So *can* no fountain both yield
> salt water and fresh.

As James points out, a very small piece of metal can control a horse,
a relatively small piece of wood or metal can turn a ship, and a very
small spark can burn a forest. Just so, a very small comment can
destroy a testimony or hurt a friend or brother.

Proverbs 6:2 warns, "Thou art snared with the words of thy mouth, thou art taken with the words of thy mouth." Evil words, those words that would ensnare us, come in many forms. First, there are those words characterized as "grievous" words that stir up anger (Proverbs 15:1). These are words that are earthy, or painful, or disrespectful, or hateful. Then there are the talebearer's words, those words that seek to hurt, or to break in pieces, or to cause division. These can include things like back-stabbing, cutting remarks, and insults. That is why Proverbs 18:8 and 26:22 both say, "the words of a talebearer are as wounds." A talebearer's words assault the spirit of another in much the same way that the thieves abused the man found along the road by the Samaritan. The talebearing Christian has more in common with those thieves than with the Good Samaritan.

The tongue's power to destroy is manifested in more than one way. First, it devours reputations. That's what the injunction against tattling refers to—telling tales that hurt the reputation of the one about whom we are reporting. We have often made the error of assuming that such gossip is not *sinful* as long as the story is true. But that is not the case. Telling *false* hurtful stories falls into the categories of "maliciousness," "deceit," "inventors of evil things," (see Romans 1:18-32), not to mention making one a liar and a false witness. The concept of *tattling* assumes the story is true, but that the tattler reported it to an inappropriate party or was motivated by selfishness.

Besides devouring reputations, the tongue can also destroy unity, which is what "backbiting" implies. In addition to talebearing, this includes griping. Griping is best understood as "complaining about a problem to someone who is not a part of the problem or a part of the solution." Of course, some people seem to complain for the simple joy of being miserable to get along with, caring nothing for a solution. There are also those who advise that if you are upset, you may feel a need to express your irritation by telling someone about it just to help you feel better. That is psycho-nonsense. "Talking it out" may well be sinning against God and your brother. Talk to God about it, not your neighbor. If it is important enough to repeat, your obligation by God's command is to talk only to those involved, at least in the first stage of reconciliation. If it is not significant enough to talk to them, then you sin by harboring a grudge or repeating gossip. The problem is that most people lack the character to handle problems properly, and they create greater problems and commit greater sins by the abuse of their tongues.

Other evil words are described in Ephesians 4:29 as "corrupt communication." This refers to rotten and worthless speech. It includes dirty talk, off-color remarks or jokes, crude or rude talk or words, children sassing their parents, and other such speech. Similarly, Colossians 3:8 condemns "filthy communication." This is like "corrupt communication," but includes a condemnation of lying, improper teasing, and hateful, hurtful, or malicious speech.

Our society has come to accept even children using the most shockingly vile language. Many families in most churches need to clean up how they let their children talk to their parents, to each other, and to others in authority. It is neither cute nor funny for children to make sarcastic, snide retorts to parents and peers, despite the "laugh tracks" and audience responses to nearly every television comedy today. Despite the prevalent opinion of our culture, dirty jokes, dishonesty, sexual innuendoes, and smart-mouthed children are not funny. To the degree that we join in the laughter, we condone and even encourage the kind of speech God condemns.

The bad news is that your tongue is powerful, destructive, wicked, hard to control, and hypocritical. Even worse, this matters a great deal to God. But the good news is that there is hope. Peter writes, "For he that will love life, and see good days, let him refrain his tongue from evil, and his lips that they speak no guile" (1 Peter 3:10). The Spirit-controlled tongue should be characterized by the healing, strengthening, and encouraging it brings its hearers. By the grace of God, the tongue of the Christian can use its power for great benefit.

A generation of church members is being affected by the world's speech habits. In many cases, the quality of the vocabulary and tone of the way God's people talk is barely distinguishable from that of unbelievers. For many believers, to cultivate Christian courtesy in speech will require significant changes in the way they habitually communicate. If you are uncertain about whether or not it is wrong to speak in a particular tone or to say something a particular way, it may help to ask yourself, "Would I speak this way to the Lord Jesus?" or "Would Jesus Christ speak to a parent, a spouse, a child, a co-worker, an employee, an employer, a neighbor, as I have just spoken?" But this will only help if you actually know enough about Jesus Christ to understand what He would and would not do or say.

We know that Jesus would never, could never, say anything evil. He could only speak good words. Matthew 4:4 says, "Man shall not live by bread alone, but by every word that proceedeth out of the mouth of God." Therefore, God's words give life. And Ephesians 5:1 tells us, "Be ye therefore followers [imitators] of God, as dear children." That is, we are to emulate God in everything, including our speech. Proverbs 8:8 describes what our words should be like when it says, "All the words of my mouth *are* in righteousness; *there is* nothing froward or perverse in them."

The Scriptures have a lot to say about how God's people ought to talk. We are told that soft words, as opposed to harsh ones, turn away wrath and make peace (Prov. 15:1). We learn that pleasant words bring delight and encouragement to the hearer and the speaker, making both of them better spiritually, emotionally, and physically (Prov. 15:26; 16:24). Our words are to be acceptable in God's sight, whether or not they are acceptable to man (Ps. 19:14).

Paul tells us that our words are to be edifying (Eph. 4:29). That means we should say only those things that would build others up, making them stronger, more stable, and more courageous Christians. Our speech should help others learn and grow. Our words are also to be "always with grace, seasoned with salt" (Col. 4:6). If our words are like salt, then they will be helpful. They will have a purifying effect. They will be appetizing, in that they will stimulate a taste for the Bread of Life, and they will also create thirst for the Water of Life. Finally, Paul says that we should speak only "sound speech, that cannot be condemned" (Titus 2:8). This is a command to say only those things that are true and righteous, that could never be used to condemn you.

But we must be careful not to make any individual's response to our words the ultimate test of acceptable speech. If we do that, we will begin to say only those things that please others, or even only those things that can be described as politically correct. It is much more important that our words be acceptable to God. "Let the words of my mouth and the meditation of my heart be acceptable in thy sight, O LORD, my strength and my redeemer" (Ps. 19:14). Paul advised

Titus that those who opposed his ministry would "be ashamed, having no evil thing to say of you" if Titus would "in all things show thyself a pattern of...sound speech, that cannot be condemned" (Titus 2:7-8). Titus was to make sure his speech was acceptable to God, so that even his enemies would not be able to accuse him of evil.

It is likely that most Christians, and perhaps all Christians, could stand a little mouth washing once in a while. We must guard our speech well. At stake are both one's testimony before a lost and dying world and his relationships with the brethren in Christ Jesus. Many folks think that everybody ought to be able to overlook the tactless, thoughtless, and sometimes downright awful things *they* say, yet woe be unto those who would say similar things to *them*. God expects to demonstrate His power in us by helping us control our tongues. "If any man among you seem to be religious, and bridleth not his tongue, but deceiveth his own heart, this man's religion is vain" (James 1:26). One of the more reliable indicators of the genuineness of a man's faith is whether or not his speech gives evidence of being Spirit-controlled.

Are you truly courteous in your speech to others and about others? If at church next Sunday the pastor were to play back a recording of every word you spoke the week before, what would the congregation hear? Would they hear only words that are soft, pleasant, acceptable, edifying, gracious, and sound? If not, maybe you need to change your heart attitude and clean up your speech. We are committed to demonstrating Christian sensitivity by cultivating "Christian sympathy in feeling and Christian courtesy in speech." Each church member must determine to "rejoice with them that rejoice and weep with them that weep," being "of the same mind one toward another." Each must also "refrain his tongue from evil, and [let] his lips...speak no guile."

---

[1] In our politically correct verbiage, those who speak out against the evil of homosexual behavior can expect to be told that they need "sensitivity training." Thus, "sensitivity toward others" is often used as a euphemism for condoning sin. It has not been too long ago that "sensitivity toward others" referred to a sort of vague sense of being alert to people's moods and emotions. However, in this context the word is used in a more specific sense to describe the portion of our covenant in which we pledge "to cultivate Christian sympathy in feeling and Christian courtesy in speech."

CHAPTER 23
FORGIVENESS OF OTHERS

A few years ago I picked up a book on forgiveness that had an intriguing subtitle: *How to Get Along with Everybody All the Time!* The second chapter, "What Is Forgiveness?", ends with the following story:

Years ago I took some clothes to a local dry-cleaners. Not only did I take clothes to the cleaners, I got taken to the cleaners on the same trip! After getting home with the clothes, I discovered the pants were torn and a necktie was wrecked. "No problem," I thought, "I'll just take them back and get reimbursed." So I gathered up my damaged clothes and went back to the dry-cleaners. I showed the clerk my ruined garments and expected repayment. However, the clerk informed me that the manager took care of these incidents, and he was not available. "No problem," I said, "When will he be in?" She gave me a time and I went back, but he still was not in. I am a little slow in catching on, but after five return visits I began to see an emerging pattern! They intended to beat me out of any reimbursement and I was furious! My first thought was to take out a newspaper advertisement warning the public against that business establishment. Then I found out that was illegal. Next, I thought about printing up a handbill and warning all potential customers by stationing myself on the sidewalk immediately outside the cleaners. But I didn't have time for that, so I contacted the Better Business Bureau. By now you can

see that I was angry, very angry. I had been cheated. I was getting nowhere on the human level so I decided on a spiritual attack.
The verse came to mind, *"Vengenace is mine, saith the Lord, I
will repay."* So I prayed, "Lord, let them have it!" Every time I
drove by, I would glance over to see whether the place had been
struck by lightning the night before! I was really mad. I had
sought justice but did not find it. That is often the case in this
fallen world. There is nothing wrong with seeking justice, but
most often you will not find it. I was left with two choices: get
bitter or forgive. Being bitter is sin, so I chose (I didn't feel like
it) to forgive. I released that debt and turned them over to God. I
never got reimbursed and I never received an apology, but that
does not matter now. That decision to forgive released me from
my prison of bitterness.[1]

Unfortunately, this story did *not* describe *biblical forgiveness.* It
illustrates, quite properly, how a believer needs to relinquish expecta-
tions of restitution in order to avoid becoming bitter, but mistakenly
identifies that as *forgiveness* while actually describing *forbearance.*
While the author's forbearance is commendable, he omitted the vital
matters of repentance and restitution on the part of the offender as the
condition for forgiveness and the full restoration to the former relationship on the *basis* of forgiveness. Believers who read his book and
accept his definitions will come away confusing similar but distinct
concepts. Such misunderstanding impacts one's view of salvation.
God is forbearing toward *all* mankind, ready to forgive and never bitter. But God only *forgives* and establishes fellowship with those who
admit their guilt and ask to be forgiven on the basis of Christ's sacrifice. He will still condemn all others.

A similar incident with a different ending better illustrates true *forgiveness.* It was Saturday afternoon, and my family and I were headed to Puerto Rico to visit a mission work we supported. Our airline
tickets from Harrisburg, PA, required us to change planes in Detroit.
Our flight from Detroit was delayed by a severe thunderstorm that
struck the airport about the time we boarded, so we sat on the plane at
the gate for over an hour waiting for the weather to relent. We finally
arrived in San Juan in time for a late supper before being dropped off
at the home where we would be staying. As we began to unpack our
bags, we discovered that almost everything was soaked. Apparently,

the storm had hit Detroit so suddenly that the baggage cart with our luggage had been left standing in the rain on the tarmac. We borrowed our hostess' iron and did the best we could to straighten out our clothes. The next day, I would be preaching in two different mission churches, speaking through an interpreter for the first time in my life. I was nervous enough, without the added distraction of a stained white shirt and a light-weight wool suit that no longer fit properly.

When we returned to the States at the end of the week, I immediately contacted the airline to register a complaint. I discovered that they required notification within twenty-four hours of the incident. When I spoke with a supervisor and explained the situation, he told me I would have to bring the clothes to be inspected to the airline desk at the Harrisburg airport—sixty miles from where I lived. He told me when he would be there, and we agreed to meet on Thursday. When I arrived at the appointed time, the ticket agent at the desk told me the supervisor I was looking for didn't work on Thursdays. I was mad. I told the ticket agent my story and explained that I had not driven all the way to the airport only to be turned away without speaking to someone in authority. The agent made a quick phone call, and a few minutes later another airline representative took me to his office. I told him why I was there, and started to open the suitcase full of damaged clothing. He apologized, and told me that an inspection would not be necessary. He promised that if I would put my complaint in writing, along with an itemized list of the damaged items and their estimated value, and fax it to him, he would see that I was reimbursed. I left his office feeling a little better, but not convinced I would actually get a check.

Had the story ended there, I would have had a choice between bitterness and forbearance—the same choice that the author of the earlier story had to make. As a Christian, I ought to be forbearing and absorb the loss without becoming bitter. But I'd never fly that airline again. However, about a week after my meeting with the airline official, I got a reimbursement check and a letter of apology, along with discount vouchers for future travel to compensate me for time and trouble expended in getting the matter resolved. Now the way was open for real *forgiveness*. The airline had acknowledged responsibility and done even more than I asked to make reparations. The only thing that would keep me from flying that airline again would be an unforgiving spirit.

While the word *forgiveness* does not appear in our church covenant, it is the underlying principle when we pledge "to be slow to take offense, but always ready for reconciliation, mindful of the rules of our Savior to seek it without delay." The Apostle Paul tells us how we are to both forebear and forgive in his epistle to the church at Colosse.

> But now ye also put off all these; anger, wrath, malice, blasphemy, filthy communication out of your mouth. Lie not one to another, seeing that ye have put off the old man with his deeds; And have put on the new *man,* which is renewed in knowledge after the image of him that created him: Where there is neither Greek nor Jew, circumcision nor uncircumcision, Barbarian, Scythian, bond *nor* free: but Christ *is* all, and in all. Put on therefore, as the elect of God, holy and beloved, bowels of mercies, kindness, humbleness of mind, meekness, longsuffering; Forbearing one another, and forgiving one another, if any man have a quarrel against any: even as Christ forgave you, so also *do* ye. And above all these things *put on* charity, which is the bond of perfectness. (Colossians 3:8-14)

Paul first reminds us of our own sinfulness, then tells us that we are new creatures who must emulate Christ by the power of God. He charges believers in the church to love one another so much that we are willing and ready to forgive one another "even as Christ forgave" us. That is quite a challenge.

Forgiveness Defined

Much of the difficulty of practicing forgiveness is that many people have only a vague idea of the biblical concept of forgiveness, and many who think they know what it means have a distorted view. Depending on what source you check, you may find a variety of definitions. The Oxford American Dictionary (New York: Oxford University Press, 1980 ed.) offers this definition: "To cease to feel angry or bitter toward (a person) or about (an offense)." The World Book Dictionary (Chicago: Thorndike Barnhart, 1989 ed.) does a little better. It says forgiveness means, "To give up the wish to punish or get even with; not have hard feelings at or toward…to give up all claim to…" Harold Vaughan and T. P. Johnston offer a thumbnail definition of forgiveness as "a deliberate choice to release people from the debt[s] they owe you."[2]

While each of the above definitions includes the key idea of relinquishing hard feelings or anger or release from a debt, none of them gives a complete and accurate biblical definition. Each of these has omitted any reference to the *conditions* for and the *results* of forgiveness. Starting with the same basic concept included in the other definitions, the New Compact Bible Dictionary (Grand Rapids: Zondervan Publishing House, 1967 ed.) says that forgiveness is,

> the giving up of resentment or claim to requital on account of an offense. …Forgiveness is conditional on repentance and the willingness to make reparation or atonement; and the effect of forgiveness is the restoration of both parties to the former state of relationship. The ground of forgiveness by God of man's sins is the atoning death of Christ (p. 180).

Forgiveness Among Men

According to the Lord Jesus Christ, if one is to be forgiven he must first *seek* forgiveness.

> Therefore if thou bring thy gift to the altar, and there rememberest that thy brother hath ought against thee; Leave there thy gift before the altar, and go thy way; first be reconciled to thy brother, and then come and offer thy gift. Agree with thine adversary quickly, whiles thou art in the way with him; lest at any time the adversary deliver thee to the judge, and the judge deliver thee to the officer, and thou be cast into prison. Verily I say unto thee, Thou shalt by no means come out thence, till thou hast paid the uttermost farthing. (Matthew 5:23-26)

The Lord says that if you have wronged someone and know it, you must attempt reconciliation to be accepted by God. Admitting your guilt and seeking forgiveness is more important than offering sacrifices. He adds that anyone who fails to seek forgiveness will be held fully accountable for his transgressions. Other passages elaborate.

Take heed to yourselves: If thy brother trespass against thee, rebuke him; and if he repent, forgive him. And if he trespass against thee seven times in a day, and seven times in a day turn again to thee, saying, I repent; thou shalt forgive him (Luke 17:3-4).

Moreover if thy brother shall trespass against thee, go and tell him his fault between thee and him alone: if he shall hear thee, thou hast gained thy brother. But if he will not hear *thee, then* take with thee one or two more, that in the mouth of two or three witnesses every word may be established. And if he shall neglect to hear them, tell *it* unto the church: but if he neglect to hear the church, let him be unto thee as a heathen man and a publican. Verily I say unto you, Whatsoever ye shall bind on earth shall be bound in heaven: and whatsoever ye shall loose on earth shall be loosed in heaven. Again I say unto you, That if two of you shall agree on earth as touching any thing that they shall ask, it shall be done for them of my Father which is in heaven. For where two or three are gathered together in my name, there am I in the midst of them. Then came Peter to him, and said, Lord, how oft shall my brother sin against me, and I forgive him? till seven times? Jesus saith unto him, I say not unto thee, Until seven times: but, Until seventy times seven (Matthew 18:15-22).

We find several elements necessary in the granting of forgiveness revealed in these two passages. First, we see that a prerequisite for forgiveness is the repentance of the offender. He should come willingly, because he recognized his sin and wants to clear his conscience and be restored to fellowship. But if he does not, some form of disciplinary action is necessary. A private rebuke may be sufficient. But the disciplinary authority of the church, discussed in Chapter Eighteen, can be an important factor in convincing a transgressor of his need to repent in order to be forgiven and restored. The escalating publicity of the offense, eventually leading to expulsion of the unrepentant from fellowship with the church, is all intended to put increasing pressure on him to acknowledge his sin and ask for forgiveness. While forgiveness is always *available* to the repentant, forgiveness cannot be *applied* without his confession and request for restoration.

A second vital element of forgiveness taught by Jesus Christ is that when the transgressor confesses his guilt and asks to be forgiven, he is to be restored to a relationship of fellowship with the brethren. He is to be treated with the same affection he would have been shown had there been no offense.

Further, forgiveness may require restitution by the offender. Nowhere in Scripture, either in the Old Testament Law or in New Testament practice is there any provision for forgiveness without restitution. When Zacchaeus, the tax collector, acknowledged his sin and turned to Christ, he promised to repay anyone he had wronged four times the amount he had taken improperly (Luke 19:8-9). Exodus 22:1-9 established the penalties for stealing. If the thief's conscience smote him so that he turned himself in and offered to restore what he had taken, he was to repay the full value of that which he stole plus an additional 20%. If he were caught with the property, and then confessed under duress, he was to repay double the value of the goods taken. If he were found to have been guilty, but the property was destroyed or consumed, he was to repay four times its value. Zacchaeus volunteered to go well beyond the 120% required under the law for voluntary restitution. He was doing exactly what Jesus had said in Matthew 5 should be done when one acknowledges his transgression against another—he was announcing his intention to make right his wrongs as a prerequisite to God's acceptance of his offering.

It is, of course, the prerogative of the one to whom the debt is owed to extend mercy by waiving his right to restitution or accepting it at a lower level than that to which he was entitled. It is often best, though, to allow the offender to make restitution of at least 100-120%. If you don't, there is a human tendency both to be proud of your mercy, and to think of the waived restitution as an unpaid debt to be called in or used as a guilt club if the offender dares wrong you again. Further, paying restitution teaches the offender the cost of offenses, and allows him to be confident that he has really satisfied the offended one so the relationship can be restored.

Consider a hypothetical situation. Suppose I were to lend a book from my reference library to a man who asked to borrow it for a few days. I don't do that very often, because my books are my tools and

among my most valued possessions. I can't always anticipate from
one week to the next which books I might need, so I don't like to let
them out of my study. But supposing I did lend the book, and a couple of weeks went by without its being returned. It would be perfectly appropriate for me to ask my friend to return my book. What if,
during the days he had my book, he spilled coffee on it and stained
most of the pages and warped the cover? If he returns a damaged
book and says, "Sorry I messed up your book. I'll try to be more
careful next time," you can be sure there will not be a next time. I'll
not loan him another book, because he still owes me the one I loaned
him the first time. But if he says, "I'm sorry; I destroyed your book.
I've ordered a new one for you, and it will be here in a couple of
days." Fine. Bring me the new book when it arrives and all is well.
If he does not offer to replace the book, I have a choice: I can behave
properly and forebear his offense, or I can sin by becoming bitter
toward the offender. I should not feel anger or resentment every time
I think of the lost or damaged book, but my friend still owes me a
replacement volume. Of course, if he offers to replace the book, I
have other options: I could allow him to replace the book, in which
case he has paid his debt, and our fellowship is restored. Or, I would
have the right, and in some cases maybe even the obligation, to show
mercy by telling him that replacing the book would not be necessary;
I would buy another copy myself. If I do that, I have released him
from his debt by paying it for him. In either case, I cannot hold the
debt against him any longer, because he owes me nothing. That is
forgiveness, and it can only be applied to the repentant offender. To
offer "forgiveness," as a canceling of debts and restoration to the former relationship, when the offender is unrepentant, is not *biblical* forgiveness. It is *indulgence*—permission to leave debts unpaid without
consequence.

Forgiveness from God

We must not become confused by the fact that God offers to forgive
the sinner *freely*. God's forgiveness is *free* in the sense that it is available to all who believe and ask to be forgiven. But God's forgiveness
is only offered on the ground of the shed blood of His Son, the Lord
Jesus Christ (Ephesians 1:7; Colossians 1:14; Hebrews 9:22). When
God's forgiveness is applied on the basis of Christ's shed blood, the
burden of God's wrath is removed. This is true, not because God

changes His mind about our sin, but because His justice has been satisfied. The debt has been paid. That makes God's forgiveness very
costly indeed. However, the principle of sowing and reaping (2
Samuel 12:13-14; Galatians 6:7) is not suspended by forgiveness. For
instance, a young person may throw away his or her virginity in an
illicit relationship before marriage, then repent and ask God to forgive. He will certainly do so, but the young man or woman will never
again be a virgin. Even though God's righteous wrath has been satisfied, the consequences of sin remain.

Restitution must be made for every offense, and forgiveness is only
applied to the repentant. The Scriptures even demand evidence of the
genuineness of one's repentance. Real repentance is demonstrated by
obedience. The Lord Jesus challenged his audience to "Bring forth
therefore fruits worthy of repentance" (Luke 3:8).

Real repentance is also demonstrated by *forgiving others*. Matthew
6:12-15 makes that very clear.

> And forgive us our debts, as we forgive our debtors. And lead us
> not into temptation, but deliver us from evil: For thine is the king-
> dom, and the power, and the glory, for ever. Amen. For if ye for-
> give men their trespasses, your heavenly Father will also forgive
> you: But if ye forgive not men their trespasses, neither will your
> Father forgive your trespasses.

Believers must forgive in the same manner and by the same measure
by which we were forgiven. That forgiveness must be offered freely,
without vindictiveness and without restriction, but it must be applied
only to a repentant offender.

Jesus went so far as to tell His disciples that if a transgressor refuses
to repent when confronted by the church, he is to be treated as "an
heathen man and a publican" (Matthew 18:17). That is, the unrepentant church member is to be removed from the roll of the church and
treated as if he were an unbeliever—not as one who is cursed and to
be avoided, but as one who needs to be won to Christ. And a man is
won to Christ by repenting of his sin and seeking God's forgiveness.
That is why Jesus said that an unforgiving spirit was evidence of an
unforgiven heart. If we understand the magnitude our own guilt
before God, and the price that Christ paid to settle our debts, we

should have no trouble forgiving anything others do to us. Those offenses are petty in the shadow of our transgressions against God.

Peter asked "Lord, how oft shall my brother sin against me, and I forgive him? till seven times?" (Matthew 18:21). The rabbis had taught for centuries that everyone must forgive the first time an offender repents, and the more spiritual would forgive a second offense. The extraordinarily merciful might forgive a third time, but offering forgiveness beyond that would be inappropriate. So Peter was being quite generous. But the Lord Jesus told Peter that would not be enough. He would need to be willing to forgive "seventy times seven" offenses (Matthew 18:22). His point was that offenses would abound. The disciples should expect people to wrong them, because people are sinners. In fact, there would be a multitude of disputes and offenses even among themselves. If they were to be successful in the mission that Christ was going to entrust to the church, they would need to demonstrate a level of forgiveness approaching the divine.

Forgiveness Applied

In order to understand forgiveness, there are three ideas we need to keep in mind. First, *forgiveness* involves restoring to fellowship a repentant offender when wrongs have been made right, either by the offender paying his own debt or by a third party paying his debt for him. *Mercy* is demonstrated when the victim does not require the full measure of restitution or the injured party absorbs the cost himself. *Grace* is showing favor to the offender that he does not deserve.

As we learn to forgive others, we must insist that it is *not unforgiving* to expect the wrongdoer to be genuinely repentant. Further, it is *not unforgiving* to expect full restitution for wrongs committed. A person who is truly repentant will *desire* to make restitution. But it *is* unforgiving to hold a grudge against and refuse to restore to fellowship someone who has truly repented and made appropriate restitution where possible.

In our relationship with God, we must never forget that God's *forgiveness* required Christ's bloody death in order for the eternal judgment for our sins to be satisfied. We must remember that God's *mercy* may grant happiness by removing the temporal consequences of our sin, but that it does not demand it. But God's *grace* imparts

eternal life. When we are forgiven, we receive that promise.
Regardless of the immediate consequences of our sins, the ultimate
benefit of God's forgiveness is eternal.

---

[1] Harold Vaughan and T. P. Johnston, *Forgiveness: How to Get Along with Everybody All the Time!* (Vinton, VA: Christ Life Publications, 1992), pp. 17-18.

[2] *Forgiveness: How to Get Along with Everybody All the Time!*, p. 15.

CHAPTER 24
FIDELITY TO YOUR COVENANT

A man in my church once came to tell me that he was considering a job offer that would take them out of the area. This was a couple who was actively involved in our church ministry, and we would miss them if they left. When he asked my advice, I was tempted to tell him, "Forget it. We need you here." But, admitting that such a move may be the will of God, I tried to give him some guidance in how to understand God's leading. Among other things, I encouraged him to take a careful look at the local churches in the vicinity of his potential employer. Later, he came back to tell me he had decided to take the new job. While they were selling their property and looking for a new home, I reminded him to keep his family's spiritual needs in mind. He said, "I know," but added that his top priority was to find property with the space and facilities they needed for their hobbies. They eventually bought such a place, and made their move without having found a good local church. Over the next couple of years, cards and letters told us of their unsuccessful search for a satisfactory church anywhere near their new home. When they visited our church some time later, he and his wife told us through their tears that they had only attended church services a couple of times over the last several months. They were experiencing spiritual struggles which they attributed, in part, to lacking the contribution of a church home.

We live in a very mobile society. While not every family has as much trouble finding a good church as the one I've described, situations like theirs are not uncommon. When people relocate, it usually takes them a while to reach a comfort level in their new community. Just finding a satisfactory doctor, dentist, hair stylist, or dry cleaners can be time consuming and even frustrating. So can finding a new church home. But making contact with and settling into a church family is one of the most important decisions an individual or family can make. What kind of church should you look for?

The church is, in some respects, a living entity. Its vitality and ministry are dependent upon its individual parts. There is an old cliché that says "everything rises or falls according to the leadership." That is only partly true. Leadership certainly has an impact on the character and practice of a local church. The Scriptures have much to say about the negative influence bad leaders exert, with pronouncement of judgment upon such evil shepherds (Zechariah 10:2-4; Ezekiel 34:1-16; John 10:1-21). Good leadership is commanded (Colossians 4:17; 1 Timothy 3:1-13; 4:12-16), and believers are expected to heed such godly shepherds (1 Timothy 5:17; Hebrews 13:7). But most of the instructions to the church are addressed to the believers at large, usually in the context of their own local assemblies.

We have considered many aspects of the believer's relationship with his church. The benefits that are available to the individual believer through membership in a good local church are real and varied. The believer's active participation in the ministry of such a church provides manifold opportunities for personal growth in Christ as we all learn to contribute our gifts, skills, energies, and other resources to the good of the church and the glory of Christ.

All of us will, throughout our lives, enter into many different relationships. Most of these will be *casual* relationships, such as those with friends and neighbors. Although benefits and obligations may be assumed in these relationships, they are by nature non-binding. Other relationships we enter into are *contractual*. These would include lease or mortgage agreements, credit agreements, employment agreements, etc. They would be established more rarely and with more careful consideration, because they include binding both parties to particular obligations and benefits to be fulfilled during a specified period, and invoking certain penalties if either party fails to fulfill his obligations. But occasions in which one would enter into a *covenan-*

tal relationship are very rare. While a covenant may include provisions for judicial consequences for those who do not keep their vow, our accountability to *God* is more direct than in any of the other relationship types. Those who join a church by covenant become participants in a relationship more like a marriage than a mortgage. Like a marriage vow, our church covenant is *unconditionally* binding—all of the promises are made by the one taking the vow. Nowhere does it say, "If the church will...then we will." We simply say "we will" assume certain obligations toward one another and toward Christ.

In its first paragraph, the membership covenant of our church identifies itself as a vow, and the Scriptures abound with commands to keep our word and to fulfill our vows (i.e., Numbers 30:2; Deuteronomy 23:21; Ecclesiastes 5:4; Colossians 3:9). Further, our covenant invokes "God, angels, and this assembly" as witnesses. This echoes the words of the Apostle Paul as he addressed Timothy in 1 Timothy 5:21, "I charge *thee* before God, and the Lord Jesus Christ, and the elect angels, that thou observe these things...". The statement in our covenant actually reads, "...we do now, in the presence of God, angels, and this assembly, most solemnly and joyfully enter into covenant with one another as one body in Christ." This makes our covenant a very solemn oath indeed.

There is one final statement in our covenant that makes it clear that our vow goes beyond our responsibilities to one another within our own congregation and community. Our covenant closes with a promise that defines the *duration* of the covenant:

> We moreover engage that, when we remove from this place, we will as soon as possible unite with some other church where we can carry out the spirit of this covenant and the principles of God's Word.

Paul encouraged Timothy to "continue...in the things which thou hast learned and hast been assured of" (2 Timothy 3:14). A marriage covenant's life-long duration is established by clauses like "till death do us part" and "as long as we both shall live." The promises made in our church covenant are also made for life, and we are bound to a particular congregation until "we remove from this place," but only until "we remove from this place." Our continuance "in the things which we have learned" is not restricted to a particular location. We are to continue in these things no matter where we are.

Removing from Your Local Congregation

Our covenant emphasizes the obligations we share while we are members of this particular congregation, but it recognizes that we are not bound to remain a part of a particular congregation until we die. Members can "remove from this place," yet still be bound by the principles of this covenant.

There are a number of reasons one might have for leaving one congregation for another. First, you might move out of the area. In most of the world today people are much more mobile than ever before in history. But transitions from one location to another were not unknown in the first century. In 2 Corinthians 3:1 Paul makes a general reference to the church's practice of sending letters of commendation with members who left one community for another—"Do we begin again to commend ourselves? Or need we, as some *others*, epistles of commendation to you, or *letters* of commendation from you?" Luke makes a similar historical comment concerning the endorsement of the church at Ephesus, particularly of Aquilla and Priscilla, for the evangelist Apollos—"And when he [Apollos] was disposed to pass into Achaia, the brethren wrote, exhorting the disciples to receive him: who, when he was come, helped them much which had believed through grace" (Acts 18:27). Paul sends to the church in Rome a glowing recommendation that they receive a believer named Phebe who is coming from the church in Cenchrea (Romans 6:1-2). It is clear that when the early believers left one region for another they joined themselves to the group of believers in their new locale. Today people sometimes leave a congregation because they move out of the area or are called of God to go serve in another church of like faith.

Another reason for leaving one congregation for another is that the local church where you are a member might change its character. Proverbs 19:27 says, "Cease, my son, to hear the instruction *that causeth* to err from the words of knowledge." One should *not* leave a church simply because it does not offer your favorite programs or activities. No church in the world is going to do everything the way you want. And if they did, you can be sure they would not be doing

everything right. One should not leave a church over matters of personality or taste, but one *must* leave when a church forsakes the truth.

A church may depart from the truth by *forsaking doctrinal fidelity*.
This can occur when a church begins to teach doctrines that are contrary to Scripture, or begins to fellowship with those who do. But
such doctrinal infidelity may be evidenced more subtly by a church's
introduction of ministry programs or methods that violate Scripture.[1]
In the early stages of such doctrinal drift, concerned members may be
able to correct the digression. But when these errors become established positions or practices, it is time to find another church.

Another evidence of departure from the truth is seen when a church
forsakes moral purity. This may be evidenced in many ways, some
more obvious than others. Some churches make no pretense of standing for biblical morality, publicly endorsing sins like homosexuality
and abortion. Such errors are easy to recognize. Others take an official stand against immorality, but may have officers or teachers who
retain their positions despite known moral digression. This departure
from truth may not be as obvious, because it is often covered up by
the leadership. An even more subtle evidence of moral impurity in a
church is simply in its refusal to exercise proper discipline in cases of
immorality (adultery, drunkenness, lying, stealing, etc.) among its
membership. It is time to leave a church when it compromises with
immorality rather than practicing what it preaches.[2]

A third way in which a church may depart from the truth is by *forsaking ethical integrity*. This may be evidenced in several ways. For
instance, ethical integrity is violated by improprieties in the raising
and/or handling of funds, tendencies of the leadership to mislead or
manipulate people, unnecessarily harsh criticism of good people with
whom they disagree, political maneuvering for position within the
membership, or unbiblical leadership attitudes. Any one of many
such ethical violations might be grounds for a member concerned
about his own faithfulness to his covenant to look for another church
to join.

A fourth evidence of departure from truth is seen when a church *forsakes a biblical philosophy of ministry*. One sign of this is attempting
to stimulate church growth by adopting worldly methods. This may

include the surrender of standards in music, dress, grooming, or deportment in order to make the church more appealing to the lost or the sensual. It may include using give-away gimmicks, or side-show theatrics to try to attract a crowd. It may include trying to draw people to the church by promoting celebrity-status musicians or speakers without regard to the quality of their Christian testimony. Philosophical differences such as these may be reason enough to move to a new church.

Bear in mind that no church is perfect. Thorough scrutiny of any church will reveal inconsistencies. Flagrant violations of Scripture or programs designed to systematically move the church away from its biblical moorings may require your departure. More subtle violations or philosophical shifts may need time to address and correct. Much discernment will be needed in any given setting to determine what you ought to do when confronting such issues. The point is, there are some cases in which it is perfectly legitimate for a church member to transfer his membership to another local church. In situations like the ones just described, leaving would not *violate* the covenant we make at our church as much as it would *validate* it. Faithfulness to the Scripture must take precedence over fellowship with a particular congregation.

However, more often than not, people's reasons for leaving one church for another are not so honorable or biblical. Church members occasionally just stop attending. Without necessarily thinking of it in these terms, they decided that they are simply unwilling to keep their covenant. Sometimes believers get distracted by the cares of this world and drift away. That seems to have been the case with Lot (Genesis 19:1-36; cf. 2 Peter 2:7-8) and with an unnamed fellow in the church at Corinth (1 Corinthians 5). These should be treated like the prodigal son who is prayed for, looked for, and welcomed back when he repented. But there are others who leave because they were never really saved. That may have been the case with Demas, one of Paul's traveling companions and "fellowlaborers" (2 Timothy 4:10; cf. Colossians 4:14 and Philemon 1:23-24). It was certainly the case of those John mentions in 1 John 2:19—"They went out from us, but they were not of us; for if they had been of us, they would no doubt have continued with us; but they went out, that they might be made manifest that they were not all of us." There may have been a show of faith, a demonstration of faithfulness for a while, or even a high level of spiritual activity. But Demas was a missionary, and the ones to whom John refers were ministers who were not truly saved. The only absolute evidence of the genuineness of a person's salvation is *not* the words of his prayer of repentance, nor his works of service in the church, but his perseverance to the end.

There are also those church members who refuse to keep their covenant and are also unwilling to leave the church. These must be dealt with by disciplinary removal from the fellowship (1 Corinthians 5:1ff).[3] One may violate the covenant of the church through an overtly evil act for which he will not repent and make restitution. Another may forsake his covenant by his continued neglect of his promises despite the church's best efforts to encourage him. Members like these can and should be removed from the church roll. Again, the covenant is not being violated, but validated by the church.

Joining with Another Congregation

Let's assume that you would only leave your church if there were due cause—the Lord has moved you out of the area, or your church has forsaken the truth either by doctrinal infidelity, moral impurity, ethical impropriety, or philosophical carnality. Our covenant would demand that you continue your Christian life in another church. That church should be like the one described in the covenant, whether or not the church you left is still living by the promises made in it.

You should not delay. The writer of Hebrews warns all believers against "forsaking the assembling of ourselves together, as the manner of some is" (Hebrews 10:25). If you are moving from one church, you should find a group of like believers with whom you can worship. You should join them in the fellowship of ministry within that new local church as quickly as is practical. Granted, it may take some time to locate a sound church, and there are several things you should examine before joining. But as you visit other churches it should be with the intention of finding one where you can settle in and contribute to its ministry.

So how do you find the right kind of church? You should be more concerned about the *character* of the church than about the *name* of the church. Check its Constitution and By-laws. This document should include a statement of faith that is clear and biblical (2 Timothy 1:13-14; cf. 2 John 1:7-11). It should also give you a pretty good idea of whether or not the church's organizational structure is consistent with Scripture—if it is set up to function as a church should. Also, check its membership covenant. It may not look exactly like the covenant of the church you just left, but since you vowed to adhere to the same principles in any church you join there should be nothing in it that would violate the covenant of the church you are leaving. You should also check the church's policies and practices. Simply attending services for a while will teach you much. You will want to know how they plan to carry out their responsibilities as a church and whether or not what they actually do is consistent with the Bible and with what they say they intend to do. Additionally, you should check the church's affiliations. Find out what guest speakers they like to host, what mission boards they support, what colleges they recommend, and with what other churches they associate.

Having decided you must "depart from this place," you immediately begin to search for a church of like faith with which to worship and fellowship. Once you've determined which church that will be, you should officially join the membership of that church. Of course, changing churches should never be for the purpose of infiltration and take-over. Finding a church in which to serve the Lord is not the same as finding a place that needs you to come straighten it out. Trying to do the latter usually leads to much grief for you and the church, and much dishonor to the name of the Lord in the community. Rather, finding a church should be for the purposes of fellowship, worship, and ministry.

If you are a member of a local church that makes a covenant like the one examined here, you have vowed to be faithful to and serve in that church "until you remove from [that] place," after which you would join another like church. You break your vow if you leave over petty issues or personality conflicts. But if you have a good reason for leaving, your vow obligates you to join another church as soon as possible where you can keep the same promises. Your covenant does not necessarily bind you to a particular location or congregation, but it does bind you to a particular set of biblical principles that will help you live by the faith you profess.

Active participation in a good church will aid in your own spiritual growth and provide you with opportunities to contribute to the evangelistic work of that local church and the spiritual growth of its members. God has promised that all believers are "*more than conquerors*" (Rom. 8:37) over all the challenges of life, but too many Christians are content to be *merely spectators*. Spiritual maturity does not come simply by watching other people be Christians. Each of us must "walk worthy of the vocation" to which we are called (Eph. 4:1). We must not be satisfied with "those things which are behind," but must reach forward to "those things which are before," pressing "toward the mark of the prize of the high calling of God in Christ Jesus" (Phil. 3:13-14). We are called to be MORE THAN SPECTATORS, active in Christ's body, the Church, so we "may grow up into him in all things, which is the head, even Christ: from whom the whole body fitly joined together and compacted by that which every joint supplieth, according to the effectual working in the measure of every part, maketh increase of the body unto the edifying of itself in love" (Eph. 4:15-16).

> *Yea, a man may say, Thou hast faith, and I have works: show me thy faith without thy works, and I will show thee my faith by my works.* (James 2:18)

---

[1] See Chapter Three.

[2] Not every church will handle such issues identically, but a good church will attempt to consistently follow Scriptural methods for dealing with such.

[3] This was discussed at length in Chapter Eighteen.

APPENDIX

WHY CLING TO A CONSERVATIVE/TRADITIONAL MUSIC STANDARD?

The music used in our churches and schools should provide a high-quality, meaningful alternative to the high-pressure worldly influence of popular music. We need a biblical and philosophical basis for rejecting populism in our music in favor of a conservative tradition. While the text is important, it is by no means the only criterion by which our music should be evaluated. There are at least three general principles we need to consider:

1. Making music is essentially an activity of the spirit.
2. Everything we do, including our music, is to be done for the glory of God.
3. God has told us what should occupy our minds.

Making music is essentially an activity of the spirit, not the flesh, and each of us lives with an ongoing battle between the two. We must not allow the music industry to dictate our terminology. We have grown accustomed to making a distinction between "sacred" and "secular" music. That is a false delineation that emphasizes only the texts of vocal music or the context for which instrumental music was written. The distinction we make needs to be between the *spiritual* and the *sensual*. Galatians 5:17 says, "For the flesh lusteth against the Spirit, and the Spirit against the flesh: and these are contrary the one to the other: so that ye cannot do the things that ye would." Several passages establish a link between the spirit and singing, like Ephesians 5:18-19—"...be filled with the Spirit; Speaking to yourselves in psalms and hymns and spiritual songs, singing and making melody in your heart to the Lord." (See also 1 Corinthians 14:15 and 2 Chron. 5:13-14).

A large part of the problem we have with evaluating our music is that we insist on using a *carnal* measure of enjoyment rather than the *spiritual* measure of edification that the Scriptures demand. When we criticize our traditional church music as "boring," we reveal a great deal about our spiritual condition. How could an honest, sincere believer say that the words to "Amazing Grace" are boring? What we call "exciting" or "boring" usually has little or nothing to do with its spiritual content, and everything to do with our physical response to the music. We define ourselves as carnal Christians if we make our personal tastes the only criteria for determining what music we use.

The Scriptures abound with passages exhorting us to use music in our worship. It seems that music springing from a worshipful heart is the very "language" of worship. Psalm 100:2 tells us that each one of us personally must "come before His presence with singing." Colossians 3:16-17 tells us to teach and admonish one another in "psalms, hymns and spiritual songs, singing with grace in your hearts to the Lord. And whatsoever ye do in word or deed, *do* all in the name of the Lord Jesus, giving thanks to God and the Father by him." Our music should instruct and correct one another with the goal of bringing praise to God being the motive of our hearts. In 2 Chronicles 5:13-14 we are told that at the dedication of the Temple built by Solomon the special music prepared for the celebration was so effective that the presence of God filled the place and the priests had to omit their planned ministrations of other rituals. But the service did not end there. They went straight to the preaching, with the Word of God being read by Solomon (identified in Ecclesiastes as "the Preacher.") Even the instrumental music served a spiritual purpose.

The world at large knows that music has a powerful impact on one's mind and spirit. That is why advertisers use music to create interest in a product and to boost sales. Businesses use music to influence behavior. Even the medical profession is involved. Ten years ago a surgical team in Cleveland's St. Luke's Hospital began using music by Vivaldi, Mozart, and Brahms to help relax the patient and reduce staff tension in the operating room. It even reduced the amount of anesthesia needed by the patient. [1] Others who are using soothing music as part of their treatment strategy include Tallahassee Florida Memorial Regional Medical Center's newborn ICU and Dr. Raymond Bahr of Baltimore's St. Agnes Hospital's coronary care unit. Others are using it to treat pain, anxiety, depression, mental handicaps, emotional handicaps, physical handicaps, and neurological disorders. The University of Georgia is one of many schools that now offer degrees in music therapy.[2]

Music also evokes an emotional response. People tend to insist that teachers have no right to tell them what kind of music they ought to like. That sounds like the alcoholic who insists that you have no right to tell him he ought not to drink. He likes the stuff, and that is good enough for him. A drunkard's enjoyment of alcohol does nothing to reduce its damaging effects, any more than enjoyment of tobacco makes it less dangerous. David's sin with Bathsheba is not mitigated by the fact that she was attractive. Why then should we claim that enjoyment is the only valid criterion by which we may evaluate our music? The very strength of the emotion leading to such illogical conclusions ought to warn us to be careful in our music.

A significant part of the problem is that we fail to take seriously the triune enemy of the soul: the world, the flesh, and the devil. Most of us at least give lip service to warnings about the influence of the world. We screen our children's television and literature and don't let them listen to blatantly wicked music. We also recognize at least some of the dangers of temptations of the flesh. But we have forgotten the reality of the Devil's enmity. Even if we do think of him as a real adversary out to devour our children and ourselves, we still forget what the Bible tells us are Satan's greatest gifts. We know that he is the "father of lies" (John 8:44) and that he seeks our destruction (1 Pet. 5:8). We tend to forget that he appears as "an angel of light" and a "minister of grace" (2 Cor. 11:13-15). It is even said of him in Ezekiel 28:12 that he "sealeth up the sum, full of wisdom, and perfect in beauty." But few have considered the significance of the next two verses. According to Ezekiel 28:13-14, Lucifer was heaven's master musician, created for the express purpose of making music—"...the workmanship of thy tabrets and of thy pipes was prepared in thee in the day that thou wast created. Thou *art* the anointed cherub that covereth; and I have set thee *so*."

It would be incredibly foolish to think that Satan would ignore the weapon at which he is most skilled at a time in history when it can have the greatest impact. It is even more foolish to assume that we would immediately recognize the Devil's music and that we would not like it. Even *Time Magazine* entitled an article discussing Contemporary Christian Music "New Lyrics for the Devil's Music" (March 11, 1985). Music is essentially spiritual. Satan, our great spiritual enemy, is the greatest musician God ever created. He is also a master of deception. There is ample cause for caution in our standards of music.

Everything we do, including our music, is to be done for the glory of God. First Corinthians 10:31 says, "Whether therefore ye eat or drink, or whatsoever ye do, do all to the glory of God." This principle applies whether we are at church, at home, or driving down the road. If we are selecting our music to bring glory to God, then *it is our responsibility to choose only music that reflects the character of a holy God.* God has commanded that we evaluate everything in creation in the light of His revealed Word, clinging to the good and abstaining from evil wherever we find it (1 Thessalonians 5:21).

We apply this principle in a number of ways. For instance, we are to eat and drink only those things that are good for us, and avoid those things that would do us harm. It is on the basis of this principle that we reject the use of tobacco products, marijuana, and other drugs. We are to look at only those things that will do us good, not those things that would harms us. So we reject those things that are sensually suggestive as well as those things that are blatantly pornographic. We are to participate in activities that are good for us, and not in activities that would harm us, so we reject many things that would feed fleshly lusts.

It should follow that we would select only music that would make us *better*, and reject any that might bring us harm. But in this area we tend to argue that there is no way to evaluate music objectively. We ignore the teaching of Scripture. Instead of looking outward to *inform* our taste, we look inward to clarify or *discover* our taste. Instead of trying to develop a taste for that which is good, we try to convince God that we should be able to use whatever we want. We insist on doing that which pleases ourselves, listening to that which we like. We have made our desires the yardstick by which we measure what we will accept. We forget that the only enticement to sin is the satisfaction of some desire or other. The fact that you like something does not necessarily make it wrong, but it certainly does not guarantee that it is right. The song popularized by Debbie Boone over twenty years ago was wrong when it claimed "it can't be wrong when it feels so right" ("You Light Up My Life"). Inordinate love is sin, even when it makes you feel good. *We need to remember that the primary purpose of our music must be to please God, not ourselves.*

Even those outside the circle of fundamentalism are beginning to call attention to the problem. In the introduction to an essay entitled "How Shall We Sing to God?" Leonard Payton writes:

> We are in a runaway train headed straight for a broken bridge....
> [I would] encourage ecclesiastical authorities and thoughtful laity
> to reflect soberly on the crisis before us. My prayer is for a deep
> reformation in church music—that all alike will be led to insist,
> within their own spheres of influence, that comprehensive biblical
> principles be brought to bear on every detail of worship music.[3]

Calvin Johansson insists that church music must reflect godly traits of discipline, modesty, and balance. He contrasts that with music based on disunity, rebellion, and immodesty which is inappropriate for church. Johansson even says, "that entertainment-driven worship remains just that—entertainment. Few would say that amusement should be the goal of the worship of Almighty God, he argues."[4]

The unbelieving world has a hard time following the rationale of Christians who try to "launder" music that is essentially sensual by adding words that sound spiritual. The music industry defines *Contemporary Christian Music* as "indistinguishable—except for their lyrics—from their secular counterparts" ("New Lyrics for the Devil's Music," *Time Magazine*, March 11, 1985). Top performers are equated with their secular music counterparts. A few years ago the *New*

York Times called Amy Grant "the Michael Jackson of Gospel." Back in the mid-80s the "Christian Rock" band Styper (heavy metal) did a concert in Charlotte, NC. They invited then-popular Jim Bakker, of PTL infamy, to come and pray for the band before the concert. The next afternoon, the Channel 9 News (Charlotte's local station) started running their story "teasers" to get the public to tune in to their broadcast. Their lead story was "Jim Bakker attends heavy metal concert. Details at 6:00." During the interview, which I watched, they asked him how he could justify such music, since he represented a Christian organization. He found himself trying to convince a skeptical reporter that there is a difference between "regular heavy metal music" and "Christian heavy metal music." He tried to explain that the musical style was to attract a crowd who would then be given the message of Christianity hidden in the words, with Bibles being thrown to the crowd at the conclusion of the concert. When the reporter pointed out that most of the Bibles were left trampled on the floor, Mr. Bakker had no reply.

The world seems to intuitively recognize the biblical principle of the clean and the unclean (Haggai 2:12-14). It is professing Christians, not unbelievers, who try to argue that you can use any kind of music as long as it has Christian words. But Paul tells us that "the weapons of our warfare are not carnal" (2 Cor. 10:4). Paul also warned against those who try to evangelize by using "enticing words" rather than preaching (1 Cor. 2:4 with 1:21). We are not to use illegitimate means to spread the gospel on the grounds that it will attract a crowd. You could do the same with a circus or a belly dancer. You do not make pornography "Christian" by adding Bible verses to dirty pictures.

An incident in the life of King David vividly illustrates the importance of doing God's work God's way. In 1 Chronicles 13 we are told that David wanted to have the Ark of the Covenant returned to the Tabernacle. It had been missing since the Philistines stole it in war during the tenure of Eli, while Samuel was a child. When the Philistines realized that it was not a help to them, but a curse, they decided to return it to Israel. Not knowing what else to do with it, they put it on an ox cart and let it find its own way back. The oxen pulling the cart had stopped when they entered Israel's territory, and the Ark had been unloaded there. David now wanted to bring it back to where it belonged. The book of Leviticus had given details of how

it was to be moved, using poles run through rings on its sides and carried on the shoulders of a particular family of Levites. David decided
to ignore these instructions in favor of a more practical and effective
method, one recently employed by the Philistines. However, when he
tried to move it using the Philistine method of transport on an ox cart,
it cost a man his life. While they thought they were being successful,
making rapid progress toward the Tabernacle, they found that God
was not pleased. When David asked God what was wrong, he was
told that they must do God's work God's way. What worked for the
Philistines would not work for God's people. Too many of us are
making excuses for using "Philistine" music to train God's people,
and God is not pleased.

Unfortunately, much music that is overtly "Christian" is technically
shoddy. While God is not glorified by a technically excellent rendition of sensual music, neither is He glorified by a technically inept
rendition of a spiritual song. According to 1 Chronicles 15:22,
besides several people appointed to sing and play instruments,
Kenaniah was the chief *instructor* in song because he was *skillful.*
The worship music of ancient Israel was not done by a few volunteers
who rarely bothered to rehearse, asking people to "pray for us, 'cause
we ain't practiced much." No, their music was led skillfully, by paid
professionals. Psalm 33:3 commands us to sing and play "skillfully,"
which is the translation of a Hebrew word that means "beautiful,
praiseworthy, or lovely." God is truly glorified when we produce
music that is both consistent with the principles of God's Word and
skillfully done.

God has told us what should occupy our minds. Philippians 4:8
says, "Finally, brethren, whatsoever things are true, whatsoever things
are honest, whatsoever things *are* just, whatsoever things *are* pure,
whatsoever things *are* lovely, whatsoever things *are* of good report; if
there be any virtue, and if *there be* any praise, think on these things."
The word "music" is based on the root "to muse" or "to meditate." It
has its foundation with our innermost selves. It is a medium of communication designed to cause one to ponder, think, or meditate upon a
message. That is why a more common term for a singer or songwriter
used to be "muse." And Philippians 4:8 has told us what we are to
"muse" upon. Paul is merely elaborating on what Psalm 33:3 says

should characterize our music—it should be beautiful, praiseworthy, or lovely.

Our music, then, must be excellent music, true music, honest music, righteous music, pure music, beautiful music, reputable music, virtuous music, admirable or praiseworthy music. We should not waste our time or talents, not to mention harm our spirits, with music that is false, dishonest, unrighteous, impure, ugly, disreputable, licentious or shameful. We need to stop asking "Will people like this music?"— meaning, "Does this music appeal to sinful men?" We need to ask instead, "Is this music acceptable to a holy God?"

The fact that much of Israel's music was instrumental is also important. Just as music need not have a sensual text to be sensual music, neither must it have a spiritual text in order to be spiritual music. To glorify God the music itself must be excellent in the technical aspects of melody, harmony, and rhythm, without having an inordinate sensual appeal.

Musicians tend to assume that Israel's worship music was essentially the popular music of the day, and that they used any and all instruments at their disposal. Those notions are debunked by Hebraist and musicologist Suzanne Haik-Vantoura, who spent over thirty years deciphering the musical notations that permeate the Hebrew Old Testament. She writes, "Israel was not innovative in this art. It was content to utilize, but in a particular way, the elements that culture placed at their disposal. And it made choices. For example, it did not use…gigantic instruments, like certain Egyptian harps that were only played by two persons….Later, when decadence set in, the prophet Amos (8th century B.C.E.) raged against the voluptuous people and their 'noisy songs' (Amos 6:5). So a distinction was made between healthy vigor and squalling" (pp. 119-120). Her citation of Amos relates to the French translation. She might have added that Amos condemned sensuality by those who "invent to themselves instruments of music" (KJV). Haik-Vantoura also pointed out that Israel's music was "untouched by the pervasive influence of Hellenism" (p. 5), and that their "melodies were piously conceived according to revered norms….No one had the individual right to innovate" (p. 24). [5]

Leonard Payton provides an important observation.

> Many Christians who appropriate the goods of popular culture
> cite Luther as a precedent. A common claim is that Luther used
> tunes 'from the bar.' However, musicological research since 1923
> is weighing in heavily for Luther as the composer of his own
> melodies. Luther did use a musical form called a 'bar' form. But
> this is a technical term referring to the architecture of music, not,
> as would normally be expected, a place where alcoholic beverages
> are consumed. Others mistakenly cite Luther's famous question,
> 'Why should the devil have all the good tunes?' When Luther
> spoke of the devil metaphorically, it was directed at the pope, not
> the pub. To rephrase what Luther was saying, 'Why should we
> leave the great old hymns to the Roman Catholics?' It was an
> apology for the traditional, not for the contemporary![6]

We also need to realize that when we add Christian words to sensual
music we create a sensual "double-talk." In public speaking or dramatic performance it is vital to understand multiple means of communication. Generally, the impact of our communication can be broken
down as follows: the words we say communicate 7% of the message,
our tone of voice communicates 28% of the message, and non-verbal
means communicate 65% of the message. "Tone of voice" includes
inflection as well as voice quality. For instance, whispering can communicate emotion that speaking in a normal tone does not. A rising
inflection indicates incomplete thought or uncertainty. A falling
inflection indicates completed thought or certainty. The wider the
range through which the voice travels, the greater the intensity of
emotion. A double inflection indicates sarcasm, or reversal of meaning (the insertion of an understood "not" in the idea.) "Non-verbal"
communication includes posture, facial expression, dress, gestures,
movement, and so on. Notice that of all the aspects of communication, the words are the least important. When our words agree with
our tone of voice and non-verbal expression, clear and good communication occurs. When our words do not agree with our tone of voice
and/or non-verbal expression, it creates confusion, with the listener
discovering that they must believe the tone and non-verbal message
while rejecting the misleading words.

When our music expresses a sensual message through tone of voice and non-verbal communication, adding words that are spiritual does not make the music spiritual. Rather, it makes a mockery of the message by adding the understood "not" of sarcasm or the obvious hypocrisy of words that say one thing while everything else communicates a contrary message. Ultimately, the message communicated is the message of the music, not the text.

Many people are guilty of a subtle form of idolatry in their misdirected affection. They devote themselves to mediocre and awful music as if it were truly great. Kyle Henderson, former bass player and singer for the rock group "The Producers," has described the pop music of our day this way:

> Like a stunningly dressed prostitute who is alluring but defiled, music can be beautifully packaged and skillfully marketed, but intrinsically rotten. And, just like the wanton woman's customer, many music consumers regularly give their hearts to something grotesque, something unworthy of love, something destructive to the soul....

> [T]o the degree that music ignores God's taste and degenerates into a wild play of fantasy, its value necessarily diminishes. To the degree its value diminishes, it becomes less worthy of our affections. To the degree we unduly love such music, we sin. And sin is always destructive to the soul.[7]

We need to stop trying to convince God that He ought to accept the music we love, and begin allowing God to teach us to love that music which brings Him glory.

As pastors, administrators, and music teachers, we have an opportunity to exert a profound influence on those for whom we are responsible. Our church and school music programs must reflect a biblical philosophy of music, teaching people that the purpose of our music is to glorify God, not entertain ourselves, much less the unbelieving world. We have considered three general principles: 1) Making music is essentially an activity of the spirit; 2) Everything we do must be done for the glory of God; and 3) God has told us what should occupy our minds. All of our music, whether it is for public performance or private enjoyment, must be evaluated in the light of these principles.

We will one day give an account to a holy God for the choices we make and the influence we exert. May God be pleased to say, "Well done."

1 *Readers' Digest*, "Music's Surprising Power to Heal," August, 1992.

2 Numerous studies and experiments conducted by believers and unbelievers alike have indicated music's power to influence the spirit. Sixteen-year-old David Merrill, a student at Nansemond River High School in Suffolk, Virginia, experimented with the effects of music on mice. He took 72 mice and divided them into three groups: one to test a mouse's response to hard rock, another to the music of Mozart, and a control group that would listen to no music. He played music ten hours each day. During the experiment, he put each mouse through a maze three times a week that originally had taken the mice an average of 10 minutes to complete. Over time, the control mice cut their time to about half. The mice listening to Mozart cut their time by 85%, to an average of only 1.5 minutes. The group listening to rock music tripled their time to an average of 30 minutes. This was the second time Merrill had tried the experiment. The first time he had not isolated the mice within their groups, but allowed all the mice in each group to stay together. "I had to cut my project short because all the hard-rock mice killed each other," he said. "None of the classical mice did that" (*Insight*, 9/8/97).

3 *The Coming Evangelical Crisis*, John H. Armstrong, gen. ed., (Chicago, Moody Press, 1996), p. 189. Dr. Payton serves on ministry staff as chief musician at Redeemer Presbyterian Church in Austin, Texas.

4 AgapePress, 7/23/01. Dr. Johansson is a professor of music at Evangel University, an Assemblies of God school in Springfield, MO.

5 Quotations are taken from *The Music of the Bible Revealed*, Translated from the French by Dennis Weber, (Berkeley, CA: BIBAL Press, 1991). This translation is based on the 2nd French edition published by Dessain et Tolra, Paris (1978).

6 *The Coming Evangelical Crisis*, John H. Armstrong, gen. ed., (Chicago, Moody Press, 1996), footnote 10, p. 205.

7 "A Wild Play of Fantasy: How Music Can Be Destructive to the Soul", an article in a devotional periodical published by Ligonier Ministries, Orlando, FL. Henderson is now an editor at Walk Thru the Bible Ministries in Atlanta, GA.